Annie Oakley

ANNIE OAKLEY

by Shirl Kasper

University of Oklahoma Press : Norman and London

Library of Congress Cataloging-in-Publication Data

Kasper, Shirl, 1948–
    Annie Oakley / by Shirl Kasper.
        p.   cm.
    Includes bibliographical references and index.
    ISBN 0-8061-2418-0 (alk paper)
    1. Oakley, Annie, 1860–1926. 2.   Shooters of firearms—United
States—Biography. 3. Entertainers—United States—Biography.
I.   Title.
GV1157.03K37   1992
799.3′092—dc20
[B]   91-50864
                                                                     CIP

The paper in this book meets the guidelines for permanence and durability of
the Committee on Production Guidelines for Book Longevity of the Council on
Library Resources, Inc. ∞

This book is dedicated to all the little girls who grew up in the 1950s, as I did, looking for a heroine. We found her in Gail Davis, who starred in the ABC television show "Annie Oakley," which was released in January 1954. Davis's Annie could outride, outdraw, and outfight any villain. She wore the white hat and did the right thing.

Contents

CONTENTS

Illustrations

ILLUSTRATIONS

Acknowledgments

I was a graduate student in journalism at the University of Kansas when I learned that history can be a lot of fun as well as a scholarly pursuit. I have Professor Calder Pickett to thank for that. In the spring of 1980, in a journalism history seminar, Calder Pickett spoke names that sounded like magic to me: Jesse James, Pretty Boy Floyd, and Pancho Villa. How, he asked, did newspapers contribute to their legend? If this was history, it was for me. When I told him he had just given me the idea for my thesis, Pickett scowled. "If you're going to make a legend of somebody," he said, "make it someone who is worthy of it." Well, what western character could that be? I thought as I walked across the street to Watson Library that same day. Only one name came to mind—Annie Oakley. Like most Americans, I knew her name, but little more.

Thus began this journey, which has been assisted by numerous people along the way. Professor and author David Dary, then at the University of Kansas, read my initial drafts, showed me how to organize, and, most important, told me the secret of good biography—fact mixed with feeling. The interlibrary loan staff at the University of Kansas's Watson Library helped enormously in the early stages by ordering countless newspapers on microfilm, which enabled me to follow Annie Oakley on her travels with Buffalo Bill's Wild West. Toni Seiler, director of the Garst Museum in Greenville, Ohio, shared my enthusiasm for Annie Oakley. She welcomed me to Darke County, steered me in the direction of Annie's birthplace, and answered numerous questions.

ACKNOWLEDGMENTS

Dr. Paul Fees, curator at the Buffalo Bill Historical Center in Cody, Wyoming, put one of Annie's very own Francotte shotguns in my arms and rolled a rare film clip for me of Annie at the Mineola fairgrounds in 1922. Ann Close, an editor at Alfred A. Knopf, went out of her way to suggest ways to strengthen the manuscript, and historian Don Russell lent me his insight that Annie Oakley's main stroke of genius "was to pick that name." And then there was Si Brandner, a coworker at the *Topeka Capital–Journal* who set up some tin cans in his backyard and let me try out his shotgun.

The late Rush Blakely, Annie Oakley's nephew by marriage, invited me into his house on Chippewa Street in Greenville and showed me a silver tea service, which he said had belonged to Annie Oakley. Annie's niece, Irene Patterson Black, in her nineties and living in Florida, graciously endured a lengthy telephone conversation.

And, of course, without the help of the staffs at numerous libraries and historical societies this book would not have been possible. In particular, I would like to thank: Eleanor M. Gehres, Denver Public Library, Western History Department; John F. Steinle, Cincinnati Historical Society; Mildred B. McIntosh, Given Memorial Library, Pinehurst, North Carolina; James L. Murphy, The Ohio Historical Society; Greg and the late Bob Parkinson, Circus World Museum, Baraboo, Wisconsin; Michael Kelly, Buffalo Bill Historical Center, Cody, Wyoming; British Library, Department of Printed Books; Susan W. Persak, Nutley (New Jersey) Free Public Library; John R. Claridge, Erie County (Pennsylvania) Historical Society; Trapshooting Hall of Fame, Vandalia, Ohio; Greenville (Ohio) Public Library; Kathleen Stavec, The New Jersey Historical Society; Archibald Hanna and Cindy L. Balaska, the Beinecke Rare Book and Manuscript Library, Yale University Library, Western Americana Collection; Dorothy L. Swerdlove, The New York Public Library; Minnesota Historical Society; Harold B. Lee Library, Brigham Young University, Provo, Otah; Academy of Motion Picture Arts and Sciences, Beverly Hills, California; Sarah Pritchard and Paul T. Heffron, the Library of Congress; Emmett D. Chisum, University of Wyoming, American Heritage Center; Seth Purdy, Jr., Amityville (New York) Historical Society; the Board of County Commissioners, Butler County, Ohio; the Court of Common Pleas, Hamilton County, Ohio; Judge Fred J. Borchard of the Tenth Judicial Circuit of Michigan; and Nicholas R. Amato, surrogate of the County of Essex, New Jersey.

ACKNOWLEDGMENTS

I also would like to thank friends who believed in me and understood my commitment to this project.

SHIRL KASPER

Kansas City, Missouri

Introduction

At the height of her career, Annie Oakley was called the most famous woman in America—some said, the world. Her legend took root in the dusty arena at Buffalo Bill's Wild West, the great outdoor show that was the forerunner of today's western movies and television programs. For seventeen years Annie Oakley performed as a star sharpshooter, shattering clay targets under the bright summer sun from Boston to Denver and Duluth to Macon. By the turn of the century her name was on the lips of every man, woman, and child in America.

Despite her great fame, four biographies, and a lingering legend, much misinformation remains about the facts of Annie Oakley's life. Biographers have mistaken the dates of her show career and of her marriage to Frank Butler, and have misunderstood the circumstances that motivated her to join the struggling Wild West show in the first place. They have wrongly disputed her claim to have been adopted by the famous chief Sitting Bull, yet repeated a story without foundation that said her hair turned white in seventeen hours after a train wreck. Biographers have painted her as a sweet little girl, when in fact she was a resolute, competitive woman, intent on making her way in a man's world. And perhaps the biggest falsehood of all is the legend itself, which portrays Annie Oakley as a swaggering cowgirl, when she really was no such thing. She was a petite woman, standing only five feet tall and weighing about 110 pounds. She was prim and proper, conservative in her views, an Ohioan who probably had never been west of the Mississippi—until she went with a circus train.

INTRODUCTION

It is the intent of this biography at last to paint an accurate portrait of Annie Oakley. This work is based largely on newspaper accounts of her life, which are about the only historical documents extant. Much of the information related here was taken from Annie Oakley's own scrapbooks, eight of them in all, filled with articles cut and pasted by Annie Oakley and Frank Butler themselves over a period of forty years. Within their pages the woman who became one of the most beloved folk heroines of all time is portrayed, not as legend would have her, but as she seemed to the men and women who actually met her.

Annie Oakley

1.

A Darke County Girl

Darke County, Ohio, is a tranquil farmland, carved from what once was a thick, virgin forest stretching from horizon to horizon. That was in the early days, before General ("Mad") Anthony Wayne built his formidable fort at Greenville and defeated the Indians at the Battle of Fallen Timbers. White settlers flocked in after that. They cleared the lush forests to plant corn and graze cows.

They were men like Jacob Moses, who came west from the hills of Blair County, Pennsylvania, with his wife Susan, his three young daughters—and his old Kentucky rifle. Jacob was a pleasant, athletic man, who even at age fifty-six could outjump anyone in the county and hunt as well as the next. In those days, a man had to know how to use a gun, even if he was a Quaker, as Jacob Moses was.

Jacob arrived in the woodlands of Darke County in about the spring of 1855 and settled just outside a tiny village called, appropriately, Woodland. The community was only eighteen miles from the county seat of Greenville, but it might as well have been eighty miles. There was no rail service, and the post office was a half mile south of town. In time, Woodland would boast a buggy shop, an ice house, a saloon, a restaurant, and a cream station, but the day Jacob arrived, it didn't even have a general store.[1]

Determined to make his living from the land, he set about clearing a plot just northwest of town. He cut the trees and piled the logs in windrows, then took a broadax and hewed them smooth so they fitted at the corners. He built a cabin, making the roof out of rough timbers and the fireplace and chimney out of sticks plastered with a thick coating of clay.

3

ANNIE OAKLEY

In Jacob's rough cabin cut from the Darke County forest, Susan Moses gave birth to another daughter on August 13, 1860. Susan called her new baby Phoebe Ann, but the name didn't stick: the baby's sisters called her Annie.[2] She grew into a small child, strong despite her size, with thick, dark hair and eyes that people noticed, for they were blue-gray, large, and bright with a direct gaze. Annie was a vivacious girl, an admitted tomboy who took no interest in her sisters' ragdolls. She palled instead with her father and her brother John, who was born two years later.

They picked brush and built fences around the little farm. They butchered a young cow and tanned the hide to make shoes. They smoked ham, pickled beans, and tucked away apples before the winter set in. Annie spent hours wandering through the woods, listening to the birds and tracking rabbits. The woods were full of hickory nuts, walnuts, and wild cherries. Roses grew unchecked, and the wild ducks and geese flew free.[3]

It was during her forays into the Darke County woods that Annie Moses learned to shoot a gun. It must have seemed a natural thing to an independent little girl who already knew the ways of the forest and its creatures. Her father had taught her to make traps out of cornstalks, and by the time she was seven, Annie already was trapping quail and rabbit for the family table.[4] Eager to learn to shoot, she was drawn with an uncontrollable curiosity toward the old Kentucky rifle that Jacob had brought from Pennsylvania. It hung, forbidden, over the fireplace.

The day that Annie Moses took that rifle down and fired her first shot has become an ingrained part of the Annie Oakley legend, though the facts are long lost. Annie herself told the story on occasion, though she, like everyone else, romanticized the moment. "I was eight years old when I took my first shot, and I still consider it one of the best shots I ever made," she once said. "I saw a squirrel run down over the grass in front of the house, through the orchard and stop on a fence to get a hickory nut." She ran into the house, climbed on a chair and slid the rifle down to the mantel. She lugged it outside, rested the barrel on the porch railing, and took aim. "It was a wonderful shot, going right through the head from side to side," she said.[5]

Even historians couldn't resist the urge to tell a good story. In the *History of Darke County*, Frazer Wilson wrote that Annie's brother was so angry she had used the rifle that he secretly put a double load in his shotgun and handed the gun to Annie, hoping the kick would discourage her from ever shooting again. He threw up his hat as a target, but to

4

his surprise, the hat too was quickly pierced, "and the sister, undaunted, won the day." [6]

That the sister won the day was, of course, the very foundation of the Annie Oakley story. Girls weren't supposed to shoot guns, let alone hit what they aimed at. It was Annie's gender that made her stand out, even as a girl of eight in the Darke County woodlands. "My mother . . . was perfectly horrified when I began shooting and tried to keep me in school," Annie said, "but I would run away and go quail shooting in the woods or trim my dress with wreaths of wild flowers." [7]

Annie's carefree childhood ended on a snowy day early in 1866 when Jacob Moses set out by buckboard to take his corn and wheat to the local mill, fourteen miles away. He was gone all day, and as the hours passed, a blizzard set in. It was past midnight, the snow still coming down, when an anxious Susan Moses, surrounded by her children, heard the creak of wagon wheels pulling up to the cabin.

"Mother threw the door wide open into the face of the howling wind," Annie recalled. It was a scene she never forgot. Her father sat upright in the buckboard seat, the reins around his neck and wrists. His hands were frozen and his speech gone. The doctor came, but there was little he could do. That March, Annie's father died. [8]

The destitute family moved to a rented farm, but life did not improve. Annie's oldest sister, Mary Jane, came down with tuberculosis and died, and Susan Moses sold Pink, the family cow, to pay doctor and funeral bills. She tried to earn a living by nursing in the county but made only $1.25 a week by taking maternity cases. Susan was so poor that she let a family named Bartholomew take her youngest child, Hulda, born in 1864. [9] And Annie fared no better. About 1870, when Annie was ten years old, Susan sent her to live at the county poor farm. The hard times would leave an indelible imprint on Annie Moses and perhaps were the beginnings of a deep and abiding pride that would mark her character for the rest of her life. Though she never denied her early struggles, she was too proud—or perhaps too hurt—ever to admit that her mother sent her away from home to save money. [10]

The county poor farm, or the Infirmary as everyone called it, was a three-story brick building that spanned the Greenville and Easton pikes, just two and one half miles south of Greenville. In 1870, Greenville was a booming town of three rail lines, four pike roads, and two newspapers, the *Democrat* and the *Journal*. Life revolved around the public square, which stood within the boundaries of old Fort Greenville and extended down Broadway to Third Street. As the name suggested, Broadway was a wide street, bordered on both sides by a score of businesses. There was Farmer's Bank, Tomilson & Sons' saddle shop, and Juddy & Miller's furniture store. A man could get a drink at Gutheil's saloon or take a room at the Broadway Hotel. There was a bookstore, a hardware store, a baker, and a fur trader, Allen LaMott.[11]

Before Annie had much time to become acquainted with Greenville, an area farmer came by the Infirmary looking for a girl to serve as a companion for his wife and new baby. It was a common practice in those days to farm out poor children, and it was not unusual that Annie went with the farmer, whom she described later as a "wolf in sheep's clothing." The farmer, whom she never would identify, made a slave of her.

"I got up at 4 o'clock in the morning, got breakfast, milked the cows, washed dishes, skimmed milk, fed the calves and pigs, pumped the water for the cattle, fed the chickens, rocked the baby to sleep, weeded the garden, picked wild blackberries and got dinner," she said. "Mother wrote for me to come home. But they would not let me go. I was held a prisoner." The couple also physically abused her, although to what extent is not known. The only mention Annie ever made of it was in her autobiography, when almost in passing she talked of scars and welts on her back and said that one night the farmer's wife threw her barefoot into the snow because she had fallen asleep while doing some darning. Annie said she would have died had not the farmer come home and let her in. Life became intolerable with the couple Annie forever afterward called "The Wolves," and one spring day, probably in 1872, the already independent and resolute Annie Moses ran away.[12]

She went back to the poor farm, where she lived with the new superintendent, Samuel Crawford Edington, and his wife, Nancy Ann, who Annie said was a friend of her mother's.[13] They treated her as a daughter and let her stay in their living quarters. She made friends with the Edington children and began attending school with them. They called her "Topsy" because when she smiled she showed all of her teeth, just like the little girl in *Uncle Tom's Cabin*. In time, the Edingtons paid Annie to work as a seamstress, and she sewed dresses and made quilts for the Infirmary inmates. She learned to embroider and stitched fancy cuffs and collars to brighten the orphans' dark dresses. Annie was such a responsible youngster that the Edingtons put her in charge of the Infirmary dairy. She milked the twelve cows, saved the cream, and made butter for the kitchen. One day she got a raise and, just as she would always do, began to save her money.[14]

Annie was about fifteen when she returned to her mother, who had remarried and was building a house near the North Star crossroad, not far from Woodland. Annie had big plans for the future. As she left Greenville, she stopped at the Katzenberger brothers' grocery store at the corner of Main Street and the public square. She had probably been there dozens of times before on errands for the Edingtons, so she knew that hunters and trappers could trade their wild turkeys and rabbits there for flour, wheat, and ammunition.[15] According to Annie's autobiography, G. Anthony and Charles Katzenberger had purchased game from her before, back in those early days when she was just learning to trap and shoot. And now, fed up with being poor, Annie proposed a new business deal. She was going home, she said, and planned to hunt and trap again up in the north county woods. She wanted the Katzenbergers to buy any small game she shipped to town. When they agreed, Annie took them at their word, went home, and launched her trade. For the rest of her life she would earn her living with a gun.

"I donned my linsey [dress] and hied me back to the deep, quiet woods," she wrote in her autobiography. "Oh, how grand God's beautiful earth seemed to me." She studied game lore, set her traps, and hunted. She learned that the rabbits hid in the hedgerows, the ruffed grouse in the wooded gullies and ravines, and the quail in the stubble fields. They flew from their covert so fast that one barely caught a glimpse of them. She had to be quick, aiming by intuition. She never could bring herself to shoot sitting game, as some people did. "I always preferred taking my shot when the game was on the move," she said. "It gave them a fair chance, and made me quick of eye and hand."[16]

Annie Moses became a familiar, though odd, sight around North Star. She was a slender girl of sixteen dressed in coppertoed boots and long yarn stockings. She wore a short, sturdy dress with knickerbockers, and heavy mittens with a trigger finger stitched in. She spent countless hours in the woods and the fields, enjoying nothing more than the crunch of leaves underfoot and the smell of burnt gunpowder. "I guess the love of a gun must have been born in me," she once said.[17] Her ability with firearms was uncanny: her eye was true, her hand steady, her rhythm natural. To Annie Moses, shooting was as easy as pointing her finger at the object and pressing the trigger. "Nothing more simple,

I assure you," she once said. "But I'll tell you what. You must have your mind, your nerve and everything in harmony. Don't look at your gun, simply follow the object with the end of it, as if the tip of the barrel was the point of your finger." [18]

The Katzenberger brothers took a liking to Annie, and one Christmas they sent her a very special present: one can of DuPont Eagle Ducking Black Powder, five pounds of shot, and two boxes of percussion caps. It was Annie's first can of high-grade powder, a gift she treasured so dearly that it was days before she could bring herself to break the seal and use it. "I was assured by the merchant that it was the best powder made," Annie said, "and I never again expected to own another can of such a grade." [19]

Around the same time, Annie was given what she called her first real gun, a Parker Brothers 16-gauge breech-loading hammer, complete with one hundred brass shells. [20] Annie's new gun was a testament to the great strides being made in the development of firearms. The breech-loading shotgun, which swept over America in the late 1870s, enabled the shooter to load his shells at home and simply slip them into the barrel in the field. It was quicker, more convenient, and more reliable than the old muzzle-loaders. No longer would Annie have to carry a powder horn, use an unwieldy ramrod, or worry about damp or rainy days, when the powder might get wet and fail to ignite.

With her new gun, she shot more game than ever. She wrapped them in bunches of six and twelve, then shipped the packages by mail coach to the Katzenbergers, who in turn shipped the game to hotels in Cincinnati, only eighty miles from Greenville. Legend has it that hotelkeepers preferred the quail and rabbits Annie killed because they always were shot through the head. That way, guests never complained of buckshot in their dinner meat—a charming story that cannot be verified.

In those days, Annie Moses would have been called a market hunter. Unusual as it was for a girl, the occupation itself was nothing out of the ordinary. The country still teemed with game, and a farmer armed with an old muzzle-loader might kill two or three thousand prairie chickens a year for the market. Unthinkable though it seems now, conservation was not a public issue, and there were no game limits. Around the Great Lakes, for example, a competent hunter could kill 150 to 200 white-tailed deer in one autumn and get between fifteen and twenty dollars for each. Money like that was more than the average lumberjack, farmer, or miner could earn in a year. [21]

In later years when the public conscience was raised and game limits

Annie Oakley's mother's house, just below the North Star crossroads in Darke County, Ohio. The unidentified man and woman (center) lived in the house when the photograph was taken, probably in the 1950s. The woman at left was a friend of the photographer. The house eventually was torn down, but the marker still stands. (Courtesy of the Garst Museum, Greenville Ohio)

were set, Annie was embarrassed when Charles Katzenberger showed her his old account books, listing the amount of game he had purchased from her. "I won't say how much, as I might be called a game hog," she said.[22] She never said, either, how much money she made, though it was enough to pay off a two-hundred-dollar mortgage on her mother's house at North Star. That Annie paid off the mortgage with her gun became a famous piece of the Annie Oakley legend, one that undoubtedly was true. Annie was proud of the story, just as she always would be proud of her self-sufficiency and her earning power. She was fond of saying that from the time she was ten years old, she never had a dollar that she did not earn.[23]

By the time Annie Moses was in her late teens she had shot so much game and entered and won so many local turkey shoots, a popular entertainment of the time, that she finally was barred from entering them.[24] This local reputation led to the most important shooting match of her life.

2.

The Fancy Shooters

While Annie Moses was growing up in Darke County, Americans were talking about another shooter, one Captain Adam H. Bogardus. Annie was only nine years old when Captain Bogardus made a name for himself by killing one hundred pigeons without a miss. That same year, 1869, he also bet a Mr. R. M. Patchen a thousand dollars that he could kill five hundred pigeons in 645 minutes. The captain did it with 117 minutes to spare. By 1871, Bogardus had defeated the champion shooter in his home state of Illinois and taken the national title from Ira Paine. And that was only the beginning of the captain's career. By the time Annie Moses was fifteen years old, Bogardus had been to England, challenged any man there, won eighteen matches, and come home with a medal declaring him the champion of the world.[1]

Champion shooters, though, were plentiful in the 1870s and 1880s, and Captain Bogardus was just the most famous of a growing string of exhibition shooters. His most celebrated—and flamboyant—rival was Doc Carver, who tried to outdo the captain on a bright summer morning in 1878. Doc looked very western as he made his way to Deerfoot Park in New York City that day. He carried a shiny Winchester rifle at his side, and wore a broad sombrero on his head and a silk scarf around his neck. He tucked his pantaloons inside his boots and fastened his belt with a gold buckle that the newspapermen said was nearly as large as a railroad frog. They chuckled at Doc's long hair and his velvet shirt, but they found nothing funny about his plans: Doc said he was going to break 5,500 glass balls in 500 minutes, a feat never before attempted with a rifle.[2]

The curious gathered round as Doc took his post at the top of a little lane, formed by barrels of feather-filled glass balls and boxes of metallic cartridges. Precisely at eleven o'clock, Doc's assistant, Colonel Horace Fletcher, grabbed a ball from a barrel and tossed it into the air; Doc waited until it reached its apex, then fired, breaking it cleanly and sending feathers drifting in the wind. As fast as Fletcher threw the balls up, Doc shot them down. He fired so fast that the fing, fing of the bullets sounded loudly and monotonously, forcing some spectators from the park. Those who stayed were soon white from the feather shower.

As fast as Doc emptied one gun, he was handed another, freshly oiled and loaded. The empty guns, still smoking, were plunged into a tub of ice water to cool. By early evening the rifles were so fouled that a tongue of fire accompanied each shot. Doc's buckskin gloves were perfectly black, perspiration poured from his face, and his eyes were terribly inflamed from a combination of dirty water, glass dust, feathers, and sulphurous smoke. Carver paused and pressed a handkerchief filled with ice to his eyes.

"For God's sake boys, how much more have I got to do?" he cried. The answer, "Just 100 more, and 18 minutes to do them in," seemed to revive him. Doc made his quota that day, and with ten minutes to spare. His score: 5,500 out of 6,208.

"He calls himself the 'Champion rifle shot of the world,'" the *New York Times* wrote. "He is 38 years old, 6-2 in his stockings, of magnificent physique, an iron constitution, iron nerves and iron will." But despite his iron constitution, Doc was put to bed, where he suffered all night. The pain in his eyes was so great, he said, that all the wealth in the world would not tempt him to try such a feat again.[3] But it wouldn't be many years before Doc Carver would eat those words. Exhibition shooting was a jealous, competitive business, and a man had to stay on top of his rivals, even if it meant nights of pain.

Other shooters in turn staged various feats. One was a man named John Ruth, who showed up at Deerfoot Park on a summer day in 1880 with his wife. He surprised everyone when he handed her a pistol weighing about six pounds. She took it, aimed, and broke a glass ball he threw in the air. A series of fancy shots followed, in which Mrs. Ruth proved that a woman could handle a gun, too. She broke glass balls while holding her pistol sideways and upside down and then stood with her back to the target, took aim in a small mirror, and shot a ball swinging to and fro on a string. John Ruth, thirty-seven, wasn't a bad shot himself. In 1879, he broke 979 (some accounts say 990) balls out of 1,000 at a county fair in Oakland, California. Good as his shooting was, John Ruth never became as famous as Carver or Bogardus.[4]

Neither did Charley Austin, who was one of the earliest exhibition shooters to perform on the stage. He used a Winchester rifle to shoot potatoes from the fingers of his assistant, a Frenchman named Duchene. Austin shot cigarettes from Duchene's mouth, extinguished candles with a bullet, and cut the spots out of playing cards.[5] Annie Moses wasn't yet a teenager when Charley Austin came on stage, leaned over a crate backwards, and smashed targets. Perhaps Mrs. Ruth copied her fancy mirror trick from Charley, who slung a rifle over his shoulder, sighted in a mirror, and shot an apple off Duchene's head.

Another fancy shooter, Ira Paine, was a specialist with the pistol. He was a well-built, calm man who was said to handle a gun like a machine, lifting or lowering it with precisely measured movements. He appeared on stage in a simple suit of tight trousers, black coat, and a sports hat, and was assisted by his pretty wife. She held a cardboard target with a bull's eye measuring about one inch. Paine hit it from an amazing distance of sixty-five feet.[6]

A number of the fancy shooters in those days performed with a woman. Captain Frank Howe, for example, took Miss Tillie Russell as his partner. This was about 1881, when Howe, a tall, muscular man, was about thirty years old. He dressed in gray chamois leather trousers and high patent boots. His waistcoat was decorated with white and red stars, and his jacket was made of leopard skin. On his head was a big, wide-brimmed sombrero. Miss Russell, who wore tights, impressed the audience more by her good looks than by her marksmanship. Her best feat was shooting a big potato from Howe's hat—at a distance of all of four paces.[7]

Fancy shooters were becoming so common by the 1880s that even a twelve-year-old girl was calling herself the champion rifle shot of the world. Her name was Miss Lillian F. Smith of Watsonville, Santa Cruz County, California. She held out a five-hundred-dollar wager that she could break 1,000 glass balls in 50 minutes.[8]

Exhibition shooters were not a new phenomenon; they dated to the early 1800s, when shooters performed with circuses. But it wasn't until the 1880s that they achieved the height of their popularity. It was a time when the public liked a good show, and when guns were a familiar part of American life. The feats of a Bogardus or a Carver made the pages of newspapers big and small, and people remembered their names. The men of the hour, in fact, were the shooters on the American Rifle Team, who had astonished the nation by upsetting the world-famous Irish shooters at the old Creed farm on Long Island on September 26, 1874. "A Victory for America," rang the page-one headline in the *New York Times*. The victory had astonished a nation that considered Wimbledon and Monte Carlo the hotbeds of good shooting, not the American range at Creedmoor. Barely a year old, it had been established by a newly formed club called the National Rifle Association. The club had only 760 members that year, but the great victory at Creedmoor would change all that. It placed American sharpshooters in the spotlight and spurred great interest in rifle shooting.[9]

Perhaps it was at Creedmoor that Frank Butler first took an interest in shooting. He was an Irish immigrant, who as a boy had worked his way across the ocean by paring potatoes and helping on the deck of a ship. After arriving in New York City, he begged and did odd jobs. He dipped milk from the back of a wagon, sold newspapers, cleaned a livery stable, and tried to learn the glass-blowing trade. He worked on a fishing boat for two years, got married, and had two children.

Frank Butler was a nice-looking man, about 24 years old. He was slightly below average in height, and had dark hair, a trim mustache, and a sense of humor. He liked to tell stories and to play jokes on his friends. He enjoyed people and could strike up a conversation with almost anyone. And Frank Butler was a sentimental man. He liked to write poetry about nature and friendship and the passage of the seasons. If there was a blot on his life, it was the failure of his marriage sometime in those early days when he was just getting started.[10]

His life headed in a new direction when he joined an amateur show, a type of theatrical group that was very common in the 1870s. Frank trained a troupe of dogs and went on stage. He later laughed at himself when he told about a theater he had once played in Philadelphia. The theater was next door to a fire station, and one of his newly trained dogs was an old fire dog. When the fire alarm rang just as Frank was getting ready to go on stage, the old dog instinctively took off for the fire, and the rest of Frank's canine troupe followed.[11]

Better times were ahead. Sometime in the mid-1870s, Frank learned to do trick shooting and eventually scrubbed his dog act for a new shooting act along the lines of Charley Austin's.[12] He learned to shoot while

13

sighting through a mirror and to fire a rifle while bending over backwards. He found a couple of partners, though neither was a woman: one was a man named Baughman; the other a poodle named George. They began performing in the variety theaters, which were so numerous in New York City in 1875 that the *New York Times* confessed it couldn't hope to keep a record of all the program changes.

Variety theaters offered as many as eighteen acts on one bill, each act lasting about twenty minutes. Some theaters offered two or three shows a day, running continuously from ten in the morning until eleven at night. Admission was a nickel, and patrons dropped in or left as they chose. Besides fancy shooters like Baughman and Butler, variety theaters featured acrobats, ventriloquists, wire walkers, jugglers, boxers, magicians, quartets and duets, and the always popular song-and-dance man. [13]

Though Baughman and Butler billed themselves as "the champion marksmen," and though legend would build them as great stars who packed opera houses at every performance, the truth was that they weren't very famous at all. When they played Cincinnati in the spring of 1881 they barely got a mention in the Cincinnati *Enquirer*. And then, the notice said only that Baughman and Butler had decided to join the Sells Brothers Circus. [14] Evidently, they were having a hard time making it on the stage and had decided to try a different life; the circue would assure them of steady bookings and a regular income.

They did well to hook up with Sells Brothers. The show had been touring for almost ten years and was one of the largest and best known on the road. Traveling by rail, it comprised fifteen gondolas, seven stock cars, two elephant cars, a baggage car, and three sleepers. The Sells brothers, Ephraim, Lewis, Peter, and Allen, were hard-working Ohio boys who billed their circus as the "Big Millionaire Confederation, the Biggest Amusement Enterprise on Earth." [15] Baughman and Butler grew in stature upon joining the Sells Circus. They now were billed as the "Biggest Creedmoor Champions, the Champion Rifle Dead-Shots of the World."

"The great snap-shot sensation," the circus couriers read. "For the first time under canvas, Baughman and Butler . . . in their original and unrivaled off-hand, snap-shot, bulls-eye programme of startling, dexterous, critical hits." Baughman and Butler shattered glass balls, shot backwards while sighting in a mirror, and at fifteen paces knocked apples off each other's head. [16] They were told to report to Columbus, Ohio, where the circus would begin its new season on April 25, 1881. That month, Baughman and Butler packed their bags in Cincinnati, where they had been staying in a hotel frequented by farmers. While there, Frank Butler had a conversation that would change his life. "Some of the guests heard we could shoot and soon I was tackled by one who wanted to know what I could do," Frank said. "I told him I could beat anything then living save Carver or Bogardus. He said he had an unknown who would shoot me at Greenville ten days from that time for $100 a side." Greenville was a good eighty miles from Cincinnati, but Frank Butler knew a sucker when he saw one. He laughed and took the bet. "It seemed a shame for me to take the money from those country people," Frank said. "I thought there were some country people who thought someone could shoot a little and were ready to lose money, and as I needed it, I went out." [17] Of course, the someone whom the country people thought "could shoot a little" was Annie Moses.

3.

Butler and Oakley

A late spring storm had dumped twenty inches of snow in Greenville, and the roads undoubtedly were muddy when Frank Butler arrived in town. But even the mud couldn't dampen Frank Butler's spirits. Counting on an easy hundred dollars, he was cheerful as he hopped off the train at Greenville and started on his way to North Star, where he would face the country folks' unknown.

The shooting match that followed and later was immortalized in the Broadway play *Annie Get Your Gun* has never been documented. The lack of information, in fact, has perplexed historians and undoubtedly gave rise to the legend, which says the match was shot in Cincinnati on Thanksgiving Day of 1875. That is pure fiction. Frank Butler probably didn't even begin his shooting career until a year after that.[1]

The true story of the famous match is found in much later newspaper accounts, quoting Frank Butler himself. On three occasions—once in 1903 and twice in 1924—Frank told inquisitive reporters how he met the famous Annie Oakley. According to Frank, the match took place in the spring of 1881 in a little town near Greenville, "18 miles from the nearest station." That could only be the North Star–Woodland area, where everyone was familiar with Annie Moses.

"I got there late and found the whole town, in fact, most of the county out ready to bet me or any of my friends to a standstill on their 'unknown,'" Frank said. "I did not bet a cent. You may bet, however, that I almost dropped dead when a little slim girl in short dresses stepped out to the mark with me." The little girl was Annie Moses, wearing her linsey dress and knickerbockers. If she was nervous, she never admitted it, and with a confidence she would display her entire life she stepped to the mark with the crack shot Frank Butler.

"I was a beaten man the moment she appeared for I was taken off guard," he would say. "Never were the birds so hard for two shooters as they flew from us, but never did a person make more impossible shots than did that little girl. She killed 23 and I killed 21. It was her first big match—my first defeat."[2]

Embellished though Frank's story may have been, there is no question that the shooting match that day was the beginning of a lifelong relationship, born of business and a mutual love of guns. Before leaving North Star, Frank invited Annie to a theater to see his act. She went, and there made friends with Frank's poodle, George, who sat still while Frank shot an apple off his head. When George picked up a piece of apple and laid it at Annie's feet, the romance began.[3] That the dog became the cupid in the love affair may say how bashful Annie Moses was toward courting, though she already was twenty years old. If there had been any other suitors in her life, she never talked of them. Frank eased into the relationship. When he left to join the circus, he sent greetings to Annie via George. At Christmastime, George sent Annie a box of candy. Letters came, and one time, a poem Frank had written. He called it "Little Raindrops."

> There's a charming little girl
> She's many miles from here
> She's a loving little fairy
> You'd fall in love to see her
> Her presence would remind you
> Of an angel in the skies,
> And you bet I love this little girl
> With the rain drops in her eyes.[4]

If Annie Moses seemed like a little girl to Frank Butler that spring, he must have seemed a man of the world to her. He had crossed the ocean and played in theaters and honky-tonks from the Bowery to the St. Louis riverfront. But there was nothing hard about Frank Butler. He was a kind man, and he didn't smoke, drink, or gamble, facts happily noted by Annie's family.[5] And above all, Frank loved the same things that Annie Moses loved—a good gun and a fast bird.

Though their love would last a lifetime, its beginnings leave us with questions that cannot be answered. When, for example, did Frank and Annie wed—and where? The date of the marriage not only has puzzled

Frank Butler, Annie Oakley, and the poodle George in 1883, as the shooting team of Butler and Oakley. (Courtesy of the Circus World Museum, Baraboo, Wis.)

Frank Butler, in the early days with Annie Moses, probably about 1883. (Courtesy of the Garst Museum, Greenville, Ohio)

historians, but also was a mystery to Annie's niece Fern Campbell Swartwout, who spent a great deal of time with the Butlers in their later years. "I never heard my aunt or uncle speak of it," Fern wrote, "except that Uncle Frank would tease her by saying that when he married her she had only a gingham dress."[6]

That Annie was ticklish about the marriage date was proved years later when she was visiting another niece, Bonnie Patterson Blakeley. Annie, in her sixties then and apparently thinking of posterity, pulled a marriage certificate out of a box and handed it to Bonnie for safekeeping. Keep this in case questions are raised, Annie told her.[7] The certificate, issued to Frank Butler and Annie Moses of Saginaw, Michigan, was dated June 20, 1882, in Windsor, Ontario, Canada. That marriage certificate, which is the only one known, raises the prospect that Annie Moses left Darke County with Frank Butler before she was married. Of course, that would not have been a proper thing for a young woman to do in 1882. Perhaps that explains why the Butlers—who cared a great deal about their public image—always were so vague about their marriage date. Possibly, Frank's divorce from his first wife was not yet final, and Annie and Frank had to wait to marry—or they may have had a second ceremony. According to Bonnie Blakeley's husband, Rush, Annie gave the 1882 certificate to his wife for fear that questions would come up after her death, and if people couldn't find a marriage certificate, they might assume that she and Frank had never been married. "They didn't want that," Rush Blakeley said of the Butlers. "There's lots of misinformation. [Biographers] claim she married when she was sixteen, but she was about twenty-two."[8]

Publicly, Annie and Frank said no more than they said to family— just that the marriage took place about one year after they met and that shortly after the ceremony, Frank put Annie on a train and sent her to Erie, Pennsylvania, to attend a Catholic school while he traveled. By then, Frank had completed his contract with the Sells circus and had a new partner, John Graham. Interestingly, John Graham hailed from Erie, where his mother, Catherine, ran a boardinghouse, called Park Place. Annie may well have stayed there while Graham and Butler toured the variety circuit. Records do show that Frank Butler was a visitor there during 1882, but whether Annie really attended a Catholic school is not known.[9]

Graham and Butler billed themselves as "America's own rifle team and champion all around shots." They wore tall black boots, tight pants, and coats with tails. They sat on chairs and shot an apple off

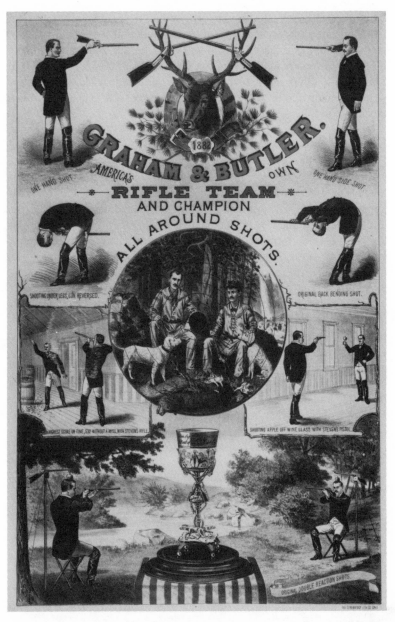

A poster for Graham and Butler, 1882. (Courtesy of the Cincinnati Historical Society)

each other's head. Frank fired while bending over backward, and John Graham shot with his rifle upside down between his legs. The *Annals of the New York Stage* place Graham and Butler at the Volksgarten during the week of March 6, 1882, and on May 1 they played Crystal Hall in Springfield, Ohio. No one by the name of Annie Oakley was mentioned, which undoubtedly means that her persona had not yet been created. That, however, was soon to change.[10]

It probably was in late 1882 or early 1883 that Annie left Erie and joined Frank and John Graham on tour. According to her autobiography, she was not a part of their act until John Graham became ill. Needing a partner, Frank asked Annie to hold objects while he shot. He said it was his habit to miss his target intentionally a couple of times to work up the interest of the audience. But one day, try as he might, he could not hit the mark. He had missed about a dozen times when a burly spectator staggered to the ring and pointed at Annie. "Let the girl shoot," the man shouted. Annie had never practiced the shot, Frank said, but she picked up a gun, fired, and hit the target on her second try.

"The crowd went into an uproar," Frank said, "and when I attempted to resume my act I was howled down, and Annie Oakley continued." Quick to recognize a good act, Frank made Annie his new partner, and the shooting team of Butler and Oakley was born. "From that day to this," Frank said, "I have not competed with her in public shooting." And he never would. Frank's name was up front in the new team of Butler and Oakley, but it soon became Annie Oakley at the fore. Frank taught her what he knew, and then he stepped aside. "She outclassed me," he would say.[11]

Indeed, she did, just as she would outclass every rival she ever faced. There were scores of sharpshooting acts—but Annie Oakley was different. She didn't brag boldly like Lillian Smith or wear sexy tights like Tillie Russell. Annie Oakley dressed simply in a dark dress with a starched white collar and pretty cuffs at the sleeve. She stood only five feet tall and weighed about 110 pounds. She looked innocent and above reproach, a sweet little girl—yet a sharpshooter of matchless ability. That paradox was part of her appeal. She had a pleasant, wide smile, and thick, dark hair cut close around her face and worn long in back, falling over her shoulders. There was magnetism in the way she smiled, curtsied in the footlights, and did that funny little kick as she ran into the wings.

There was something, too, about that name, Annie Oakley. It possessed some unexplainable magic. How Annie Moses thought it up, no one knows for sure. Some say, though doubtfully, that it was an old family name. Others say that she took it from the Cincinnati neighborhood of Oakley. Or perhaps Annie simply picked it out of a hat. All she ever said about it was that she took it in 1882 as a stage name.[12] She took it, and she would keep it always. She became Annie Oakley to herself and to the world, burying Annie Moses forever.

She had evidently never liked the Moses name anyway. In fact, she insisted the family name wasn't Moses at all, but Mozee. Annie was stubborn. She changed it in the family bible and began a lifelong feud with her brother when she went so far as to have "Mozee" engraved on the headstones when two of her nephews died. According to Annie's niece Fern Campbell Swartwout, the name was a quirk of Annie's. But Annie herself never budged on the issue. Interestingly, the 1860 census records spell Jacob Moses's name as Jacob Mauzy, indicating either that the census taker couldn't spell or that "Moses" was pronounced with a distinct accent. Perhaps Annie was so stubborn about the name because she honestly thought it should be spelled as pronounced, "Mozee." But popular thinking, including a fictional account called *The Secret Annie Oakley, A Novel,* holds that a very modest Annie, and a very proud one, disliked the name Moses because as an impoverished child she may have been teased with rhymes such as "Moses Poses, Moses Poses, no one knows where she gets her clothes-es."[13] There simply is no way to know what the truth is.

Little is known of Annie Oakley's early days on the stage, except that she and Frank played variety theaters and skating rinks, lived out of a trunk, and stayed in inexpensive hotels and boardinghouses along the way. One account says they played in the Midwest and along the Great Lakes that first year of 1883.[14] Traveling was a way of life for performers then. Even famous actors like Edwin Booth and Sarah Bernhardt were on the road, though Bernhardt had a private railroad car and employed private servants. Annie and Frank, on the other hand, consulted train schedules and looked for the cheapest fare.

"We never rode in Pullmans those days if we could make a day trip," Annie said. "That extra money meant gloves, hose and pretty hair ribbons so I could look neat at rehearsals."[15] She spent the nights at theatrical boardinghouses and the daytime hours practicing the fancy shots that Frank taught her, though he never took any credit for himself.

"I didn't teach her to shoot, because she could have taught me even then, although I was supposed to be a crack shot myself in those days," he would say. "I simply got her a position and she did the rest." The hardest part of learning to shoot on the stage, Annie said, was mastering the artificial lights, which were insufficient and uneven—and sometimes went out entirely. The border lights were operated by levers that sometimes slipped, and the footlights were produced by jets of flame blown against two pieces of lime. The lights hissed, sputtered, cracked, and dropped red-hot sparks on the stage. Not only was it hard for a sharpshooter to see, but also the gas lights consumed oxygen, making the theater intensely hot and fouling the air.[16]

Through it all, Frank seemed content to take a back seat as Annie's manager. He was the one who placed ads in the trade papers, talked to theater managers, made bookings, consulted train schedules, and counted the money. "That part was always in my husband's hands," Annie would say, "and I owe whatever I have to his careful management. Of course, we were poor when we started, and I remember him saying to me, 'Well, Annie, we have enough this week to buy you a pretty hat.'"[17]

They eventually tired of the financial worry and decided to rejoin the Sells Brothers Circus, where they would have a free ride and a fair salary to boot. They signed a forty-week contract, set to begin in mid-April 1884 from the Sells circus lot in Columbus, Ohio. They could do a couple of shows a day, then sit back and watch their savings grow. But first, they had a few last bookings to fulfill. One was an engagement at the Olympic Theatre in St. Paul, Minnesota, a booking that led to one of the most celebrated moments of Annie Oakley's life.

4.

Little Sure Shot

Of all the stories that would grow up around the legendary Annie Oakley, the one that told how she was adopted by the Sioux chief Sitting Bull was most open to question. The adoption, though never documented, was mentioned over and over again in Buffalo Bill's Wild West press literature, which said Annie met Sitting Bull in a St. Paul, Minnesota, theater in 1881, and that he was so impressed with her shooting that he dubbed her "Watanya Cecila," or Little Sure Shot. It made a good story, almost too good a story. Knowing how press agents liked to fabricate, one of Annie Oakley's biographers went so far as to conclude that the meeting never happened.[1] But the meeting did indeed happen, and it happened in a St. Paul theater, just as the legend said.

The story began in March 1884, when Annie Oakley still was struggling for recognition. She and Frank needed all the bookings they could get that winter, so they took a job with a traveling show called the Arlington and Fields Combination. With money always on her mind, Annie supplemented her income by competing in shooting matches during the day and playing theaters at night. She apparently was too busy to care much about the big goings on in St. Paul as the traveling show pulled into town that week.

The most distinguished prisoner of war in Dakota Territory was in town: Sitting Bull, who was blamed for the murder of General George Armstrong Custer at the Little Big Horn just eight years before. The good citizens of St. Paul stood on the streets watching for Sitting Bull, not sure whether to nod or hiss. Most just stared at the stout man with the round shoulders and the deep chest. In their eyes, he was not a handsome man. His face was round, his eyes full, his hair long and black. It was parted exactly in the middle, each half plastered and bound with otter skin in a strand that fell to his waist. He wore a calico shirt, a waistcoat of plush brocade, and blue trousers bordered with fancy braid and dotted with brass buttons. His feet, which looked remarkably small, were thrust into moccasins with india-rubber soles.[2]

Trips were nothing new to Sitting Bull, who made his home now at the Standing Rock Reservation at Fort Yates. He had been to Bismarck to celebrate the opening of the Northern Pacific Railroad and had gone along on the last great buffalo hunt, in September 1883. He was in St. Paul this March with Major James McLaughlin, the agent at Standing Rock, who accompanied Sitting Bull on a full-blown tour of the city.[3]

They went into Charles Fetsch's cigar plant, where Sitting Bull sampled a cigar made right before his eyes. He expressed his delight "with some very significant" puffs. At the *Pioneer Press* newspaper office, workers turned Sitting Bull "onto the telephone eavesdropping racket," and he grunted in admiration, "Waukon," which meant "the devil." Later that Monday, Sitting Bull and his nephew, One Bull, walked from room to room in St. Paul's schools, listening to children recite lessons and watching them do calisthenics. At Franklin School, the principal rang the electric fire alarm and a delighted Sitting Bull watched the building empty in one minute and forty-five seconds.

Everyone seemed to go all out for Sitting Bull. The school board president, a Mr. Oppenheim, took him on a tour of his large millinery house, where the chief was greeted by the forty women who worked there. They shook Sitting Bull's hand and decorated him with ribbons and artificial flowers.[4] Sitting Bull didn't seem so ferocious after all. There was something admirable about him; perhaps it was the way he looked you in the eyes and spoke deliberately and forcefully.

At night, Sitting Bull took in the theater. He watched "Muldoon's Picnic" at the Grand Opera House one evening, and another night laughed at the Rex Reed show, in which he seemed especially to like the hugging scene between Dick Smythe and Nell. On Wednesday night, March 19, Sitting Bull went to the Olympic Theater on Seventh Street near Jackson to see the Arlington and Fields Combination, billed as "the greatest aggregation of talent" ever to appear in St. Paul. Sitting Bull walked to the parquet and sat down in a prominent seat in Box B. From there, he watched the Wertz brothers do acrobatics, heard Miss Allie Jackson sing a medley of songs, and saw Flynn and Sarsfield in their burnt-cork minstrel act. He sat attentively through the afterpiece, "St. Patrick's Day in the Evening," and was there, too, when Annie Oakley bounded on stage and snuffed a burning candle with a bullet from her rifle.[5]

Though the St. Paul newspapers did not mention Sitting Bull's reaction to the performance of Butler and Oakley, the chief must have watched in fascination as the vivacious Annie snuffed candles and knocked corks from bottles and cigarettes from Frank's mouth. Here was a tiny woman with flowing brown hair who could do rifle tricks that even he could not have performed. "He was about as much taken by my shooting stunts as anyone ever has been," Annie said. "He raved about me, and would not be comforted. His messengers kept coming down to my hotel to enquire if I would come and see him. I had other things to do, and could not spare the time."[6] She was busy, of course, with a shooting match and didn't dare miss it or she would have to forfeit her entry fee. Money meant a lot to Annie Oakley, and it was only when Sitting Bull started talking money that he finally got her attention. He sent sixty-five dollars to her room in hopes of obtaining a photograph of her. "This amused me," Annie said, "so I sent him back his money and a photograph, with my love, and a message to say I would call the following morning. I did so, and the old man was so pleased with me, he insisted upon adopting me, and I was then and there christened 'Watanya Cicilla,' or 'Little Sure Shot.'"

Annie Oakley was much too practical to see the romance in the exchange. She made light of her adoption and chuckled at the "privileges of her rank as a chieftain's daughter." Though she laughed at the thought of ever taking up residence in Indian country, she didn't fail to note the material value if she did: "I am entitled to receive five ponies, a wigwam, no end of cattle, and other presents of live stock," she said.[7] That was Annie, her eye always on a dollar. The businessman in Frank Butler was no different. He recognized the story as good advertising for Annie's career, and on April 5, 1884, just two weeks after the incident, he put an advertisement in the trade publication, the *New York Clipper*. Frank Butler knew how to promote Annie Oakley. "The Premier Shots, Butler and Oakley, Captured by Sitting Bull," Frank wrote. The advertisement said Sitting Bull had given Annie a picture of himself, a large feather from the head of a Crow chief, and the original pair of moccasins he'd worn in the Custer fight. There had been witnesses, not the least of whom was Major McLaughlin, and from the Arlington and Fields Combination Tin-pan Fields, the Sunlin Brothers, Heffern and Professor Morrison, Ace Levoy, Sarsfield and Flynn, and Miss Allie Jackson. "P.S.," Frank added at the bottom of the advertisement, "Finest shooting-act ever seen here," according to the St. Paul *Daily Globe*.

Sitting Bull and Annie Oakley parted in St. Paul that March, but their paths would cross again. He headed west, back to Standing Rock. She went east, toward Ohio, to begin a tour with the Sells Brothers Circus. On her way, as she would do so often between engagements, she stopped at the little house just below the North Star crossroads for a visit with her mother.

5.

A Whole World of Wonders

The coming of the Sells Brothers Circus was all the talk in Ottawa, Kansas. For days the circus had been running its big advertisements in the town newspaper, the *Daily Republican*. Sells was coming to town, the paper said, "in all its towering and overpowering greatness." It was coming on its "own great trains," drawn by its "own locomotives." It was "a whole world of wonders" never before exhibited. "Greater than the greatest! Larger than the largest! Better than the best!"[1] Sells was coming with fifty cages of live wild animals: "Just 50. No more, no less, embracing every known type of beast, bird, reptile and Deep sea monster." Sells boasted the biggest and only $57,000 pair of stupendous living hippopotamuses, the biggest and only full-grown living giraffe, a $22,000 two-horned rhinoceros, the biggest and only $50,000 arctic aquarium of amphibious monsters. The only small thing about the Sells circus was Chemah, the Chinese dwarf, "the smallest adult body that contains a soul." The star of stars was Emperor, a giant elephant, who led ten teams of elephants drawing ten golden chariots.[2]

Hundreds of people turned out for the street parade, which began promptly at ten. They cheered as three brass bands played and the stars of the show rolled by. There was the famous horseman James Robinson, "the laurel-crowned emperor of the arena"; Frank H. Gardner, "the astounding high and lofty leaper"; and Adelaide Cordona, "the greatest lady horseback rider ever beheld." If Annie Oakley and Frank Butler rode in the street parade that day, as surely they did, no one bothered to mention them. As it was, they barely made the newspaper advertisements, billed in small type as Butler and Oakley, "the champion rifle shots." Far from a star, Annie Oakley also rode side-saddle in the Rose Garland entrée and doubled as Mrs. Old One-Two in a pantomime in which Frank played Quaker Starchback. It was a comic act, starring the clown, Humpty Dumpty, and the pantaloon, Old One-Two.[3]

Annie played Old One-Two's wife that whole season of 1884 as the circus train wound its way from Ohio, Illinois, and Kansas into Missouri, Arkansas, and Texas. All told, Annie Oakley would play to big crowds in 187 cities in thirteen states that season, but her name would not become as famous even as that of Emperor, the giant elephant. Yet within three years she would be shaking hands with the prince of Wales and her name would be known across the nation.

The most fateful turn in Annie Oakley's career came late in 1884 as the Sells circus train pulled into New Orleans to wind up its season at the World's Industrial and Cotton Exposition. The city was decked out in flags, bunting, and flowers that November as New Orleans made ready to celebrate the one-hundredth year since America had exported its first cotton. Exhibits from every state and territory already crowded the floor in the main exhibition building at the fair. Texas alone had shipped 360 varieties of grasses and 21,000 plants. Philadelphia was talking about lending the Liberty Bell, and Dakota had shipped a carload of wild animals. The fair director, a Mr. Dabney, was in a dither because he had no place to keep the bears and the wolves.

Twenty-five thousand visitors streamed into town. They took furnished rooms for seventy-five cents a day and looked for things to do. "Around the World in Eighty Days" was playing at the St. Charles Theatre, the Cal Wagner Minstrels were at the Academy of Music, and "Ranch No. 10" at the Grunewalk Opera House. And on a lot just off Canal Street, the Sells Brothers Circus had set up, hoping to cash in on the crowds. The circus played every day, but attendance varied with the weather. It rained often and hard that December, and if the Sells brothers had hoped to stay in New Orleans at least until the cotton exposition opened, the persistent rain changed their minds. They closed the circus after only two weeks and packed their bags for home.[4]

That left Butler and Oakley without a job. They renewed their circus contract—which Annie duly noted was at an increase in salary—but the contract did not start until April in Ohio, and this was December in Louisiana.[5] Always watching their finances, they had no intention of remaining idle over the winter. In fact, Frank had begun looking for work within days of arriving in New Orleans. As he sometimes did, he took out an advertisement in the trade publication, the *Clipper:* "Butler and Oakley, premium shots," it said, "will close a 40-week season with Sells Brothers' enormous shows in New Orleans, La., shortly, and will have a new and novel act, for Variety Theatres, Combinations or Skating Rinks, Never Before Introduced. Address Frank Butler, Sells Bros' Show, New Orleans, La."[6]

Only days after Frank placed that advertisement, he got word of just the job he was looking for. Always a keen reader of newspapers, he must have devoured eagerly a small story about a new show that was getting ready to open in town. The story appeared in the New Orleans *Picayune* of December 4, 1884: "Mr. E. W. Woodcott," it read, "general agent for the Buffalo Bill Wild West Show, reports progress on 'Buffalo Bill's Wild West Park'—an original American amusement enterprise." The show included horse races and shooting matches. In addition, it was setting up right off Canal Street, probably within walking distance of the Sells circus lot. The Honorable William F. Cody himself, better known as Buffalo Bill, was scheduled to arrive in New Orleans in just a few days, and word had it that he planned to set up his show for the entire winter. The ad must have sounded ideal to a couple of sharpshooters looking for a winter job. The timing, in fact, could not have been better. Buffalo Bill arrived in New Orleans on Monday, December 8; the Sells circus closed on Saturday, December 13.[7]

It was sometime during that week, Annie Oakley said, that Buffalo Bill paid a visit to the Sells circus lot, and she and Frank were introduced to him.[8] They took the opportunity to ask for a job, but much to their disappointment, Cody turned them down. His show already was heavy on shooting acts, he said, and he simply had no room for them on his bill. Annie consoled herself when she learned that Cody's bill included, of all people, the famous Captain Bogardus, who was performing with his four sons, Eugene, Edward, Peter, and Henry. On top of that, Bogardus was a part owner in the show. "The knowledge of this fact put my wounded vanity 'kind of straight,'" Annie said later.[9] And so, with the chance of a job seemingly gone, she and Frank packed their bags and headed north, where they spent the winter playing the variety theaters.

Cody's show went on in New Orleans without them, though that winter was the toughest the Wild West show would ever know. Troubles began on the Mississippi River, when the steamship transporting the show down the river collided with another steamer and sank, losing animals, wagons, camp equipment, guns, and ammunition. Captain Bogardus lost all his equipment in the disaster and headed back to Cincinnati to try to find the owners of the steamboat and regain damages.[10] Cody had trouble reorganizing in New Orleans and pushed the opening date back three times, from December 17, to the twentieth, and finally to the twenty-third. To complicate matters, the weather was miserable. Violent showers flooded the streets and turned the lot off Canal Street into a virtual mudhole. At one point, Cody was so discouraged that he talked of giving the outfit away.[11]

Captain Bogardus also was discouraged, so much so that on Sunday, March 9, he quit the show, announcing that he was returning home with his sons, whom he wanted to enroll in school. Without Bogardus, Cody himself was forced to pick up the slack in the program by doing more shooting stunts.[12] When Annie and Frank heard the news, they jumped into action.

"I wrote to Colonel Cody right away, and asked for an engagement," Annie said. Cody responded, but balked at the salary she asked. He "expressed an opinion that my terms were 'too steep,'" Annie said.[13] She never revealed what "her terms" were, but judging from the salary she later drew, she probably had asked for at least five times what the cowboys were making. It made Cody stop and think, especially since the Wild West show was suffering financially after the long, wet winter in New Orleans. The show already was sixty thousand dollars in debt, and taking on a new high salary was the last thing he needed. Cody also was worried that Annie couldn't handle the rigors of the job. He'd sized her up. He thought such a tiny woman might not have the strength to fill Captain Bogardus's shoes. After all, the captain's Scott shotguns weighed ten pounds each. How was a woman of 110 pounds going to bear up under weight like that day in and day out in the arena?

"At first, Colonel Cody entertained a grave doubt as to whether I should be able to withstand the recoil from a shot-gun," Annie said. But Cody's fears never seemed to faze her. Always confident when it came to a gun—and always so proud—you could almost hear her snort, years later, "I think I have pretty successfully demonstrated . . . that I have been able to bear up against it."[14] To prove that she was worth every penny she asked, and that she could do the shooting Bogardus had done, she agreed to a three-day trial. If Cody wasn't satisfied, she would leave the show, no questions asked. Cody liked the deal and invited her to join the Wild West in Louisville, Kentucky, where the show was to open a new season on the last weekend of April.

With Cody's offer in hand, Annie and Frank never looked back. They immediately canceled an engagement at "a little river town in Ohio" where they were playing and took the first train out to Cincinnati, where Annie spent most of April at a city gun club, practicing at the trapshooting range. To prove her stamina—as well as to gain some practice with the shotgun—Annie attempted the greatest endurance feat of her life before trying out for the Wild West. She took three 16-gauge Parker shotguns and tried to break 5,000 glass balls in one day, just as Doc Carver and Captain Bogardus had done. She loaded her own guns and stood fifteen yards from the traps. After nine hours she had broken 4,772 balls. In the second thousand, she hit 984 balls, which she said was a record for the time. It was an endurance feat to be proud of, and it is curious that Annie never talked about it much, though it commonly was listed among her records. Her only other one-day endurance feat had taken place a year earlier, on April 6, 1884. It is significant that she used a rifle then—a .22-caliber Stevens rifle—breaking 943 targets out of 1,000. A year later, with her eye on joining the Wild West, she switched to Parker shotguns.[15]

Some historians have wondered why Annie and Frank were so eager to join the Wild West, considering how down and out it seemed to be. The answer was simple: Annie Oakley wanted to get off the variety circuit. There were so many fancy shooters on the stage—all of whom used pistols and rifles—that it was becoming hard to make a living. But Frank had never heard of a female exhibition shooter who used a shotgun. With a shotgun, Annie would have a new angle for her act. She would be a female Captain Bogardus, smashing glass balls and clay pigeons on the wing. That was a sight above the corks and bottles of the variety stage.[16]

Corks and bottles were stationary objects, and anyone with a good eye, a steady hand, and a lot of nerve could learn the art of stage shooting. Hadn't the likes of Captain Howe and Tillie Russell proved that? In fancy shooting, it was the appearance of difficulty that counted, whether the shot really was very difficult or not. By 1884, so many fancy shooters were on the stage that even Annie's edge as a woman had grown thin. Frank said he knew of at least twenty women and girls in the line.[17]

Annie Oakley may have been a better, more natural shot than any of them, but what did it matter? They all could shoot a cork from a bottle—and some of them cheated.

Cheaters were so common, in fact, that the (London) *Referee* declared that at least one half of all fancy shooters accomplished their feats by "trick and device." Knocking the ashes off a cigarette, for example, which would become one of Annie Oakley's most famous stunts, was an easy trick to perform by cheating. The shooter and his accomplice simply ran a wire through the cigarette. At the report of the gun, the accomplice touched the wire with his tongue, knocking off the ashes. Even Annie's candle trick, which had so impressed Sitting Bull, could be done by cheaters. Instead of placing the candle in the open, cheaters put it in front of a block of wood. If their bullet hit anywhere within three inches of the candle, the concussion from the bullet was enough to snuff the light. Frank told the story of one faker he had seen doing a piano trick in a New York theater. The man played a tune by hitting disks that hung from each piano key. Halfway through the act his gun jammed—but the piano kept on playing anyway. The man's accomplice in the orchestra apparently had failed to see what was happening and had kept on playing.[18]

6.

Buffalo Bill and His Wild West

William F. Cody was a young man of twenty-six when he got into show business. It happened rather on a whim, when the dime novelist Ned Buntline persuaded him to star in a melodrama called *Scouts of the Prairie*. Cody, popularly known as Buffalo Bill, was a genuine prairie scout, so the role was a natural one. He had never acted before, but that didn't seem to matter as he showed up at Nixon's Amphitheatre in Chicago on a December night in 1872 for his debut on the stage. The theater was packed, though the caliber of the audience was not much to the liking of the Chicago *Tribune,* which smelled the "presence of 2,000 bad breaths and twice as many unclean feet." The play, *Scouts of the Prairie,* stank too, but the audience hardly noticed. It was too busy admiring Buffalo Bill in his buckskin shirt and leggings and "fairly bristling with revolvers, knives, and rifles." What did it matter that Buffalo Bill obviously "had never been on any but the overland stage." He *looked* like a scout of the prairie, and that was his appeal. The New York *Herald* found him a good-looking fellow, tall and straight as an arrow, but ridiculous as an actor. The New York *Tribune* found the play "idiotic" and "tom foolery," but had to confess that Buffalo Bill had his moments. When he stood, tall and stalwart in a cloud of smoke and dust, pistols blazing and a heap of dead Indians at his feet, Buffalo Bill was sublime.[1]

In moments like those, Buffalo Bill was transformed from a minor actor into perhaps the best-known and best-loved western folk hero of his time. Cody became a symbol for all the best the frontier had to offer—the freedom, the excitement, and the heroism. He was tall and

35

strong, with long dark hair and a dark goatee. Drama critic Amy Leslie called him "the most imposing man in appearance that America ever grew." She detected "a hint of the border desperado" lurking in "his blazing eyes" and a "poetic fierceness" in his "mien and coloring."[2] William F. Cody was a likable man, generous, friendly, and easy-going. His biggest fault—his heavy drinking—would become as legendary as his virtues.

During the 1870s, Cody starred in many plays similar to *Scouts of the Prairie* and was the central figure in a number of dime novels, all of which romanticized the life he had led as a scout and Indian fighter on the western plains. Though the stories became so glorified that it was almost impossible to separate fact from fiction, the man Buffalo Bill was genuine. He was born in Scott County, Iowa, on February 26, 1846, the son of Mary Ann and Isaac Cody. The Codys moved to Kansas in 1854 and settled in the Salt Creek Valley near Leavenworth. When Isaac Cody died in 1857, young Will went to work for a neighbor, driving an ox team for fifty cents a day. Before the age of twenty, Cody became an accomplished wrangler, hunter, and plainsman. He was only fourteen when he rode for a short time with the Pony Express, once covering 322 miles in twenty-one hours and forty minutes, which was said to be the third longest ride in Pony Express history. When he was sixteen, he worked as a guide and scout for the Ninth Kansas Volunteers in an expedition to the Kiowa and Comanche country, and in 1864 he enlisted in the Union Army. When the Civil War ended, he worked as an Indian scout and dispatch bearer for the army in Kansas and for a time drove a stagecoach between Fort Kearney and Plum Creek in Nebraska. In October 1867 he was commissioned at five hundred dollars a month to supply 12 buffalo a day for the Kansas Pacific Railroad, which was laying track westward across the Kansas prairie. Cody's buffalo helped to feed the crew of twelve hundred track layers. He worked for the railroad for eight months, killed 4,280 buffalo—and acquired the name Buffalo Bill.

After that, Cody found more work as a scout and guide, mostly for the U.S. Fifth Cavalry during the western Indian campaigns of 1868–76. Between October 1868 and October 1869, he took part in seven expeditions and nine Indian fights. He acquired a reputation for accurate marksmanship, total recall of terrain, knowledge of Indian ways, courage, and endurance, though some historians would question the truth of it. However, many of his contemporaries, including generals Eugene A. Carr, Philip H. Sheridan, C. C. Augur, and W. H. Emory, spoke highly of him. Cody was awarded the Medal of Honor in 1872, and fought his most famous Indian fight on July 17, 1876, when he killed and scalped the Cheyenne warrior Yellow Hair near Montrose, Nebraska.³

On the stage, Cody found a new way of life. For a decade he toured the theaters from fall to spring with his troupe, the Buffalo Bill Combination, and spent his summers guiding hunting parties or working as a scout. Though he was married and had a ranch at North Platte, Nebraska, Cody spent little time at home.

By the time Annie Oakley and Frank Butler met Cody, he was thirty-nine years old and had left his Buffalo Bill Combination behind to embark on a new business enterprise—Buffalo Bill's Wild West. The show was a combination rodeo-drama, which romanticized life in the frontier West. Cowboys rode bucking broncos, Mexicans twirled lariats, and Indians beat tom-toms and went on the warpath. They burned a settler's cabin and ambushed the Deadwood stagecoach. A prairie schooner lumbered across the show lot, and a Pony Express rider changed horses with lightning speed. Buffalo Bill's Wild West was the forerunner of innumerable western movies and television programs. Cody hired genuine cowboys and scouts and made arrangements with the government to exhibit real Indians, mostly Pawnee and Sioux. There were buffalo, elk, mountain sheep, and hundreds of horses on the show lot. The show's charm, in fact, was rooted in its authenticity, right down to the Deadwood coach, which in the old days had made the run between Cheyenne and Deadwood via Fort Laramie.

The show was inaugurated in 1883 and would last until 1913. There would be many imitators over the years, but Buffalo Bill's was the first Wild West show, and the greatest. Some have called it the greatest outdoor show in American history. "America's National Entertainment, A Visit West in Three Hours," the advertisements read. And so it was. Americans flocked to the show lot, paid fifty cents admission (twenty-five for children) and took seats in the tall canvas-covered grandstands. They formed a horseshoe around a big, rectangular arena, which stood open to the sky. Here, as the Cowboy Band struck up the "Star-Spangled Banner" and the show began, the mythic image of the cowboy, the Indian, Buffalo Bill, and the American West itself was established in the American mind.⁴

The action sprang from behind a white canvas curtain at the far end of the arena. As the curtain opened, a band of Indians in full warpaint dashed in on horseback, their yells mingling with the sound of the bells around their ponies' necks. With a quick wheel and a double turn, they pulled up short, just feet from the reserved seat section. The curtain parted again, and cowboys dashed into view, followed by a band of Mexican vaqueros. They flew down the track, waving their hats, and drew up with a sudden halt. And then, with a flourish of trumpets, Buffalo Bill himself dashed down in front of the line. He wore a buckskin jacket with fringe down the arms and a wide-brimmed sombrero that bent in the force of the wind. He rode a big gray horse that pulled up short, in a puff of dust, just feet from the center grandstand.

"Are you ready? Go!" Buffalo Bill shouted, and the line of men and animals grew animated, turning instantly into a colorful kaleidoscope. Indians, with feathers flying, rode full tilt around and around the arena, and the cowboys and Mexicans—sometimes in the saddle and sometimes out—flew by like the wind. There were shouts and war whoops, the barking of revolvers and the cracking of turbines. It made the blood tingle and the children hide their heads.[5]

The show was beginning its third year when Annie Oakley showed up in Louisville, Kentucky, for the three-day tryout Cody had promised her. She and Frank took a car out Walnut Street to the Louisville Baseball Park, where the Wild West show had pitched camp. It was early when they arrived, and Cody was nowhere to be found. He apparently was out with the troupe in the daily street parade, and the camp was deserted. According to Annie, she took the opportunity "to get her hand in a bit" before the show began that afternoon at three. As she and Frank carried an armful of shotguns into the arena, they realized suddenly that they weren't alone.

"I noticed a man standing at a corner of the grandstand and thought it was someone who had just wandered into the grounds," Annie said.[6] He certainly didn't look like a part of the Wild West. He wore a cutaway coat and a derby hat and carried a fancy cane. Annie paid him no attention as she picked up a shotgun and began winging clay pigeons from a trap. She fired fast, with her gun upside down or rightside up, with her left hand or her right. Finished, she was laying her smoking gun on a barrel when the stranger came running across the diamond crying, "Fine! Wonderful! have you got some photographs with your gun?" Unbeknownst to Annie, she couldn't have run through her act that morning before a more important member of the show. He was Nate Salsbury, Wild West business manager. He was so impressed with Annie's practice round that, according to Annie, he hired her on the spot without even consulting Cody. A woman sharpshooter on the bill would be a novelty—especially a woman who could shoot like that. He ordered a woodcut of her and had her posters printed before they'd even signed an agreement. Annie was thrilled.

"I afterwards heard that he told Colonel Cody that I was a real 'daisy' and completely laid the captain 'away in the shade,'" she said in one of the few boastful remarks that ever would make print. According to Annie, Salsbury ordered seven thousand dollars' worth of printing about her, an impressive amount considering she was an unknown and the show's advertising rarely named performers.[7]

Nate Salsbury knew a good act when he saw one. He was a highly respected actor and playwright who had given up his successful company, the Troubadours, to manage the Wild West. He was Cody's partner, who worked behind the scenes to oversee every detail of finance and planning. It was Nate Salsbury who lined up members of the show for introductions that morning as they returned from the street parade. There was Buffalo Bill himself, his big hat in his hand as he bent over to say hello. He took to calling Annie Missie, a nickname that stuck and would be used by her intimate friends for the rest of her life.[8] She called him the Colonel and liked him right away. He "was the kindest hearted, broadest minded, simplest, most loyal man I ever knew," she would say. "He was courtesy itself, and more like a patron than an employer. . . . His relations with everyone he came in contact with were the most cordial and trusting of any man I ever saw."[9]

That day, Annie met William Sweeney and members of his cowboy band. They lined up with Jule Keen, the Wild West treasurer, and John Burke, press agent. John Nelson, who had guided Brigham Young to Utah, lined up with his Sioux wife and children. Buck Taylor, the original "King of the Cowboys," towered above everyone at a full six-four. A cowpuncher since boyhood, he could pick his hat off the ground from a speeding horse, throw a steer by the horns, and tie it single-handed. Johnny Baker, the "Cowboy Kid," looked as young as his fifteen years. He had grown up in North Platte, where he'd tagged Buffalo Bill around, hoping to hold his horse. When Cody started his Wild West, Johnny had begged to go along. Cody virtually adopted the boy, taught him to shoot, and made him a star.[10] Now Johnny was as much a part of the Wild West as the Sioux and Pawnee Indians with names like White Eagle, Dave, and Little Brave, and the cowboys, Bronco Bill, Bill Bullock, Tom Clayton, Coyote Bill, and Bridle Bill—probably the first cowboys Annie Oakley had ever met. She walked down the line, shaking hands and nodding hello to each. "Every head bowed before me and friendly rough hands covered mine," she said. "The chiefs, followed by their tribes, passed with a 'How! Washtay!' meaning 'All is good.' There was I facing the real Wild West, the first white woman to travel with what society might have considered an impossible outfit." [11]

Yes, there was Annie Oakley facing the real Wild West, a land of which she had never been a part. But legend would not remember such details. As Annie passed down the line and became a member of Buffalo Bill's Wild West, her life was set on a course that would transform the little Ohio girl into one of the most famous western characters of all time. Though Annie never lied about her Ohio heritage, and though the Wild West showbill presented her as the exhibition shooter she was, from now on Americans would know Annie Oakley as the western girl.

7.

In the Arena

Annie Oakley was a virtual unknown when she joined Buffalo Bill's Wild West. But she secured a solo spot on the program immediately and remained for seventeen years, billed simply and modestly as "Annie Oakley, the peerless wing and rifle shot." In the early years, she appeared midway through the program, after the riding of the Pony Express and Buffalo Bill's duel with Yellow Hand. But in time she secured the number two spot, a move that press agent Burke said was calculated to put the audience at ease with the continuous crack of firearms: "Women and children see a harmless woman there, and they do not get worried." [1]

Annie did ease the audience into her act, using a light load of shot at first and increasing it gradually. Her act was short; in her later years it lasted only about ten minutes. But it was an act so skillful and charming that it would endear her in the hearts of a generation, no matter what its length. She didn't just walk into the arena, she tripped in from the grandstand gangway, waving, bowing, and blowing kisses. [2] She wore a short skirt that fell just below her knees and a blouse that hung loosely about her waist. This allowed her the freedom of movement so necessary for a shooter. Her outfits were simple, but they were not plain. She embroidered flowers on her skirts and stitched ribbon trim along the hems, a skill she had learned years ago at the Darke County Infirmary. The skirts were A-line or pleated and usually blue or light brown. Her white collars were starched, giving her a wholesome, well-pressed look. She stood out, coy and sportive, among the rough characters of the Wild West. Always original, Annie pinned a six-pointed star to her sombrero

41

and laced up a pair of pearl-buttoned leggings. She was so particular about them that she cut and fit them herself, as a reporter learned one day in Toledo. "I remarked on the perfection of the fit," the reporter wrote, "and she told me that she cut and fitted every pair she wore as it was impossible to have them made to suit her."[3]

Fern Campbell Swartwout knew all about Annie's perfectionism. "If there ever was any one particular about their clothes, it was Missie," she wrote. "Every seam had to be finished just right, and everything had to match perfectly. It was very hard to get any one to sew for her that could please her." Annie's niece Irene Patterson Black said Annie was so particular you could almost call her "cranky." "Everything had to be just so," Irene said. "She was very, very particular."[4]

Annie's perfect-fitting leggings extended from her knees to the tops of her low, black shoes, which said as much about her personality as the leggings did: Annie Oakley was always practical. Low shoes permitted quick and easy movement, and their dark color served well in the dusty arena.

As her act began, she ran to the center of the arena, where she took her place by a plain wooden table, draped with a silken cover and laden with rifles and shotguns. Frank stood by, unannounced, to load the traps and release the clay birds. They came singly at first, then in pairs, triplets, and finally, four at a time. No matter, Annie broke them, never hesitating. She was a whirl of motion—notably accurate, incredibly fast. Her talent is documented in countless newspaper articles. "She rarely missed the glass balls . . . and when she did miss the first shot she invariably broke the ball with the second," said the New Orleans *Daily Picayune.* The Portsmouth (Mass.) *Times* counted her shots one spring afternoon. Her score was fifty-five out of a possible fifty-six, "and the last one only missed because she tripped over the uneven ground." The Dallas *Morning News* counted the shotguns on her table. There were ten, and these "she loaded and discharged with faultless accuracy and great rapidity."[5]

In addition to being fast, she was ambidextrous. She took a pistol in her left hand and one in her right, fired them simultaneously, and broke target after target. She smashed balls, firing a rifle held upside down over her head or while she was lying on her back across a chair. Sometimes she broke balls fastened on the end of a rope as Frank twirled it around his head. "Miss Annie Oakley ruined more glass balls within a given time than I would like to pay for in a week," said the New York *Evening News.* "She slammed a rifle through the air in almost any old direction, and when she snapped the trigger there was a broken ball falling ground ward . . . As fast as the target flew upward, so fast did Miss Oakley bring about their destruction. She shot from almost every conceivable position."[6]

Annie was more than a dead shot: she was an athlete, quick and agile. She grabbed a glass ball and threw it up herself, surprising anyone who thought that women couldn't throw. The ball sailed high, and Annie picked up her gun, fired, and hit it in midair. Then she tossed up two balls at a time, smashed the first, twirled completely around, and smashed the other before it hit the ground.[7] She was "so wonderfully quick" and her shots were so "swift and true" that the New York *Tribune* decided she had a "finger touch on the trigger which must be finer than the pressure on a hairspring in a watch." "Her quickness and accuracy of aim were astonishing," said the Providence (R.I.) *Journal.* "The ease with which she loaded, aimed and fired was most marvelous," said the Fall River (Mass.) *Evening News.* "She handles a shotgun with an easy familiarity that causes the men to marvel and the women to assume airs of contented superiority," said the Springfield (Mass.) *Republican.* Seldom one to boast, Annie seemed at ease with her skill, and she spoke of it matter-of-factly: "I feel now and then," she once said, "as if I could not miss."[8]

A favorite with audiences was her mirror stunt, in which Annie turned her back to the target and aimed by sighting in a hand-held mirror or, sometimes, a shiny table knife.[9] Two other feats, both original, were about equally popular. In one, Annie laid a shotgun in the dirt about ten feet on the far side of her gun table. She hurried back around to the other side of the table and waited for Frank to spring a clay bird. As he released it from the trap, she ran forward, hurdled the table, picked up her shotgun, and broke the bird before it landed. That was indeed some feat, considering it took only four or five seconds from the time the bird was released for it to hit the ground.

To get an idea of just how quick Annie was, a newspaper once timed her during a feat at the Alhambra Theatre of Varieties in London. Frank stood on a chair and held out a four-inch tin disk. Annie stood with her back to him. When she called "pull!" Frank let the disk drop. Annie whirled around, fired, and nipped it before it hit the floor. The newspaper calculated that since a falling object drops sixteen feet in a second and since Frank held the disk eight feet off the floor, that Annie had to turn and sight in one half second. That, the newspaper said, is "quite a clever performance."[10]

Annie Oakley doing her famous mirror stunt. (Courtesy of the Buffalo Bill Historical Center, Cody, Wyo.)

In the arena, Annie saved her most difficult feat for last. It required one rifle, five shotguns, eleven glass balls—and just ten seconds on the clock. She laid the shotguns on the gun table, all neatly in a row. The rifle she took in her hands and turned upside down. Frank stood ready to throw the glass balls. As the first one went up, Annie broke it with a charge from her inverted rifle. She dropped the rifle, picked up a shotgun, discharged both barrels and broke two more balls in a flash. She put the shotgun down, picked up another, discharged both barrels and shattered two more balls, exchanging guns five times until she had broken eleven glass balls. The stunt, said the Toronto *Mail and Express,* was "her cleverest number," accomplished "in the wonderful short time of 10 seconds." [11]

And with that, Annie laid her last smoking shotgun on the table, kissed her hand to the audience, and took off running across the arena "like a deer," "an antelope," or "a young colt," never stopping for breath until the last moment before she disappeared behind the white canvas curtains. [12] And always, just before she ducked out of sight, she gave a humorous little kick. That little kick became as much a part of Annie Oakley's act as the glass balls she smashed. It was a mark of her showmanship, just like the silver star on her hat. Annie knew how to package herself. She was more than a sharpshooter, she was an actress. She knew how to win an audience, how to charm them, and how to make them laugh. That was something she had learned on the variety stage and in the Sells Brothers Circus ring. She won her audience over with a little-girl charm that never aged and an actor's sense of timing and humor.

Nate Salsbury wasn't kidding when he said Annie was "a daisy" who "laid the captain away in the shade." Annie's act was far superior to that of Captain Bogardus because she went beyond the simple smashing of clay birds. She injected humor, pantomime, and drama into the act amid the skillful shooting. Annie was all motion and personality. She drew the audience in with her expressions and her movements. With a particularly difficult shot coming up, for example, she gracefully tossed her long hair over her shoulder and stood, hands on hips, as if concentrating. If she missed the shot, she stamped her foot in a fit of temper and disgust. If she made it, she gave an unmistakable little kick of delight. [13]

"When she doesn't hit a ball she pouts," reported the New York *Sun.* "She evidently thinks a good deal of her pout, because she turns to the audience to show it off." When she missed a couple of shots in Kansas

City one day, she "became exasperated," the Kansas City *Star* reported. She was so annoyed that she snatched Frank's hat off his head, tossed it in the air, and "wrecked it with one shot." When that didn't change her luck at the clay birds, she tried an old gamblers' superstition: she calmly laid her gun on the ground and walked around it. The trick worked, the *Star* said, because "the next was a 'dead bird.' Only in this case it happened to be a 'mud pie.'" [14] Annie Oakley really wasn't exasperated, nor was she superstitious. She was just a performer, doing her best to entertain an audience. Walking around her gun to change her luck was an element of humor in her act, and she would do it again and again.

One day, a reporter from the New York *Sun* caught her doing a trick intended only to please the audience. She had lain down on a chair and was preparing to shoot upside down over her head when she noticed that one of her assistants had gotten in the line of fire. At the sight of him, "she jumped up and drew a deep breath as if she had just missed killing him," the *Sun* said. When the assistant noticed his mistake, he "gasped as if he had never seen a gun before," and flew out of the target area "as if he intended to drop on his knees and utter a prayer of thanksgiving." Annie and her other assistant just looked at each other "as if they had saved the nation." Then she lay down again and broke glass balls "while the audience applauded till it got as purple as Buffalo Bill's shirt." A reporter from the New York *Commercial Advertiser* caught Annie in the same act another day and told how "the careless people in the audience" laughed and "the tender-hearted" shuddered because they thought the man had escaped being shot. Of course, it was all contrived, but that was show business. [15]

The "careless people in the audience" got a laugh another day when Annie, using a "shower of small shot from her gun," tried to clear some freeloading spectators off the roof of a house across the street. [16] In Chicago one afternoon, she had fun with some birds that happened to fly over the arena. "She laughingly aimed" at the flock and "would have taken a chance shot at them," a reporter said, if Frank Butler "had not cautioned her not to break the laws and waste powder." Another day she popped a toy balloon that "a child had chanced to let slip from its fingers." [17] Critic Amy Leslie once called Annie "an actress of no mean pretensions" and said that the comedy in her act was "half the performance." [18]

Newspapers talked about Annie's frisky bits of business, her kittenish manner, her saucy antics, and her fetching ways, which never failed to elicit applause. Her popularity was apparent to anyone who ever attended Buffalo Bill's Wild West. "There never was a question that she deserved her position as star performer," press agent Dexter Fellows wrote. "She was a consummate actress, with a personality that made itself felt as soon as she entered the arena. Even before her name was on the lips of every man, woman, and child in America and Europe, the sight of this frail girl among the rough plainsmen seldom failed to inspire enthusiastic plaudits."[19] Annie Oakley was a woman in a man's world. Her femininity added to her appeal and was the initial key to her great success.

Annie Oakley's skill with a gun created her biggest problem in the arena: she shot so easily and quickly that some people thought she was cheating. "It is all so very easy and simple, and looks it, that the hardest thing in the world," she said, "is to make people believe that there is no cheating." To make them believe, she sometimes missed on purpose, a trick she had learned from Frank. "Occasionally, I have indeed missed on purpose," she admitted, "because it looks so easy if you never miss, and the spectators might think there was a trick in it."[20]

In one town, the spectators were so convinced that the targets contained some explosive that went off when Annie fired that they appointed a committee to investigate. When the committee found no trickery, some people were surprised that Annie did not demand an apology. "Did you not consider the insinuation a deliberate insult?" one reporter asked. "Did you not ask the committee to apologize?" "Oh, no," Annie replied good-naturedly. With her reputation unharmed and her pride very much intact, she was able to brush the incident off. "It is only natural that people should try to find fault," she said. "Perhaps, had I been among the audience, I might have done so myself."[21]

Annie found the French to be the biggest doubters. One time a man was so sure that her act was not fair and square that he threw his watch up for her to shoot. "He has never been able to tell the time by that watch since," Annie said. "Doubtful whether he ever picked up a hundredth part of the pieces."[22]

Another dispute centered on Annie's use of shotguns in the Wild West arena. Many people who knew little about firearms mistook her shotguns for rifles and felt cheated when they learned the truth. After all, rifles fired bullets; shotguns fired shot pellets, more than two hundred of them in a load. Logically, it seemed harder to hit a clay pigeon with a single bullet than with two hundred shot pellets. But there was a very good reason for using shotguns in the arena: They were safer. Rifles could shoot precisely for up to one thousand yards and be dangerous at distances of up to a mile. Shotguns, on the other hand, were short-range weapons, seldom effective beyond sixty yards. Rifles had grooved barrels, which spun the bullet quickly, and more accurately, toward its target. Shotguns had smooth barrels. By loading their shotguns—or smooth-bored rifles—with a light load of powder, there was little chance the shot pellets would sail very far, which was an important consideration in an arena lined on three sides with hundreds of spectators. Annie did her shooting while facing the open end of the arena, where no spectators sat. What pellets did not fall harmlessly into the arena were caught by the white canvas curtains that separated the arena from the back lot of the show.

According to Johnny Baker, who also used shot, it was just about as hard to break a glass ball at twenty yards with a light load of shot as it would have been with a rifle bullet. Baker said that Buffalo Bill and Doc Carver actually had used rifle bullets when they first started the Wild West but stopped using them after they received bills for broken glass from greenhouses eight or ten blocks from the arena. Press agent Dexter Fellows also defended the use of shot in the arena. "Their use of such ammunition in no sense reflects upon their skill with arms," he wrote. "Any one of them could put a clean hole through a coin tossed into the air or perform other spectacular stunts using real rifle bullets." [23]

Knowledgeable sportsmen like Ralph Greenwood, who wrote for *Shooting and Fishing*, were surprised to learn that anyone thought Annie smashed the clay birds with anything other than a shotgun. "Certainly Miss Oakley makes no pretense of shooting bullets," Greenwood said, "and any one who chooses to inquire will learn that no bullets are fired in Buffalo Bill's exhibition." Annie did the bulk of her work in the arena with 12-gauge, double-barreled shotguns of Lancaster, Francotte, Scott, and Parker makes. [24]

According to Fern Campbell Swartwout—who, it must be noted, was not always a reliable source on the Wild West—what rifles Annie did use in the arena were rebored for shot, just like those of Buffalo Bill. [25] He used a .44-caliber Winchester repeating rifle, 1873 model, bored out smooth and taking a long shell loaded with twenty grains of black powder and about one quarter ounce of No. 7½ chilled shot. In his performance, Cody shot glass balls from horseback. He rode slightly behind another horseman, who tossed balls into the air while Cody smashed them with his charges of shot. "It is true he is not shooting a bullet, and the public may think they are deceived; in one way perhaps they are," Ralph Greenwood wrote, "but if anyone thinks it is an easy performance to break those balls with a charge of shot, shooting from horse-back, they are mistaken. I have seen Col. Cody's act many times, and every time I see it it delights me. Whenever he misses a ball he works the lever of the Winchester the second time, and he very seldom fails to break the ball with the second shot." [26]

Although Annie was able to shoot balls from horseback, she never did so in the Wild West arena, perhaps because she did not want to upstage Cody. Johnny Baker shattered clay pigeons while standing on his head, a feat that always brought a laugh because his head invariably ended up resting on a stone. He'd stop his act and rub his head before getting down to business again. Baker's act was amusing, but according to Frank Butler, shooting while standing on one's head wasn't very difficult. Annie had tried it and done well—but only in private and after modestly buckling her skirt down so it wouldn't fall over her head. [27] Today, a woman would simply slip into a pair of jeans, but that was never an option for Annie Oakley. She had very definite opinions on what was proper for a lady—and standing on one's head in public was not, let alone putting on a pair of trousers. Indeed, the conservative and proper Annie Oakley probably never even gave the question a thought. She was a contradiction when it came to a woman's role. While she was comfortable wielding a gun and living in a masculine world, and while in later years she would be held up as an example of the liberated woman, she herself wanted most to be considered a lady. And ladies wore skirts, even if it meant some inconvenience.

As famous as she later became, Annie Oakley never claimed to be "the champion," and in fact detested the word. It was a simple matter of practicality. If she claimed to be the champion, she would have to face any shooter who challenged her, and Annie Oakley had neither the time nor the desire to do so. She had a social reputation to defend, and a living to earn. She and Frank feared that an open challenge might force her to associate with an undesirable person, such as one woman stage shooter who had killed a young girl while trying to shoot an apple off the girl's head. Instead of showing remorse, the shooter capitalized on the incident by billing herself thereafter as the "woman killer." [28] Annie Oakley wanted no part of that. She cared deeply about her reputation, almost to the point of obsession. She put herself above—and rightly so—the many fakes and undesirables in the shooting business. The less her name was associated with theirs, the better.

Annie's reputation was an issue from the moment she joined the Wild West. To her, it was no small matter that she was the only white woman with the show when she joined and that she traveled in the company of Mexican vaqueros and cowboys, who did not have the best of reputations in the 1880s. It didn't take the proper and upright Annie Oakley long to set them straight about where she stood, and they seemed to go out of their way to honor her wishes. "If, at any time they should meet me on the street, when they were with a man not of the highest character or slightly intoxicated, perhaps, they would all cross the street and avoid me." Never, Annie said, "has one of those cowboys made a remark to me which he would not make to an 8-year-old child. They were certainly very considerate of my feelings." [29]

One night nearly every member of the Wild West troupe went on a midseason binge in North Platte, Nebraska, enjoying a frolicsome night of "hard liquor" in Guy Lang's saloon. The next day, sixty percent of the boys were still "very, very tight," according to press agent Dexter Fellows. The show went off anyway, though Cody "was rocking in his saddle," and the Cowboy Band was playing off key. Fellows said a Mexican "got all tangle up in his rope," and none of the cowhands could keep his seat on a bronco. "Only two of our Western acts went off as they were intended," Fellows said. "They were those of Annie Oakley and Johnny Baker, who were in full possession of their faculties." While the rest of the troupe was "poured out of North Platte," not so Annie Oakley. Annie Oakley didn't smoke, cuss, or drink hard liquor, though Dexter Fellows said she did drink an occasional beer—when someone else paid the bill. [30]

8.

A Season with Sitting Bull

It was late on a Friday afternoon when the Atlantic Express pulled in at the train depot in Buffalo, New York. A large-bodied man sporting a bushy mustache and a diamond in his lapel stepped out of a car and planted his feet squarely on the coach steps. There could be no mistaking John Burke. He was chief promoter of Buffalo Bill's Wild West, and its most conspicuous worker. Was there a notice to be published in the Podunk *Gazette?* Burke got it. Was there an entertainer to be hired or a government endorsement to be had? Burke secured it. Good friends said he had "nothing more than wind and brass as a stock in trade," backed by a tremendous popularity in every newspaper, railway, and theatrical office in the country. Perhaps it was his "grand simplicity" that endeared him to people. The Wild West show meant more to him than anything else in the world, and he had a way of inspiring enthusiasm in the minds of editors and reporters. Burke adopted the nickname "Arizona John" and the title "Major," though he had no claim to either. He was an easterner by birth who had made his living as a stock-company actor, the manager of an acrobatic troupe, and the agent for a number of stage celebrities. He had known William F. Cody since the old days of *Scouts of the Prairie* and now idolized the man he promoted, right down to wearing his hair as long as Buffalo Bill's.[1]

Burke was jubilant this day when he spotted a reporter from the Buffalo *Courier* standing on the depot platform. He had a story that would write itself. "He is ours. I have captured him," Burke shouted to the reporter. And then, none other than the great chief Sitting Bull him-

51

self emerged from the car behind Burke. Sitting Bull wore a bonnet of forty large eagle feathers and a buckskin tunic heavily trimmed with beads. A medicine bag hung at his side and a crucifix from his neck. In his hand he carried a bow and arrows and a long peace pipe trimmed with ribbon. Sitting Bull hopped aboard one of Miller's open carriages and rode down Michigan Street toward the driving park, where Buffalo Bill's Wild West was performing. John Burke had brought off a great coup: he had persuaded Sitting Bull to travel for a season with the show.[2]

"He is Buffalo Bill's guest. But I've had a tough time in getting him here," Burke told the man from the *Courier*. Burke had gone all the way to the Standing Rock Reservation, where Sitting Bull lived in a cabin on the Grand River. Persuading him to join the show had been a matter of money and promises, though legend would credit Annie Oakley for the coup. The story goes that Sitting Bull refused Burke's overtures time and again—until someone pulled out a photograph of Little Sure Shot and told him that if he joined the Wild West he would be able to see her every day. Within an hour the agreement had been made and sealed.[3] Touching as the legend is, it seems highly unlikely that Annie Oakley figured in Sitting Bull's decision. In fact, it appears that John Burke didn't even know the two were acquainted. And Sitting Bull certainly did not mention Annie Oakley as he rode out Michigan Street. Instead, he said he had consented to join the show because he wanted "to see the new White Father at Washington," President Grover Cleveland, who had been inaugurated only three months earlier. Thinking that the change in administration might mean a change for the Indians, Sitting Bull wanted to talk to Cleveland. The Wild West was his means to get "to the great ʿᵊpee at Washington." Sitting Bull also was interested in the money he could make. When he signed a four-month contract on June 6, 1885, he demanded $50 a week, an advance of two weeks' pay, a bonus of $125—and the sole right to sell his photographs and autographs.[4]

He arrived at the driving park in the midst of the afternoon performance and sat in his carriage in the sun, watching Buffalo Bill shoot balls from horseback and Indians attacking the settler's cabin. He apparently took an interest in what he saw because he "gave vent to frequent monosyllabic utterances of approval." As members of the show finished their acts, they came over to the carriage to get a look at the famous Indian. Among those who pressed forward, said the *Courier*, was "the clever and adept feminine markswoman Annie Oakley," who was the only one in the troupe who seemed to know the old chief. She walked right up to him and inquired about a red silk handkerchief and some coins she had sent to him. "'I got them,' Sitting Bull said through his interpreter, 'but I left them at home for safety. I am very glad to see you. I have not forgotten you and feel pleased that you want to remember me.'"[5]

The meeting this day only reinforced the truth of her statement that she had met Sitting Bull before. According to Annie, they became reacquainted as the show pressed on to Detroit, Saginaw, Grand Rapids, and Boston, and any condescension she had shown earlier seemed to disappear. He "made a great pet of me," Annie said. "He is a dear, faithful, old friend, and I've great respect and affection for him."[6]

Surprisingly, John Burke never turned Annie's friendship with Sitting Bull into a press event, which could mean he didn't know until later that they were acquainted. If he did know, it seems odd that Annie was not even mentioned the day Burke staged an adoption ceremony on the Wild West lot. Instead, it was Nate Salsbury whom Burke ushered into Sitting Bull's tent. The peace pipe was lighted, puffed, and passed around the circle, and Salsbury, much as Annie had, became a member of Sitting Bull's tribe and took the name "Little White Chief."[7]

With Sitting Bull on the show bill, promotional events were easy to arrange, though Annie Oakley never seemed to be a part of them. In St. Louis, Burke arranged a meeting between Sitting Bull and his own old army foe, General Eugene A. Carr, who happened to be in town on the same Saturday as the Wild West. Burke directed Carr to the Southern Hotel, where Sitting Bull already was seated on one of the rich divans in the hotel parlor. Beside him sat his friend Crow Eagle, dressed in a boiled white shirt with the initials W. F. C. on the bosom tab. When William F. Cody showed up with a handful of reporters in tow, John Burke's press event took shape. Carr "shook hands cordially with the Bull and the Eagle," the St. Louis *Republican* said, but there was a coolness on the Indians' part that "indicated they did not feel kindly toward the man who had interfered with their fun years ago." Reporters complained that Sitting Bull spoke "few words" and replied "in monosyllables," but Buffalo Bill came to the Indians' defense. "The Indian feels no resentment against a great foeman," he said. If Sitting Bull was a man of few words, that was just the Indian way. "The Indian is too grave for the newspaper correspondent," Cody said. "His thoughts do not run so rapidly, and he does not like a long interview."[8]

But, of course, there would be many long interviews as John Burke sought all the free publicity he could get. The meeting in the Southern Hotel was just one of many that Burke would arrange that season to promote Buffalo Bill's Wild West. Another gimmick, which he used for years, was a "frontier barbecue," rustled up by the Wild West cooks. One took place on a Friday afternoon in Boston for about a dozen reporters who arrived at Beacon Park shortly after noon. They walked past a corral full of horses and down a path toward a big tent, from which the aroma of roast beef drifted their way. As they ducked under the big canvas awning they saw cowboys turning huge joints of juicy beef over a campfire. Nate Salsbury and Buffalo Bill Cody himself implored the city slickers to take a seat on a wooden bench and spread a napkin over their knees. But that was about the extent of the table etiquette. Waiters carrying steaming pans of beef came round, and each guest took a sharpened stick, pierced a rack of ribs, and ate it "with the appliances with which nature had provided him." To wash down "such viands as stuck in one's throat," reporters drank "an abundance of delectable liquor," all provided free of charge by the Wild West.[9]

Dessert at such affairs was an interview with Sitting Bull. How did Sitting Bull like the East and its people? a reporter would ask through an interpreter. "They treated me very kindly," Sitting Bull would answer, "and when I return to my people I shall tell them all about our friends among the white men, and what I have seen." And invariably came the question, which was asked over and over again all season long: What really had happened during the Custer massacre? Regardless of how often the question was asked, Sitting Bull refused to answer. He "raised his hand and shook it warningly," one reporter wrote, and then muttered these words: "That is another day. I fought for my people. My people said I was right. I will always answer to my people. The friends of the dead pale-faces must answer for those who are dead."[10]

Years later, the same question was put to Annie Oakley, though she could shed no light on the topic. "Sitting Bull seemed to think it served [Custer] right," Annie said in an interview in 1917. "You see, he had his whole fighting force and his war chiefs in hiding, and Custer came upon three hundred or more old men and women. He charged this outfit, which of course ran, and developed the trap." In the 1917 interview, an Annie Oakley grown sympathetic with the years, repeated, in her own broad and simple way, some of the stories she said Sitting Bull had told her during the show season of 1885. A favorite trick of the white man, Annie said, was to put two men on the scales with every cow weighed for the Sioux or to count every cow twice. Another trick, Annie said, was to serve "half and half instead of sugar—the other half being sand."[11]

In 1885, not everyone felt as kindly as Annie Oakley toward Sitting

Bull and his Indians. Some Wild West patrons hissed and booed as Sitting Bull rode by in the opening processional, and the newspapermen poked fun at "the murderer of Custer." "Sitting Bull is one of the finest looking Indians who ever committed murder," wrote the Detroit *Evening Journal.* Another newspaper compared Sitting Bull's face to "a New England pumpkin pie that has been sat upon." In Grand Rapids, Michigan, Sitting Bull was called "as mild mannered a man as ever cut a throat or scalped a helpless woman." [12]

People were kinder when the Wild West swung into Canada that year for its first trip outside the United States. Sitting Bull seemed relaxed in Canada, where he had lived peacefully in exile after the Custer fight. He took a ride on the St. Lawrence River and sailed down to Lachine, Quebec, to meet Chief Delisle of the Iroquois tribe. He boarded the steamer *Filgate* and ran the rapids, and in Montreal was greeted kindly by Mayor Beaugrand. He thanked the mayor for his hospitality and, through his interpreter, asked whether he could have some of the rolls of Canadian tobacco that he had seen outside the Wild West camp. Beaugrand promised to send him some. [13]

It was Sitting Bull's way to be generous. He had been sending a portion of his salary home to Standing Rock every week to his two wives and eleven children. What he didn't save, he lavished "in the most reckless manner" upon the bootblacks, the newsboys, and the other children he saw around the Wild West camp. [14] Poverty bothered Sitting Bull, who wondered what the white man would do for the Indian when he did not care for his own people. By the time the Wild West pounded in its stakes for the last stand of the season, Sitting Bull had had his fill of the white man's world.

"The wigwam is a better place for the red man," he said that fall. "He is sick of the houses, and the noises, and the multitudes of men. Sitting Bull longs for his wives and children. When he goes out the white men gather around him. They stare at him. They point fingers at him. He likes to be alone among his people. Traveling is interesting and it pleases Sitting Bull, but the forest is better and his family pleases him more." [15]

Sitting Bull had gotten to see the Great White Father in Washington—just as John Burke had promised he would. And except for the rudeness he endured, his life had not been hard. He had worked for only moments a day, appearing in the show's opening processional and riding in the Wild West street parade that preceded it. He had been the star Indian, but Buffalo Bill had not made a spectacle of him as Colonel Alvaren Allen had done when he'd taken Sitting Bull on a tour of fifteen

Sitting Bull and Buffalo Bill Cody in 1885, the year Sitting Bull traveled with the Wild West. (Courtesy of the Buffalo Bill Historical Center, Cody, Wyo.)

cities the year before. Allen had displayed Sitting Bull among the wax-works at the Eden Musée in New York and advertised him as "the slayer of Custer." [16] Buffalo Bill had allowed Sitting Bull more dignity than that. The chief had held his head high as he rode among his people in the parade that wound down Main Street in every town. The band had played, cowboys had sauntered by, and Buffalo Bill had ridden up front, looking the "beau ideal" of a horseman.

Also riding by had been "a pretty girl on a pretty horse," who, no doubt, was Annie Oakley. [17] It wasn't surprising that newspapermen had yet to learn her name. Her first year with Buffalo Bill's Wild West had been overshadowed by a figure much larger than she. But Annie hadn't cared much about that. She had found something more important than fame; she had found a home and a steady job. As long as she stayed with the Wild West, she would never be poor again. Her first season with Buffalo Bill had been a happy one, marred by only one sorrow, the death of Frank's poodle George. He had been caught in the rain, come down with pneumonia, and died while the Wild West was playing in Cleveland, Ohio. It had been a sad day for the whole Wild West camp. A company carpenter built a small wooden coffin for George, and Indian girls made wreaths and chanted hymns over him. A friend in Cleveland offered his lawn as a resting place, and two Wild West cowboys dug a grave. [18]

Annie and Frank covered George's body with the satin and velvet table cover they had used in their old act. They wouldn't need it any-more. George's life on the stage was over—and so was that of the shooting team of Butler and Oakley. Frank Butler had put away his guns and his high-top boots and already had stepped back into the shadow of his talented wife. Though Annie Oakley's name had yet to take hold, John Burke and Buffalo Bill were saying that she had brought good luck to the show. It finally was out of debt, and Cody boasted that the Wild West had made more money in 1885 than any other show on the road. Annie Oakley wasn't famous yet, but her star was on the rise.

9.

Summer in New York

New York was the richest city in the United States in 1886. Manhattan already had an impressive skyline, electricity, and thousands of telephones. The new Brooklyn Bridge spanned the East River, and architects were planning the first skyscraper with a steel skeleton, the eleven-story Tower Building at 50 Broadway. The city's population already had reached one and a half million.

Hoping to tap that huge populace, Erastus Wiman, president of the Staten Island Amusement Company, built an open-air arena and amphitheater on Staten Island that summer. He called it Erastina. Wiman strung electric arc lights around the field and set up a row of refreshment stands. Then he signed a summer contract with Buffalo Bill's Wild West, which chipped in by building an eight-thousand dollar dock at the new town of St. George and laying four miles of track to Erastina's gate. The Wild West had everything to gain from Wiman's venture. All summer long it would play under the wide, blue sky, and within sight of the largest city in America.[1]

Erastina was only a short, breezy ride across New York Bay from Manhattan, and soon the "land of the red man and the mustang" was the talk of the city. "Big red letters on every dead wall in town announce that it takes thirty-five minutes to get to the grounds, and that the Wild West is brought right to our doors," reported the New York *Herald*. Ferries ran from Brooklyn, Jersey City, Newark, Elizabethport, the Battery, and points along the North River. New Yorkers sailed out into the bay and past the new Statue of Liberty, which was to be dedicated

58

that fall. They docked at St. George, boarded a train, and rode the new rail line straight to the Wild West ticket booth. "How they did swarm in!" the *Herald* said. "Train after train packed full of sweltering humanity." It didn't take long for the big grandstands to fill with people, who didn't seem to mind the crush or "the bull-dozing of police." New Yorkers were so eager for a glimpse of the wild and lawless West that they "trod on each others' corns with glee." But, oh, it was worth it, the *Herald* said, because Buffalo Bill's Wild West "'whooped things up' in a way that made good its name."

"Staten Island Trembles Beneath the Tread of Painted Warriors on the War-Path," read the headlines. "Just Like Real Fighting, Indians Fall from Horses and Look Like Dead Men." New Yorkers liked the show so much that they came even on Sundays, when it did not play. They found entertainment enough just walking about the campgrounds, which were situated in a little patch of woods only five hundred yards from the water's edge. Here were the tents of the "long-haired cowboys" and the "greasy Mexicans," and that of Buffalo Bill himself. His tent was the biggest of the lot and "furnished in a most civilized manner" with Brussels carpet, easy chairs, and knickknacks.[2]

Here, too, was Annie Oakley's tent, which Amy Leslie described as a "bower of comfort and taste." Knickknacks and portraits sat on a table, and a folding chair stood by the entrance. Satin pillows, buffalo horns, cougar skins, and buckskin trappings were laid about "in artistic fash-ion," and on the floor was a bright Axminster carpet. And, of course, there were "guns, guns, guns everywhere," including a rack full of them in one corner. The tent, like the feminine shooter herself, was an incongruous mix of hard guns and soft pillows.[3]

Beyond Annie's tent and deeper in the woods stood the "rude habi-tations" of the Indians, which came in for the greatest share of publicity. After all, explained the New York *World*, "the sight beats anything that was ever pictured in a story book." A woman brought out her baby for admiration, and someone in the crowd chucked it under the chin and gave it a nickel. A little boy permitted a party of young ladies to swing him about to their hearts' content, and the New York boys found amusement in lifting up the edges of the tepees to peer inside.[4] The Wild West Indians were a constant focus of interest, and stories of their exploits, big and small, made the pages of the New York newspapers all summer long.

One Sunday morning the Indians astonished the congregation of a Baptist church by solemnly filing down the aisle and taking up a row of pews. When the organ played "Nearer, My God, to Thee," the Indians joined in singing, though they knew no English. They sang in the guttural Sioux tongue, but strictly adhering to the tune and meter. "Where they picked it up I cannot imagine," John Burke said, "but probably from some frontier missionary." New Yorkers smiled another day when they read that Nate Salsbury had treated the Indians to a feast of five hundred pies. No one revealed what kind of pies they were, except that they were "Yankee pies," and that the Indians, never having tasted such delicacies, devoured them with delight.[5]

Stories like that kept the Wild West in the news and the crowds at the gates. Within four weeks, the Wild West had attracted 360,000 visitors, an average of almost 14,000 a day. On Saturday, July 24, nearly 28,000 people showed up, so many that the Wild West couldn't seat them all. Four thousand were turned away at the gate, and the Wild West carpenters set to work building additional seats. No other attraction in New York had ever enjoyed such popularity.[6]

Annie Oakley was excited about the stand on Staten Island. She wanted to make a good impression, especially since Cody and Salsbury had added another woman sharpshooter to the troupe: Miss Lillian Frances Smith, "The California Huntress and Champion Girl Rifle Shot." Annie didn't much like Lillian, and with good reason: Lillian was going around bragging "that Annie Oakley was done for" now that she had joined the show.[7]

Lillian was about as good at bragging as she was at breaking glass balls. She'd been doing both since she was a girl back in California, where she was born in the fall of 1871. According to the Wild West program, Lillian was only seven years old when she "expressed herself as dissatisfied with 'dolls,' and wanted a 'little rifle.'" Her father, Levi Smith, bought her a .22-caliber Ballard rifle and became her biggest promoter. He entered her in local turkey shoots, where Lillian acquired a local reputation, much as Annie had done. At a turkey shoot in San Benito County, California, during the holidays of 1883, Lillian reportedly killed so many turkeys that the managers arranged with her "to drop out and give the boys a chance at the turkeys, too." When Lillian was only ten, she performed at Woodward gardens in San Francisco, "her marvelous accuracy and extreme youth creating the greatest sensation." She once broke 323 glass balls in a row and held a score of 495 of 500. Levi Smith was so sure of his daughter's talent that he held out a standing challenge to back her against anyone in the world for five thousand dollars. She claimed to be faster than Captain Bogardus and went so far as to challenge Doc Carver to a match at Pope's Theater in St. Louis. When the hour came and no Doc Carver with it, the St. Louis newspapers laughed. "The young lady," said the St. Louis *Republican,* "has every right to say that she frightened off 'the Evil Spirit of the Plains.'"[8]

There is no doubt that Lillian was a decent shot. In the Wild West arena, she broke twenty-five glass balls in a minute, struck a plate thirty times in fifteen seconds, and shot two balls revolving rapidly on a string around a pole. She had received press notices every bit as favorable as Annie Oakley's. The St. Louis *Republican* found her "graceful and skillful" in the handling of a rifle and revolver and said her performance was "one of the most catching features" of the show.[9]

Annie Oakley was in for some competition, and just how anxious she was about it has long been overlooked by biographers. Notably, it was after Lillian Smith joined the Wild West that Annie began lying about her age. The truth was that Annie was going on twenty-six, while Lillian was only fifteen. Competing against Lillian with guns was one thing, but what of Annie's youthful image? The short skirts, the loving kisses she blew, the way she ran lightly into the arena and gave a little kick on the way out endeared Annie to the public as a kind of schoolgirl-next-door, full of life and vigor. Youth was an important part of her image, and she must have felt very threatened indeed by the arrival of a fifteen-year-old competitor.

Though she never would admit it, Annie dealt with the problem quickly and decisively: she simply lopped six years off her age. From now on she would tell interviewers that she was born in 1866, not 1860.[10] Instantly, little Annie Oakley was a youthful girl of twenty again. The lie wasn't hard to cover because Annie was so tiny, and because she did look young. Even when she was a mature woman of forty, people would mistake her for a young woman of twenty-five. The lie became so entrenched that it would follow Annie to her grave, where the date of birth was left off her tombstone. It was a lie, pure and simple, but one that spoke worlds about Annie Oakley and Frank Butler. They would do what they had to, in order to survive in a tough, competitive world. Annie Oakley had a career to protect, and she would not let the likes of Lillian Smith destroy it.

Few people ever realized just how much Annie resented Lillian Smith, although signs of her resentment surfaced now and then. In her autobiography, Annie sneered at Lillian's "ample figure" and her "poor grammar" and insinuated that her appearance—and the inferiority of her shooting—would bring about Lillian's downfall. But Annie was much too polite to name Lillian outright, and theirs became a quiet, in-camp feud, kept from the press and the public.

The ongoing conflict proved just how proud and competitive Annie Oakley was. She would not let Lillian outshine her, even if it meant working while she was ill, which is exactly what she did during the big opening-day parade that summer in New York. Annie was determined to be in the parade, though she was running a high fever, caused by an insect that had flown into her right ear and lodged near her eardrum shortly before the Wild West set up camp on Staten Island. Frank had tried unsuccessfully to wash the bug out with oil. On the morning of the parade, Annie hurried to a doctor, who gave her a leech to draw out the bug. She took it and headed back to camp. As she entered the gate at Erastina, she found the entire Wild West company lined up for the trip to Manhattan and the big parade. Afraid she'd miss the train, Annie was frantic. She ran to her dressing room, unfastening her dress as she went. She yelled to a groom to saddle her horse, changed clothes in a flash, leaped on her horse and caught the train when it was a half mile down the track. She hopped on and then caught the boat to the city.

"That parade in New York meant everything to me," Annie wrote. She had sewn a new costume for it with everything to match, right down to the vocaros—the cloth trappings for her horse—which had the name "Oakley" stitched on either side. There'd be no mistaking Annie Oakley for Lillian Smith. "This outfit had cost a large sum of money . . . and to think that I could not use it!" Annie said.[11] No fever was going to stop her. She landed with the troupe at Twenty-Third Street and, though feeling weak, joined the parade. It went up Eighth Avenue to Forty-Second Street and over to Fifth Avenue, where the Indians, fierce with war paint and gay with feathers, rode down Murray Hill "with all the pomp and ceremony of conquerors." They swept down the length of Manhattan Island to the Battery. Buffalo Bill led the procession, followed by cowboys in woolen shirts and a general trimming of revolvers, and Mexicans with broad-brimmed sombreros and fringe down their trousers. Annie Oakley, her new vocaros shining in the sun, waved at the stockbrokers, nursemaids, dudes, and "other such civilized people" who lined the way. By the time the procession reached the Battery, an immense crowd had collected to watch the Wild West board the ferry-boats for the trip back to Staten Island.[12]

The cowboys reined in their horses and dismounted, but by now,

Annie Oakley was too weak even to slide down off her pony. Frank and Nate Salsbury rushed over, lifted her up, and carried her to the boat. At the showgrounds they tucked her in her cot and waited for a doctor to come. Frank applied the leech the doctor had given her; blood spurted, and the ear bled for five hours. The next morning the doctor came. "Blood poisoning," he said.

Annie Oakley was bedridden, so weak she couldn't sit up. Every afternoon that week, the show went on without her. During the performance of Wednesday, June 30, the Sioux chief American Horse walked by her tent and heard her moan. When he went in to comfort her, the newspapers had a story. American Horse, they wrote, had shown "that there is pathos in the Indian, after all." Why, he had bathed Annie's face "while tears ran down his cheeks."[13]

For four days Annie tossed and turned in her tent. On the fifth day, though her face was still swollen, she decided she had to perform. She made her way into the arena, but was so weak she had to lean against her gun table while she shot. Nothing ever went further to prove how dedicated and competitive she was. She had missed four performances—and they were four of only five that she would miss in seventeen years with the Wild West. Her attendance record was extraordinary, especially considering the long schedules the Wild West played. There was nothing of the pampered star about Annie Oakley. For years she would remain as steadfast and as hardworking as she was that summer at Erastina.[14]

So popular was the Wild West and so good was its press that summer that even Phineas T. Barnum came down from Bridgeport, Connecticut, to see the show. It was the first time in forty years that Barnum, now seventy-six, had gone to see a show other than his own. He came, even though he had the gout and his foot was wrapped in bandages, and he liked what he saw. "It is the coming show," Barnum said. "It don't want no 'spangles.' It is a show where no foreign language need be spoken. It is life and movement, and all people can catch the effects."[15]

What better endorsement could the Wild West receive than one from the great showman himself? Barnum had dazzled the world with his midget Tom Thumb and made a folk heroine of singer Jenny Lind. And it was he who had opened the Great Roman Hippodrome in New York's Madison Square, which was the center of all that was fashionable and exciting in the New York of the 1880s. Charles Delmonico's elegant restaurant was in Madison Square, as were all the fashionable hotels—the

Brunswick, the Victoria, the Fifth Avenue, and the twin marble palaces, the Albemarle and the Hoffman House.[16] The old Madison Square Garden itself still stood, a massive building of brick, masonry, and marble, which filled the block between Madison and Fourth avenues. Over the years, the Garden had featured horses, dogs, bands, circuses, and the brightest star in town—heavyweight boxing champion John L. Sullivan. The biggest star of all, though, had been Barnum's Jumbo, the gigantic and lovable elephant.

As the summer of 1886 wound down, Madison Square prepared to play host to New York's latest hero, Buffalo Bill and his Wild West. The show had been such a success on Staten Island that Cody and Salsbury decided to move it indoors for the winter. They hired the playwright Steele MacKaye to transform the rough-shod Wild West into an elaborate indoor pageant complete with stage sets. The revamped Wild West opened on the day before Thanksgiving to a house crowded to the roof. "Fully 6,000 people were present," said the New York *Herald*, "and the whole circle of boxes was gay with men and women in evening dress." Among those present were clergyman Henry Ward Beecher, sportsman and horse breeder Pierre Lorillard, and Erastus Wiman.[17]

The dusty spectacle under the Staten Island sky had been transformed into a four-act play christened the *Drama of Civilization*. Annie Oakley did her usual target work, and then showed off a brand-new stunt. She tied a handkerchief around her horse's pastern, then untied it as she rode side-saddle at full speed around the tanbark floor. "She and many others believe that this was never before done from a side-saddle by anything in the semblance of a woman," reported the New York *Clipper*.[18] The Ladies Riding Club of New York was so impressed that its members gave Annie a gold medal, her fourth since the Wild West opened in New York. Another day, without rehearsal, she filled in during the Virgina Reel for a rider who quit the show unexpectedly.[19] Annie was a good rider, and she was proud of her skill. Sketches of her on horseback, drawn by Dorothy and Steuard Hardy, were among her most treasured possessions. The sketches showed Annie shooting while her horse jumped a hurdle; leaning from her saddle and picking a handkerchief from the ground; and lying on her back and shooting while the horse galloped through a field.[20]

Riding a horse came easily to Annie Oakley, who was very fond of animals. She owned a number of horses and dogs during her lifetime and took pride in training them. When it came to dogs, she was particularly fond of Gordon setters. Among her favorite horses was Gypsy, whom Annie had trained so well that he would follow her anywhere, even up a flight of stairs. One time, after a stage performance, Gypsy had to be lowered to the street in an elevator. The horse didn't want to go, so six stagehands tried to drag and push him on. When Annie heard the scuffling, she ran from her dressing room, stepped into the elevator, and said, "Come on, Gyp." As always, Gypsy followed. The stagehands protested, saying it was against the rules for a person to ride in the freight elevator. "All right, then, I will break the rules," Annie said. With that, she and Gyp rode the elevator to the street.[21] Annie told another story about a vicious but well-bred horse that never had been broken to saddle. A man in Greenville had offered to give the horse to her if she could manage to ride him in less than three days. "The challenge was fair," Annie said, "the horse was valuable, and I didn't like the notion of being beaten." So she got to work, broke the horse to saddle, and claimed her prize. "[I] have since ridden him as high as fifty miles in one day," she said.[22]

Annie had so much confidence with animals that one idle day in Madison Square Garden she sidled up to a big moose named Jerry, who had a part in the *Drama of Civilization*. It was a snowy day, and Annie thought it would be fun to take a sleigh ride around the block. She found a sled, hitched Jerry on, and hopped aboard. "All went swimmingly," she said, "until we turned a corner . . . and Jerry's beadlike eyes espied a push cart laden with nice, juicy, red apples." In a split second, Jerry upset the cart and sent apples flying in every direction. "The vendor's hair stood straight on end," Annie said. "My moose ate the apples and my $5 paid the bill."[23]

Always so conscious of money, Annie kept her pockets full during the autumn lull by entering shooting matches. The Staten Island summer had enhanced her reputation so much that organizers of the Newton, New Jersey, fair guaranteed her 75 percent of the gate receipts if she would meet the well-known English shooter William Graham in a match on October 7, 1886. Annie agreed and put up a hundred dollars.

She knew Graham would be a tough match, so on the day before the shoot, she and Frank went out to practice. Annie smashed twenty-five targets, then handed the gun to Frank so he could have a try at the birds. She walked over to the trap and slid a target in for him. As she pulled her hand out, the spiral spring flew out with a zing, striking between the first and second fingers on her left hand and cutting it deeply. It seemed to be a year of accidents. Again, she hurried to a doctor, who closed the wound with five stitches and put her arm in a sling.

But what of her match the next day at the Newton fair? Annie asked. Not only did the doctor forbid the match, but he also ordered Annie not to use her injured hand for two weeks. The next day, Frank and Annie went out to the fairgrounds to explain the predicament to William Graham. Graham took one look at Annie, expressed his sympathy, and agreed to reschedule the match—until his backer chimed in. "No, the match is won. The money is ours," the backer shouted. That was challenge enough for Annie Oakley. She ignored Frank's pleas, picked up a gun with her good hand, and walked out to the score, determined to shoot a one-handed match. "[Frank] could not stop me," she said.[24]

Annie Oakley was no easy match, even with one hand. As she grassed bird after bird with her first barrel, the crowd grew more and more excited. But then, Annie said, the eleventh bird flew from the box like "a streak of greased lightning." She fired, cutting all the tail feathers clean, but the bird kept on going. Thinking the match was in the offing, Annie pulled her sore hand out of the sling to get a better grasp on the gun so she could fire her second barrel. The weight ripped her stitches open, and blood ran down her hand. Frank dashed over, announcing in one breath that the match was over and that the spectators could have Annie's percentage of the gate receipts. "I retired," Annie said, "amid cheers."[25]

While her courage gained fans that day, acceptance at the shooting line was not always so easy to attain, especially at gun clubs where a woman at the score was considered by some to be an outrage. "When I began shooting," Annie said, "it was considered almost shameful for a woman to shoot. That was a man's business, you see." But Annie Oakley, always seeming so certain of who she was and what she was about, let nothing stand in her way, not even the disapproving looks of the refined ladies who watched her from the sidelines. When she went to trapshooting clubs she often went as the only woman in the field, tanned and vibrant, and in short skirts that set her apart. How different she looked from the women who stood on the sidelines, wearing corsets under their long dresses and using umbrellas to shield themselves from the sun. "They would look me over, oftimes disdainfully, but I would not mind them at all," Annie said. "If they wished to be friendly they could. If they did not I did not care." In time she would become so accepted that people forgot it had not been easy for her to make it in a man's world. "It was up-hill work," Annie said, "for when I began there was a prejudice to live down."[26]

So fiercely proud, she sounded almost haughty when she told of the struggles she had faced. She remembered in particular one of her earliest shooting matches, when she had competed against twenty-one entrants, all men, of course. "When they saw me coming along they laughed at the notion of my shooting against them," she said. But when Annie made a clean score and took the prize money, the men were "less amused than they had been previously," she said. "It kind o' galled me to see those hulking chaps so tickled in what was no doubt to them my impertinence in daring to shoot against them—and I reckon I was tickled too when I walked away with the prize." [27]

She liked to tell about another exhibition when she had the last laugh. It was that Thanksgiving when the Wild West was playing in Madison Square. Annie accepted a challenge from the Middlesex Gun Club, across the river in New Jersey. A month and a half had passed since the Newton fair, and her hand was healed. She and Frank drove out to Dunellen that day, only to discover that the club members, wanting to make a hard day of it for the woman shooter, had fastened the traps at the toughest notch and used the strongest spring. They wanted the clay birds to sail far and fast. They "hoped to have a good laugh at me," Annie said. But she wasn't worried because, luckily, her shells were loaded for fast and distant birds. "So I only grinned when the two tryout birds left the traps," she said, and she broke them both in an instant. Annie concluded her exhibition with a popular stunt from the Wild West arena, in which she sprang the traps herself, leaped her gun table, picked up her gun from the ground, and smashed two birds before they landed. This day, she sprang the traps as always, but as she leaped the table she lost her footing on the slippery grass. She slid on her buttocks and fired while sitting on the wet grass, hitting one bird but missing the second. And then she did what she always did when she flubbed a stunt: she tried it again. This time she caught both birds and finished with a score of forty-nine out of fifty. "That club was all right," Annie said. "They gave me a handsome medal and stated that the joke was on them." [28]

After a year in New York, Annie Oakley had become so popular that unscrupulous people were beginning to copy her, which always posed a threat to Annie's reputation. One day in New York, for example, Frank visited a dime museum, where he saw a long-haired man posing as a cowboy, and his female companion posing as "Little Sure Shot." "They will never starve if cheek will carry them through," an indignant Frank Butler wrote to *Shooting and Fishing*. "The fact that she was about a foot taller than the original 'Little Sure Shot,' made no difference to her." When Frank heard about another "Little Sure Shot" who was posing at the Wilmantic Fair in Connecticut, he was so angry that he wrote to a number of sporting magazines, asking sportsmen to let him know if they came across any other fakes posing as Annie Oakley. "As a rule I pay very little attention to these kind of people," he wrote, "for there is little to be gained by getting into a controversy with anyone who is unprincipled enough to try to do business on someone else's reputation." Still, Frank said, "I should be very sorry for anyone to think that it was Annie Oakley who was on exhibition eleven hours daily in a museum." [29]

The fakes worried Frank, especially now that the Wild West was preparing to sail to London for a long stand at the queen's Jubilee. Frank wouldn't be in the United States anymore to keep an eye on the fakes and to look out for Annie's good name. He was worried enough that before leaving for London he took out an ad in the New York *Clipper,* dated April 2, 1887. In big, bold letters, it read: "DON'T FORGET THIS. There is only one ANNIE OAKLEY. And she leaves for Europe with the Wild West."

While Frank took care of business, Annie caught a train home to Ohio to say goodbye to her mother. She hadn't seen her in almost a year, and it would be longer than that before she would be home again. Annie's second stepfather, Joseph Shaw, was eighty-five years old and near death. Annie knew it wouldn't be long before her mother was alone again. "It was a sad parting," Annie wrote in her autobiography. "I kissed the tears from mother's cheeks as I bade her goodbye." [30]

10.

The Magical Year in London

A chilly wind blew along the Hudson River docks in New York City. Buffalo Bill's Indians wrapped their blankets tight against the cold and even Buck Taylor, the "King of the Cowboys," wore a long overcoat. But the chill wasn't enough to keep the crowds away. Scores of people, including many members of New York's theatrical community, gathered at the foot of Leroy Street to bid farewell to Buffalo Bill's Wild West. The show was sailing for London aboard the steamship *State of Nebraska*, and the scene on board that morning, said the *New York Times*, "was as gay as a . . . ballet."

Tall figures of Indians, dressed in all their finery, lined the upper deck. Mr. and Mrs. Walking Buffalo were aboard, wearing apple-green flannel, and Mr. and Mrs. Eagle Horse promenaded the deck "like tigers." Seated in the steerage and shivering in the wind were Moccasin Tom, Blue Rainbow, Wounds-One-Another, Throws-Away, Rushing Bear, Arrow Mound, Returns-from-Scout, Big Leggins, Spotted Eagle, Picket Pin, Tall Medicine, Iron Good Voice, Pawnee Killer, Double Wound, and Mr. and Mrs. Cut Meat and their baby.

Buffalo Bill walked up and down the deck, carrying a sword some friends had given to him. The cowboys "gave no trouble at all." They scattered themselves over the ship with their friends and talked and laughed in high enjoyment. The lady rider Georgie Duffy "capered about the deck, talking and laughing vehemently," and Annie Oakley, as usual, "bubbled over with good spirits."

Below deck, sixteen buffalo and a couple of bears, elks, and deer were stowed away, and a dozen flossy, docile mules thrust forth their noses to be petted. The Deadwood stage, boxed, corded, and nailed, was going to London, too. It had "afforded much amusement as it was lowered into the hold with the utmost difficulty."

If the words "good luck" and "bon voyage" were said once, they were said a hundred times, until precisely at ten o'clock, with the crowd "shouting and whooping and gesticulating for dear life," the steamship slid into the Hudson. It sailed into New York Bay, past Bedloe's Island and the new Statue of Liberty, past the old Wild West dock at St. George, and through the Narrows into the Atlantic Ocean. Buffalo Bill and Annie Oakley were off on a great adventure. In just two weeks, the plainsman who once would have thought it a big deal to meet the mayor of Leavenworth, Kansas, would be cracking jokes with the prince of Wales, and Annie Oakley would be shaking hands with the queen of England.[1]

As the *State of Nebraska* moved up the Thames and into the Albert Docks, London already was plastered with posters of Indians stampeding a mailcoach and cowboys lassoing mustangs. Booksellers packed their windows with editions of James Fenimore Cooper's *The Path Finder* and *The Last of the Mohicans,* and curious Londoners ran down to the wharf to watch the ship unload. They lined up behind a rope to catch a glimpse of what the London *Times* called a troupe "the like of which has never before crossed the seas."[2]

"Red Indians" sunned themselves on the larboard rail while the steam winch whirred and crates holding live buffalo, elks, deer, and mules swung out of the holds, fore and aft. Someone counted more than 160 horses. Lady riders, Mexicans, and American cowboys, "attired in the picturesque garb of the backwoods," appeared, then boarded the North London, Midland and West London railway for a trip to the West Brompton Station and Earl's Court, where the Wild West would be playing all summer long.

Earl's Court stood on a big railroad junction in London's West End. The grounds, which comprised twenty-three acres of gardens, courts, and exhibition halls, had been secured by a group of American businessmen for a trade fair, called the American Exhibition. The Wild West was to play in conjunction with it. Horse stables, a corral, and a huge grandstand that could seat twenty thousand people had been erected, and the camp village had been set up amid a grove of newly planted trees. Each tent had a wooden floor and a slow-combustion stove inside to guard against the damp English spring.

A covered bridge spanning rows of railroad tracks led from the Wild West camp to the main exhibition hall, where a hodgepodge of American-made goods was on display. There were organs and pianos and a Davis sewing machine, with its samples of embroidered and frilled dresses. There were sweeping brushes, typewriters, stepladders, watches, cutlery, and Waterbury clocks, electric motors, canned goods, drugs, and a steam carpet cleaner.[3]

Londoners could walk in ornamental gardens, enjoy splashing fountains, listen to bandstand music, or view Thomas Sully's celebrated full-length portrait of Queen Victoria in her coronation robes. The painting was certain to come in for much attention this year of 1887, the fiftieth anniversary of the queen's coronation. Adventuresome visitors could ride on a switchback railway or hop aboard the wooden toboggan slide with its six solid oak-and-iron sleds. At the center of everything stood a fantastic diorama of New York Harbor, designed by Statue of Liberty creator Frédéric-Auguste Bartholdi and lighted by 250 new electric lights.

For all its flash and glitter, the American Exhibition did not catch the fancy of Londoners. They were tired of trade fairs, especially since the Colonial and Indian Exhibition had played in London just the year before. The American Exhibition, in fact, probably would have fallen flat on its face if Buffalo Bill's Wild West had not been secured as a side attraction. The London papers made no bones about that.

The papers were there when the exhibition opened on Monday, May 9, with a short prayer by Cannon Farrar, a welcome by Lord Ronald Gower, and the singing of the "Star Spangled Banner" and "Rule Britannia." A band struck up "Dixie," and with that, the crowd made a mad stampede—not for the main exhibition, but for the covered bridge that led over the railroad tracks to the Wild West camp. "Not a soul stayed behind to look at the false teeth, or linger over the 'ironclad bran-duster,'" reported the *Daily Telegraph*. The Wild West show was all the talk, and Londoners, who soon dubbed it "The Yankeeries," flocked to its circular grandstands from the first moment. "The crush, and fight, and struggle amongst both quadrupeds and bipeds to reach the gates of the Yankeeries, was, for some hours, something terrific," the *Evening News* reported. A mass of carriages "of every description" crawled along the Old Brompton Road, and the sidewalk was "just as bad for pedestrians." Ten thousand people were smart enough to show up early and take the best seats in the grandstand a full hour before the show was to begin.[4]

"All the world and his wife were there," wrote the reporter from the *Evening News*. It was a fashionable and distinguished throng, indeed, the cream of London society. The actor Henry Irving was there, as were Irish writer Oscar Wilde, evangelical writer Hughie Drummond, Lady Randolph Churchill (wife of the British statesman), playwright William Gilbert, and composer Arthur Sullivan. Cardinal Henry Manning was there, as well as actor Charles Wyndham, "and indeed everyone who is known in London's innermost literary and dramatic circles."

And everyone, it seemed, was heartily pleased with The Yankeeries. In the first three weeks of May alone, the show attracted half a million visitors. In London, Buffalo Bill's Wild West—and with it Annie Oakley—marked the beginning of what was to be fifteen years of enormous popularity.[5]

The Wild West was so popular in England that special performances were commanded first by former prime minister William Gladstone, and then by Edward, prince of Wales. Edward, the eldest son of Queen Victoria and the late Prince Albert, would become King Edward VII in 1901. He was below average in height and on the pudgy side. He was an eager sportsman, though, and horses from his stables won the English Derby three times. Edward took an interest in guns and hunting and liked the outdoors. The Wild West was a show he was bound to enjoy. He took a seat one day in the royal box, draped with American and English flags. Beside him were his wife, Alexandra, their daughters, Louise, Maud, and Victoria, and a royal party that included the duke of Cambridge, the duke of Teck, the comtesse de Paris, and Crown Prince Frederick of Denmark, who was Alexandra's brother. Such lists of royal personages were common in London that year as Europe's royalty came to honor the queen on her Golden Jubilee.

When the royal party was seated comfortably, Edward motioned, and on his signal the entire Wild West outfit darted into the arena from behind an ambuscade of rocks. The Indians, scantily dressed in feathers and beads, produced a sensation instantaneous and electric. "Yelling like fiends, they swept round the enclosure like a whirlwind," said the London *Daily Chronicle*. The prince, carried away by the excitement, rose from his seat, leaned over the front of the box, and remained standing for most of the performance.

Annie Oakley, "the girl shot," trotted out and "did some capital shooting at glass balls thrown from a trap by hand." She did so well that Prince Edward called her up to the royal box to congratulate her. As she approached, he extended his hand over the box, expecting a handshake.

But Annie, in a move characteristic of the resolute woman she was, ignored it for a moment. She turned instead to Princess Alexandra and shook her hand first. "You'll have to excuse me, please," Annie said to Edward, "because I am an American and in America, ladies come first."

For all that, Annie had made a terrible breach of English custom—and people noticed. The next day the *Daily Chronicle* mentioned Miss Oakley's "charming naivete," in shaking the wrong hand first. But Miss Oakley was not nearly as naive as people assumed. She intended to snub Prince Edward, who was known to be a lady's man and was rumored to have had an affair with the English actress Lillie Langtry. Alexandra, who had been married to Edward for twenty-four years, apparently had accepted the affair. She was a quiet, gentle woman who had suffered a serious illness. She was much devoted to the poor and was a favorite with the British public. Annie Oakley's heart, too, went out to Alexandra.[6]

"All I had heard of women trying to flirt with the prince while the gentle princess held her peace" ran before her as she approached the royal box, Annie said. That was the reason she broke custom and shook Alexandra's hand first. An upright and prideful Annie Oakley wasn't going to let the prince of Wales think she was a flirt like Lillie Langtry or any of those other actresses she'd heard about.

Although her faux pas would be mentioned time and again in accounts of the royal meeting, Annie didn't consider it a gaffe. She was proud of herself, especially when she told how the gentle Alexandra had turned to the prince and "looked at him as much as to say, 'That's one on you.'"[7] It is noteworthy that Annie was not the only one whom Prince Edward called up to the royal box. Lillian Smith, who also had done "some capital shooting," made the trip, too. In fact, the *Daily Chronicle* noticed no breach of custom on Lillian's part and wrote that she "proceeded with perfect self-possession to explain and show [the prince] the working of the weapon in her hand."[8]

Already, the Wild West was "upon every tongue," a Manchester newspaper said. Not since the departure of the elephant Jumbo had there been such a popular sensation in London. Londoners talked about Buffalo Bill's cowboys and Indians, who turned up one day at Westminster Abbey and another day at the Congregational Chapel in West Kensington, where the Indians again astonished parishioners by singing "Nearer My God to Thee." As always, visits to the theater were arranged. One Tuesday night, a half-dozen Indians and cowboys attended the Lyceum, where Chief Red Shirt occupied the royal box in a "blaze of barbaric splendour." He wore buffalo robes embroidered with porcupine quills and beads, and had stuck a plume of feathers in his hair. His braves "sat immovable as rocks," and Buck Taylor looked "swarthy and long-haired." [9]

The most popular of "the boys" was Buffalo Bill himself, who was admired by Londoners for his "coal black eyes," his "flowing hair," and "most splendid moustache." He seemed imposing and manly, yet spoke in a low, kindly voice and had a smile "as sweet as a woman's." When he wasn't in the arena, he wore a dark tweed suit and sleeve-links studded with diamonds. "Buffalo Bill has been enormously feted," reported the *Court and Society Review*. "Everybody is of opinion that he is altogether the handsomest man they have ever seen." [10]

Invitations came from Drury Lane, the Lyceum, and Toole's. Lady Bective invited him to lunch, a communication came from Marlborough House, and "a dozen obliging offers from enterprising tradesmen to supply him with everything from patent blacking to platinum doorhandles." And the lion of London took up his offers. He rode down the Row in his buggy with Mrs. Brown-Potter and was host in his tent to the actress, Miss Grace Hawthorne. One Friday, he dined at the House of Commons with Colonel Hughes-Hallett and Lord Charles Bereford, and one Saturday ate with Henry Irving at the Beefsteak Club, where he "charmed everybody by his modest and amusing manner of storytelling."

At the same time, though more quietly, another member of the Wild West was gaining a new-found popularity: Annie Oakley. "Miss Oakley is a great favorite here," reported an American who visited London that summer. "She is invited out nearly every day to some reception or other." [11] Her tent was full of flowers, and press and public alike seemed to adore her. "The loudest applause of the night is reserved for Miss Annie Oakley," said the *Referee*. Miss Oakley "is winning gold and fame in England," said the *Rifle*, which noted that "the sturdy knights of the quill" were bestowing "unstinted praise" on her in the columns of the press. Indeed. A reporter from the *Evening News* said she was "far and away" the best shot in the show. Another found her to be a "young lady possessed of a decidedly pretty and winsome face, of sweet and gentle manners, and a soft, girlish voice." To the *Sportsman* she was "a Western girl with quiet, expressive eyes, and a voice as soft and silvery as the rustling of a summer's breeze among the trees." The *Bat* noticed a "marked absence of the affectation so frequently assumed by music

Annie Oakley in London, 1887. She made the outfit herself, right down to the pearl-buttoned leggings. (Courtesy of the Denver Public Library, Western Historical Department)

hall and circus professional shots." Reporters commented on the "rare diffidence in one who is such a public favourite," and found that Annie would "rather discuss any other topic than herself." They found her courteous and open and were charmed when she showed them her guns and her trophies or offered them a glass of juice or a cup of tea. "Pray sit down and make yourself at home," she said to a reporter from *Rod and Gun*. "You have been to the Show? Yes? I hope you enjoyed it. Now we will have a cup of tea and a quiet talk, and you can ask me your questions. Interviewers are always full of questions." [12]

Annie answered so many questions and was featured in so many press notices, in fact, that she began to clip them and put them in a scrapbook. It is significant that the scrapbooks, which she and Frank Butler would keep up religiously for the next forty years, began that spring in London. Annie Oakley had been before the public for five years, but it wasn't until the magical year in London that her fame really took hold. She was so popular with the London newspapers that they even printed jokes about her, such as this one in the *Topical Times:*

"'What do you call that?' she asked her cavalier, pointing to the coil of hide in Buck Taylor's hands.

"'That is a lasso, my dear, but to my thinking Miss Annie Oakley is a much prettier lass (oh)!'" [13]

Four offers of marriage came through the mail, including one from an alleged French count, who threatened to commit suicide if Annie refused him. "He was the ugliest monkey you ever saw," said Annie, who wasn't swayed toward him in the least. When the count sent Annie a photograph and insisted that she marry him, Annie took matters into her own hands. She shot a bullet through the head in the photograph, wrote "Respectfully declined" on it, and mailed it back. "Of course, all my acquaintances know that I am Mrs. Butler in private life, although always Annie Oakley on the bills," she said. Confusion over Annie's marital status was not surprising. Although Frank always was by her side, his name was not connected with hers in the Wild West program. He was a man behind the scenes, whose exact position with the Wild West company never has been clear. Some accounts suggest that he worked in the ammunition wagon, where he had charge of the guns and ordered all the ammunition used in the show.

When Frank was mentioned, it usually was as Annie Oakley's manager, and many people in the public, at least early in Annie's career, apparently did not realize they were married. Annie, for example, told of one proposal she received in London from "a boy who said he had not missed one of my two daily exhibitions ever since the Wild West opened, that I was the one little girl he could ever love." When Annie broke the news to him that she already was married he said "that he had never dreamed until that day that there was another in [her] life." Brokenhearted, he left for South America, telling Annie that he could not keep away from her show tent if he stayed in London.[14]

If such incidents bothered Frank Butler, he certainly never said so. Frank was an unusual man. He was so comfortable with his secondary role that he even told funny stories about it, including this one, which happened in London that year. "We were great objects of curiosity when we first arrived," Frank said, "and the crowds were following us all about. One day a rather clerical looking man that I took to be a priest in the Church of England, after standing around for awhile, said to me:

" 'What do you do in this show?'

" 'I write Annie Oakley's autograph across her checks.'

" 'The h—l you do.'

"Of course," Frank said, "that let him out of the church all right."[15]

In later years, Frank told how he was introduced to Owen Moore of cinema fame as "Mr. Butler, the husband of Annie Oakley." Moore "rushed over to me," Frank said, "seized my hand and said, "I'm certainly glad to meet you and sympathize with you. For years I was Mary Pickford's husband.' " But the slight did not seem to bother Frank Butler. According to Fern Campbell Swartwout, he enjoyed the attention Annie got because he loved her and was proud of her. "People who knew Frank said that his attitude was one of the secrets of her wonderful success," Fern wrote. "He was able to allow her to receive the attention of the public, and not try to claim even a little share of it for himself. . . . The more applause Annie received, the happier Frank seemed to be, and the harder he worked to make a success of her act."[16]

Annie had so many admirers that summer in London that on her birthday she received sixty-seven presents, including a carriage, a clock, a silk dress, a thoroughbred English horse, a St. Bernard pup, and a photograph of the princess of Wales from Alexandra herself. Annie's popularity spanned all classes of people, from the princess down to the shoeblacks on the street. One shoeblack, on seeing her pass, was heard to say: "There goes the boss shooter."[17]

People recognized her, too, when she trotted her horse around Hyde Park. "I did not think anyone would recognize me in the park, but they

Annie Oakley and Sir Ralph, the St. Bernard given to her as a present on her twenty-seventh birthday, during the triumphant summer of 1887 at Earl's Court in London. (Courtesy of the Buffalo Bill Historical Center, Cody, Wyo.)

did," Annie said, "and some newspaper man commented upon my costume, the result being that I could start in business as a lady's tailor tomorrow, judging from the applications I have received for patterns." [18]

One woman was so impressed with Annie's riding style that she wrote to the *Society Times* and suggested that English riders copy it. "I had the extreme pleasure of meeting her in the Row a few mornings ago," the woman wrote, "and I think after watching her seat in the saddle, that this little American girl is ahead of us." Other society women wanted to shoot like Annie Oakley. Five of them got together and asked her to teach them, and, according to Annie, offered to pay "any price I asked." Not about to pass up a chance to earn a little money, Annie obliged and charged each woman one pound (the British equivalent of about five U.S. dollars) a lesson, thus beginning a little business on the side. [19]

Though Annie's indigent upbringing probably would have shocked the ladies of London society, the past was obscured by her style, her natural dignity, and her amiable manner. She possessed a certain polish and natural intelligence. After those first few years with Frank Butler there was nothing of the country bumpkin about Annie Oakley, though she was portrayed that way in the modern Broadway musical, *Annie Get Your Gun*. And although she has been confused in modern times with the rough-and-tumble Calamity Jane (Martha Jane Canary), the two women were nothing alike. Annie Oakley's reserve, politeness, and savvy went over well with the educated people she met. It was by virtue of her personality as well as her talent that she was admitted readily into a London society that seldom opened its doors to public performers.

Socialites invited her to their fashionable teas and luncheons, and Annie, in return, held monthly teas for society's children. The youngsters, ages two to nine, came with their governesses and sat on the grass and among the flowers in front of Annie's tent. Always a lover of flowers, Annie had lined her walk with them, and her little corner of the Wild West village at Earl's Court was a pleasant spot. "Two of my own daintily befrilled maids served the refreshments . . . with two 'Bobbies' standing on each side of the tent to keep the people moving," Annie wrote. "My six months in London were made happier by the teas I gave each month for my children friends." [20]

Through the elegant summer, Annie Oakley remained as simple as ever. When she was invited out, she always went in a modest dress, though the material was elegant and the cut very neat. Fashionable clothes, Annie admitted, made her ill at ease. She never spent her money on jewelry, either, and seldom wore jewelry that was given to her.[21]

Annie felt so welcome in England that for a time that summer she considered making it her home. "I like England immensely, and could talk a lot about it, but do not want to sicken you with any outburst of fulsome adulation," she said in an interview shortly before her twenty-seventh birthday. "I know this much: that if I had my mother living with me here I should be in no hurry to get back to the States. This country is quite good enough for me."[22]

The summer passed with one triumph after another, both for Annie Oakley and the Wild West. Even Queen Victoria herself appeared one day at the Wild West gate. Her visit was unprecedented. The queen, though a lover of the theater, had not attended a theatrical performance out of Buckingham Palace for almost twenty-six years. She had been so grief-stricken when her husband, Prince Albert, died of typhoid fever in 1861 that she went into seclusion and thereafter appeared only to unveil memorials to him and once, in 1866, to open Parliament.[23] Victoria at sixty-seven was a short woman, barely five feet tall. She was graceful and had a clear, high-colored complexion and a beautiful speaking voice. Nonetheless, she never lost her shyness in public. This day, she drove to Earl's Court in a closed carriage "and was loudly cheered by crowds of people who had gathered along the route to West Kensington."

The queen arrived shortly after five, and drove through the stables and around the arena to a box especially constructed for her and draped with crimson velvet. From there, she watched the Indians as they swept past at full gallop "with cries of delight" and "fought, plunged, danced, and shouted with rare spirit." Buck Taylor "dashed up and saluted," the little cowboy Bennie Irving "kissed his small hands in token of his respect," and Buffalo Bill "reined up his white mustang and waved his salutations."

The queen, who expressed "her entire satisfaction with all she had seen," was presented to Buffalo Bill and Red Shirt, and then she summoned some Indian women, who "came racing across the arena, bringing their little brown papooses on their backs." The queen also sent for the "American girls," Lillian Smith and Annie Oakley. Annie made the "prettiest of curtseys," and walked up to the queen. "You are a very clever little girl," Victoria said, words that surprised Annie. "I was not so very little, and I was a married woman," Annie explained, "but I suppose the costume gave the impression that I was shooting from the high school." Annie told how she was surprised by the queen's "prosaic appearance," but that she found her "gracious and a very womanly woman."[24] Lillian Smith curtsied before the queen, also, then showed Victoria her rifle. A sketch of the moment appeared later in the *Illustrated London News*.

Weeks later, on June 20, the anniversary of Victoria's coronation, Cody and Salsbury outdid themselves by taking the show to Windsor Castle, where they gave a command performance for the queen and her Jubilee guests. Because so many of Europe's royalty were in London for the occasion, probably no commercial entertainment ever was attended by more royal personages than attended Buffalo Bill's Wild West that day. It was on this occasion that the Deadwood stagecoach carried four kings: the rulers of Denmark, Greece, Belgium, and Saxony, along with the prince of Wales. When the prince, referring to poker, turned to Cody and said, "Colonel, you never held four kings like these before," Cody replied in his famous line: "I've held four kings, but four kings and the Prince of Wales makes a royal flush, such as no man ever held before."[25] It probably was on this occasion, also, that the prince turned to Annie Oakley and said, "Don't you feel just a bit frustrated shooting before so many crowned heads?" Annie's reply was so forthright that it must have sounded almost rude. "Why, no," she said. "I have shot before 30,000 Americans." The prince looked at her in amazement, then laughed.[26]

More important even than Annie's acceptance by British society was her acceptance by British sportsmen. They invited her to shoot at their elite gun clubs, and in time she would meet and shoot with every marksman in England of any note, professional or amateur. She didn't enter their pigeon matches just for fun—or even just to make money. She was out to prove herself in a country where shooting was considered a national sport. If Annie wanted to earn the respect of the English sportsmen, she would have to do it at the line against other skilled marksmen. That was the true test of the shooter, not a fancy performance in the Wild West arena.[27]

London had two elite gun clubs, the London Gun Club at Notting Hill and the Hurlingham Club, situated on the banks of the Thames. The club at Notting Hill was so prestigious that members referred to it simply as the Gun Club. Its grounds were said to be the finest in the world, and included a handsome clubhouse surrounded by a stone wall. The Gun Club charged an admission fee of one pound just to watch the shooting. The fee was intended to keep "certain classes" out.[28]

The Hurlingham grounds were large as well, though they were not considered quite so fine as those at Notting Hill. Besides gunning, the grounds included room for polo, lawn tennis, and other games. The Hurlingham Club was popular. It had fifteen hundred members and several hundred people on a waiting list. Shooting was a big sport in England. Besides the gun clubs, nearly all the English gunmakers—and there were a number of them—owned private shooting grounds, where a man could go to test out a new gun or try his hand at the pigeons.

Gunmaker Charles Lancaster, for example, owned a twenty-acre shooting ground on the main road to Harrow, just a few miles from Earl's Court. He gave private lessons there every Monday, Wednesday, and Friday morning for a guinea. Lancaster was one of London's best-known gunmakers. He had a knack for "fitting" a man with a gun and acquired a reputation for improvements he made in rifle barreling. Lancaster lived in London, at 151 New Bond Street, West. Just behind his home, on Little Bruton Street, stood Lancaster's Gun Factory, established in 1826.[29]

No man ever did more for Annie Oakley's shooting than Charles Lancaster did that summer of 1887 in London. The story began on a bleak day, probably at Lancaster's private grounds, when Annie first tried her hand at the English pigeons. They were called "blue rocks." The birds were smaller and swifter than American pigeons. "They go like lightning," Frank said. They were the fastest birds he and Annie had ever seen, so swift and strong that Frank contended the worst of them was better than the best pigeon in America. The blue rocks were so hard to shoot, in fact, that Frank said he knew of no one in America who would be able to kill ninety of one hundred when the best birds were in season. "I used to laugh when I heard Englishmen say no one could kill 80 out of 100," Frank said, "but now I say any one that can do it can make plenty of money coming here and doing it."[30]

Annie certainly had had no luck at the blue rocks. In her first outing, she hit only five birds out of twenty. "After I shot at a string of 24 I could have been led home easily by a lingerie ribbon," she said. She was embarrassed, for some of the best gunmen in London had been watching. Among them was J. J. Walsh, the distinguished editor of the London *Field,* who was considered an authority on shooting. As Walsh approached Annie after her poor performance, she cringed. "Miss Oakley," he said, "I certainly expected to find you a better shot than you are, but not to find you so much of a lady."[31]

Walsh's comment was the only bright spot in an otherwise dismal first day with the blue rocks. Annie took his words as a compliment, in fact, she said, the best compliment she ever had received. She knew it was only a matter of time before she mastered the birds, but to be considered a lady—that was a battle she would fight her entire life.

When Annie finally did master the English pigeons, it was Charles Lancaster she had to thank. She called him a "wide awake gunmaker," who noticed that the gun she had used against the blue rocks did not fit her as it should. It was an American gun, "all bedecked with gold" and showing a gold figure of Annie in the guard. Pretty as it was, it weighed seven and a half pounds and had too much drop, causing her to shoot under the birds. Lancaster improved Annie's aim by taking the gun and straightening the stock. He also thought the gun was too heavy for her, and he set about making her a new, much lighter one.[32]

That was the beginning of a sound friendship. Annie and Frank spent many mornings at Lancaster's private grounds, which were easily reached by taking the London & Northwest Railway to the Willesden Junction. From there, it was only one and three quarters miles by cab. They shot on Lancaster's pigeon grounds, looked over the two-hundred-yard rifle range, and tried out the running deer target. Annie even took a few lessons. Then, in the afternoon, she and Frank caught the train back to West Kensington for the Wild West performance.

When Lancaster finished Annie's new 12-gauge, double-barreled shotgun, she was well pleased. "The fit is perfection," she said later.[33] The gun had a short stock, twenty-eight-inch barrels, a light trigger pull, and weighed only six pounds. Frank called it a little beauty, a perfect gun for a petite woman. It always would be one of the Butlers' favorite guns, and with good reason. When Annie tried it out on the blue rocks that summer, her shots no longer went under the birds; they were on the mark. She soon scored twenty-three out of twenty-five starlings, and made a pact with herself to get forty out of fifty blue rocks before leaving England.

Annie ordered two more guns from Lancaster, both 20-bores, weighing only five pounds, two ounces each, which was very light for a shotgun. In all, Charles Lancaster made at least four shotguns for her that summer, and she was so pleased with them that she credited him for much of her early success.

The new Lancaster guns demonstrated their worth the day Annie was invited to give a private exhibition at the London Gun Club on Notting Hill. Though she already was a hit at the Wild West arena and a popular figure in London, she needed to do well on this prestigious turf if she wanted to prove herself as a true sportsman. Invitations, printed on three-by-five cards with the Gun Club insignia in the upper lefthand corner, went out to members. The private performance of Miss Annie Oakley "of the Wild West Show" was to begin at half past one o'clock on Saturday, June 11.

The invitations brought a large and distinguished company of ladies and gentlemen to the club. If editor J. J. Walsh was among the crowd, he could not have been disappointed with Annie's shooting this time around. She ran through the fifteen feats on the program without a hitch. For the most part, the stunts were the same ones she had been performing all summer in the Wild West arena. Here was the list, preserved by Annie herself on a page of her 1887 scrapbooks.

1. Short exhibition of Rifle Shooting, small rifle.
2. Shooting Clay Pigeons, first two straight.
3. Pulling the trap herself.
4. Standing back to trap, turning and firing.
5. The snap shot or killing bird close to trap.
6. Shooting double.
7. Picking gun from ground after trap is sprung.
8. Same shot double.
9. Standing 20 feet from the gun, running and firing after the trap is sprung.
10. Holding gun with one hand, throwing ball herself.
11. Throwing two balls herself, breaking both.
12. Throwing ball backwards, picking up gun, and breaking it.
13. Breaking six balls thrown in air in four seconds.
14. Breaking five balls in five seconds, first with rifle, others with shot guns, changing guns three times.*
15. To shoot at 25 Blue Rocks from five traps, standing at 23 yards distance.
    *Please take time from first report of gun.

Only the last stunt was new—shooting at twenty-five of those lightning-quick blue rocks. According to the *Field*, Annie did well, downing eighteen "in fine style, several of the birds falling at a long distance to the second barrel."

Annie was roundly applauded as the Gun Club president, Lord Stormont, stepped forward and handed her a souvenir of her visit, a handsome gold medal. Its face was beautifully engraved with a drawing of the Notting Hill pavilion and shooting enclosure, and on the clasps were the words, "Presented to Miss Annie Oakley by the members of the London Gun Club, June 11, 1887." The medal, said to be the first ever awarded by the club, always would be Annie's favorite. It was the one she wore at front and center in her publicity photos. It was a valuable medal, larger than a five-shilling piece. But more important than that, it told that she had mastered the blue rocks, and that she had found acceptance among the highest class of London shooters. It was on the back of the London Gun Club medal that Annie would have engraved the words she said were spoken to her by Prince Edward: "I know of no one more worthy of it." [34]

Charles Lancaster was so pleased with the work Annie was doing with the guns he had built for her that he made a bold prediction: Before leaving England, Annie would kill thirty-five of fifty blue rocks with her new 20-bore guns. Then Lancaster backed up his claim by setting up a match at his shooting grounds on September 30. That day, Annie downed forty-one of fifty birds. She had, indeed, conquered the English pigeons. [35]

Prince Edward inadvertently added to Annie's popularity when he proposed a match between her and his acquaintance, Grand Duke Michael of Russia, who fancied himself a good shot. Rumor had it that the grand duke was in London looking for a wife among the queen's granddaughters, an idea that did not go over well with the British press, which did not like the grand duke. So, when the match came off and Annie won, forty-seven birds to thirty-six, she was an instant heroine. The grand duke "retired from the contest abashed," and Annie was amazed at the press reaction. "You should have heard the howl," she said. ". . . the papers that were against his courting expedition were pink with sarcastic accounts of this dashing cavalier who was outdone at his own game by a little girl from Kokomo—of this Lockivar [Lochinvar] who was no match for the short dresses, and whose warlike career faded before the onset of the Indiana kindergarten. It was the most amazing and unexpected publicity I ever experienced." [36]

Now, the popularity of "the little girl from Kokomo" was assured, especially when it turned out that the grand duke did not win the hand of an English princess after all. Whether the match with Annie had anything to do with his failure cannot be said, but as Britons saw it, Annie had won two matches that June day—one for herself and one for England.

Of all the shooting events in England that summer, the biggest was the annual gathering on the Wimbledon Commons, a pleasant recreation ground in suburban London. Until 1888 Wimbledon was the meeting-place of Britain's Rifle Association, and every year the best shooters competed for prizes worth as much as fourteen thousand pounds.

"Rifle shooting is all the rage here now," Frank wrote home to the *American Field* that July. It was just like the old days back at Creedmoor. Frank visited the Wimbledon grounds twice in a week. On the last day of the competition, he found two thousand people present. "It was the deciding day for the Queen's Prize," which was worth about twelve hundred dollars, he explained. "Great interest is taken in shooting here." [37]

It seemed only logical to expect that the big-name shooters from the Wild West—Buffalo Bill Cody, Lillian Smith, and Annie Oakley—would show up at Wimbledon. After all, it was the main event of the year in British riflery, and Wimbledon was only a short distance from Earl's Court, where the three had been dazzling Londoners all summer with their skill. But much to the surprise of some, Buffalo Bill Cody did not show up at Wimbledon. Whatever his reason, his absence was a tactical error because some Britons took it to mean that he wasn't a good enough shot to make a respectable score at Wimbledon's popular running deer target. Lillian Smith and Annie Oakley did show up, but the events that followed only widened the rift between them.

Lillian appeared on Tuesday, July 19, accompanied by "a number of cowboys and other celebrities," including a small Indian boy, "most resplendently arrayed in a blue silk shirt, and a pair of red silk trousers." Miss Smith herself, noted the *Weekly Dispatch*, "presented a striking combination of native eccentricity and feminine slavishness to the dictates of fashion." She wore a white summer dress, "incongruously accompanied by a yellow silk Mexican sash and plug hat."

Lillian and her friends were escorted around the grounds by a Mr. Gallant, who was the brother of the Queen's Prize winner of 1884. When they came to the running deer target, Lillian's interest was piqued. Someone handed a rifle to her, and she stepped up to the mark to try a few shots. Her shooting was a disaster. The first two bullets missed the target entirely, and the next shots hit the haunch of the iron animal. "At this," reported the *Evening News*, "there was some amusement" among the spectators. They were amused because hitting the haunch was considered worse than not hitting the target at all. In real life, the deer would have escaped, only to suffer. At Wimbledon, shooters who hit the haunch had to pay a fine. Lillian apparently heard the snickers. She put the rifle down and explained that it was heavier than the one she was accustomed to using. She promised to come back that Thursday with her own rifle and try the running deer target again. However, she never did return. The damage was done. That week the *Dispatch* and the *Bat* took a swipe at Lillian, noting in their columns that she not only had hit the haunch, but had left the grounds without paying the fine. Her plug hat and Mexican sash had not gone over well, either.[38]

It was quite a different story when Annie Oakley showed up at Wimbledon the next day. Certainly, she did not wear a plug hat; Annie never would be so outrageous in her dress. By the same token, her shooting was much too accurate to hit the iron deer's haunch. What her score was, the papers did not say, except that it was "a fairly good record" and that she was "more successful at Wimbledon" than her "comrade in arms" had been the previous day. Not only did Annie make a good record, but Prince Edward happened to be watching and "pushed his way through the crowd" to congratulate her.[39]

Annie's success reflected badly on Lillian Smith, especially because Lillian was considered to be the Wild West's rifle expert. Annie was the Wild West's shotgun expert, but now she had beaten Lillian at her own game. Annie's success also reflected badly on Buffalo Bill and may have caused bad feeling between them. As one sportsman put it: If Cody was such a good shot, why hadn't he shown up to take a crack at the running deer? "It left the impression in my mind that the gallant colonel was not the champion of his own show," the sportsman wrote.[40] As far as he was concerned, Annie Oakley was the champion. The unidentified sportsman, who expressed his views in a letter to the Glasgow *Evening News*, wasn't the only one of that opinion. The London *Evening News* had said Annie was "far and away" the best shot in the show, a comment that was picked up back in the States by *American Field*. "We notice that Miss Annie Oakley is carrying off the majority of the honors," the *Field* had written. "The *News* says her marksmanship is better than Buffalo Bill's and that her shooting is phenomenal."[41]

Comments like those could only have exacerbated what apparently was a growing rift between Annie and Buffalo Bill. Because they never

Lillian Frances Smith, Annie Oakley's rival in the Wild West arena in 1886 and 1887. (Courtesy of the Buffalo Bill Historical Center, Cody, Wyo.)

discussed the problem in public or print, there is no way to know definitely what happened, but it's a good bet that Buffalo Bill was angry, and possibly jealous of the publicity Annie was getting. That the colonel "was not the champion of his own show" must have been a hard line for Cody to swallow. It was only many, many years later that Annie said in an interview that at one time in her career she had to abandon some of her stunts because Buffalo Bill complained that she was "outshooting" him.[42]

Furthermore, during that year in London, Annie was leading a life of her own outside of the Wild West arena—and she was making good money at it. She was giving shooting lessons and was being paid for exhibitions at the gun clubs. Though compensation never was mentioned beforehand, Annie said the clubs always slipped fifty pounds ($250) to Frank after a performance. One week, she made $750. According to Annie, her agreement with the Wild West allowed her to give private exhibitions, although she was not supposed to charge an entrance fee or make a public announcement.[43] The very fact that those stipulations were in her agreement with Cody and Salsbury probably meant that the issue was a touchy one. Annie's lucrative business outside the Wild West arena may have added to hard feelings or could have been the cause of them.

Whatever the true story was, the episode at Wimbledon could have done nothing to help matters between Buffalo Bill and Annie Oakley. Certainly, Wimbledon was the climax of the hard feelings and jealousies that already existed between Lillian Smith and Annie. For at last, there could be no doubt who was the better shot—even at rifle work.

Things grew ugly immediately after Wimbledon when someone who signed himself "A California[n]" wrote a letter to the *Shooting Times* attacking Annie Oakley. The letter contained "such palpably spiteful attacks on Miss Oakley," in fact, that the newspaper refused to publish it. Foiled there, "A California[n]" sent the letter to San Francisco, where it was published in the *Breeder and Sportsman*. A copy of the letter has not been preserved, but judging from the replies it drew, it said that Lillian Smith was "knocking the English shooters crazy" while Annie Oakley "was being left out in the cold." "A California[n]," who apparently was almost illiterate, told how Lillian was presented to the prince, the queen, and the grand duke, but failed to mention that Annie also had been presented. There were other omissions and insinuations, including a charge that Frank was passing himself off as Annie's brother.

The letter drew a heated reply from Frank Butler and caused enough of a stir in the Wild West camp that Nate Salsbury and Wild West orator Frank Richmond responded to it with their own letters to the *Breeder and Sportsman.* The charges were "entirely without foundation," Salsbury wrote on August 11. "In public estimation and in social preference Miss Oakley is the equal of anybody connected with our entertainment." More than anything, Salsbury was upset that the *Breeder and Sportsman* had published such camp gossip. "You will greatly favor me," he wrote, "if you will not publish either side of a story that should never have forced its way into the public press." Frank Richmond set the record straight: "I myself had the pleasure of presenting Miss Oakley to Her Majesty," he wrote on August 16. "Miss Oakley has always received a full recognition of her abilities during the four years I have had a daily opportunity of observing her career."

Interestingly, neither Buffalo Bill nor John Burke responded to "A California[n]'s" slight of Annie Oakley. Did they not want to become involved in an internecine feud, or was Cody's unhappiness with Annie, and Burke's loyalty to Cody, such that they did not want to respond?

Frank and Annie tried to laugh at "A California[n]" and did their best by framing the newspaper clipping and hanging it in Annie's tent, where it created "no little amount of amusement." But still, Frank felt compelled to reply to "that letter," for any slight to Annie's reputation always was of great concern. "Miss Oakley, as well as [operatic soprano] Madame Patti, [actress] Mary Anderson, or any other lady who distances all competitors and gets to the front has her enemies," Frank wrote, "and such letters as that have about the same effect on her as rain would have on the back of a mallard duck. That letter was written in the camp of the 'Wild West.' There was no need of the writer signing his name. All here know who wrote it. His bad English was as good as his signature. He is not a Californian; had he been so you could justly claim *the champion liar.*"[44]

"A California[n]'s" name is lost to history, but he probably was one of the Wild West cowboys whom Lillian Smith had befriended. Perhaps he was Jim Kidd, "the champion roper of Wyoming," whom Lillian recently had married.

There was no honeymoon with the press, though, for Lillian that summer in London. Besides the bad publicity about her errant shots at Wimbledon, she came in for some rough handling by the *Record Union* back in Sacramento, which laughed when it read an interview with Lillian published in London's *Topical Times.* The "highly polished language" ascribed to Lillian in the article just didn't fit the Lillian whom the *Record Union* remembered when she used to astonish all comers at a Sacramento shooting gallery operated by her parents. Why, as the *Record Union* remembered it, Lillian used to say, "Swab off the target pap, and let me bang de eye," or else, "Swing de apple dere, young fellers, an' let me bust his skin." [45]

Lillian's worst publicity came from a skeptical Wild West patron named James S. Carter who accused Lillian of cheating in the arena, and then set out to prove the charge. Carter went to the Wild West show armed with a pair of field glasses and a stopwatch. In one stunt, Lillian claimed to cover the sights on her rifle with a large card before shooting at swinging balls. However, Carter could see plainly with his field glasses that the card was cut away on one side and the sights were not covered.

Carter published his findings in a letter to the *Shooting Times* on June 3, 1887, in which he also questioned Lillian's claim that she shot at a ball revolving 3,000 times per minute. Carter took out his stopwatch and noted the revolutions of the ball. After the show, he walked into the arena and measured the length of the wire that had spun the ball. He calculated and figured that the ball had gone 362 times a minute, not 3,000. [46] It was beginning to look as if Annie Oakley had been right about Lillian Smith, when she opined that the inferiority of her shooting would bring about her downfall. But still, there was no hint that summer that Lillian Smith was on her way out.

It was Annie Oakley who was in trouble with Buffalo Bill's Wild West. The rift between her and Cody apparently had grown so big by the end of the summer that she and Frank took a drastic step: They decided to quit the show and go on their own. It was a startling turn of events. After all, any fame Annie had at this point she owed to Buffalo Bill and his Wild West. Knowing the frugal Butlers and their good business sense, they must have agonized over the decision to quit. Here, when at last they had gained renown, they risked throwing it away. The ready-made publicity that went with the Wild West would be gone, and so would Annie's good, steady income. Whatever the problem was that caused the Butlers to quit, it must have been a major one. It was a subject Annie would not discuss, saying only that the reasons were "too long to tell." [47] Surely, though, the trouble centered on jealousies and hard feelings.

The Butlers' parting came quietly, mentioned only in a short note in the *Evening News*, of October 31, 1887. "By the way," the note read, "the show . . . will lose one of its principal attractions in the person of

Miss Annie Oakley, who severs her connection with the Wild West voluntarily. . . . Her loss to the Wild West Show will be a serious one."[48] Annie and Frank did not lack for business offers. They were talking about visiting the Continent, where they already had received offers to exhibit in Paris and Berlin, and also in Monaco. Annie herself had ideas about becoming an actress.[49]

If she was downcast as the Wild West played its last stand at Earl Court's on Monday night, October 31, there was no indication of it. The show left London soon afterward for a winter stand in Birmingham and Manchester, but Annie and Frank stayed behind. They spent time on New Bond Street with Charles Lancaster, then headed to Shropshire to rest and hunt for a couple of weeks on the estate of a country squire. Annie and Frank had made many friends in London, and they would be missed. The *Topical Times* said goodbye in one stanza of a Wild West poem, which went like this:

> Farewell, dear Annie Oakley, whose great skill
> And charming manners captured hearts at will.
> Farewell to neatest tent with flowers strayed.
> Where many a visit oft to thee we paid.[50]

As Annie Oakley left London, a new book sat among the western novels in the booksellers' windows. It was called *The Rifle Queen* and was the nearest thing to a dime novel ever written about Annie Oakley. Within its sixty-four pages was the "truthful and stirring story" of Annie Oakley, published by the General Publishing Co., 280, The Strand, London.

The two-penny book told how Annie grew up in Kansas, where she had many adventures. She killed the "unscrupulous scoundrel" Darky Murrell, put a bullet through the eye of a panther, and shot a wolf. She tried to skin that wolf, but it opened its jaws and clapped its teeth on her arm. "The pain was agonizing," but the brave Annie Oakley "did not even cry out." Chapters of *The Rifle Queen* were full of Annie's adventures, in which she met up with "Mac, the desperado," bagged a bear, rode an unconquerable steed, survived a blizzard, and saved a train from robbers. There wasn't a matchstick of truth in *The Rifle Queen*, but what did that matter? Annie Oakley was becoming a legend.

11.

Riding with Pawnee Bill

Annie and Frank returned alone from London. No crowds waved from the foot of Leroy Street this time as they disembarked in New York during the Christmas season of 1887 and took a cab back to Madison Square. They settled in a cozy apartment opposite the Gardens and began looking for work. If Annie Oakley was to make a living now, she'd have to do it on her own, keeping her name before the public as best she could.

Frank, as her manager, had a number of ideas. In the spring of 1888, he placed ads in the New York *Clipper*, announcing that Annie Oakley was to star in a new melodrama called *Little Sure Shot, the Pony Express Rider*. The Butlers were business-minded people, not above capitalizing on Annie's western image or on her association with Cody's show. Frank secured a publicity agent, Den Howe of the Academy of Music in Fort Wayne, Indiana, and then sat back and waited for a "first class manager" with "capital to put it before the public in good shape."[1]

In the meantime, Frank hoped to pick up a couple of hundred dollars by arranging a series of shooting matches between Annie and Englishman William Graham, who was currently in the United States, defeating all the best shooters. Annie had a score to settle with Graham, who had defeated her at the Newton fair when her hand was in stitches. With her new Lancaster guns in tow, Annie faced Graham again on a bitterly cold Monday, January 16, 1888, in Merchantville, New Jersey.

A stiff breeze was blowing as she and Frank arrived at the grounds, and within fifteen minutes it began to sleet and the mercury dropped to zero. Frank rubbed brandy on Annie's arms and hands to warm her, then handed her the prized Lancaster 20-bore with which she had killed the swift blue rock pigeons in London. A crowd of nearly one thousand people huddled in close as Annie stepped alertly to the score. Americans had read of her feats in London and remembered her from the summer on Staten Island. They were on her side, though the wind seemed not to be. It carried seven of her birds out of bounds and she had to resort to her second barrel ten times. She lost the match, thirty-six to thirty-three.

But her fans did not desert her. They followed her two weeks later to Easton, Pennsylvania, a little city on the Delaware River, where Annie was to face Graham a second time. They came "in large numbers," Annie said of her fans, "still optimistic for the second shoot." Annie and Frank arrived early and found the city buried in snow. They took a cab through the drifts to a small hotel, where they booked a room for the night. Monday dawned cold but sunny, and workers went out to clear the snow. They attached scoops to their horses' harnesses and dug a path to the grounds. While they worked, a rumor spread that Annie Oakley was staying in Room 13 at an Easton hotel. Frantic, her superstitious fans pleaded with her to change rooms—and threatened to change their bets if she didn't. "You should have heard the howl," Annie said. "The old hands at the traps threw up their hands and said it was all off, unless I moved at once." But Annie Oakley stayed right where she was.[2]

"I go at these things from a pragmatic standpoint," she explained years later. "That is to say, I believe in what works. Now I was born on the 13th." And, she said, "I didn't believe I did such a bad job, at that. . . . So I joined William Cody for a three days trial on the 13th. This was my first and greatest trial of fortune. . . . Consequently I was ready to stand by my guns when I ran up against the question of this 13 business in my match with William Graham."[3] When Annie beat Graham that day, twenty-four to nineteen, her fans were chagrined, but no less superstitious. Annie just shook her head at their notions.

"It is easier to drive a trap shooting gang into a corral than to get them to make up a thirteenth squad," she said. She knew one shooter who refused to wear a striped blazer and another who would never fire a cartridge that he had once dropped on the ground. Annie Oakley was much too down-to-earth for such superstitions. To prove it, and perhaps out of a stubborn nature, she took Room 13 again when she faced Graham in the third and deciding match on February 22. This time the bets went three to one against her, but she beat Graham, anyway, forty-seven to forty-five, claiming a victory over a man who decidedly was one of the best trapshooters in the world.[4]

There would be many matches and many exhibitions that year as Annie and Frank tried to make it on their own. One April day, Annie took a Winchester repeating rifle and shattered 100 glass balls out of 109 thrown in the air, in just three minutes and ten seconds. Another day she defeated shooter Phil Daly, Jr., at his own tournament in Long Branch, New Jersey, and another day impressed the ladies at the Boston Gun Club in Wellington, where admirers tossed two half-dollars in the air and asked Annie to mark them. At the crack of Annie's rifle the coins vanished and "roars of laughter greeted the disappointed souvenir hunters," the Boston *Daily Globe* reported.[5]

Before year's end, Annie set an American record at doubles by scoring twenty-five pairs in a row and on another day defeated New Jersey state champion Miles Johnson, who reportedly never had been beaten on Jersey soil. Between fifteen and thirty-one thousand people watched the match (estimates of the number of spectators varied), so many that the traps had to be moved farther out three times because the crowd overflowed the grandstand and pressed toward the score. Annie missed only her forty-seventh bird, "a blue twister who went from No. 5 trap like a rocket." With the miss, Annie turned to Johnson and said, "Did you bring that bird from England?" "No," he replied. "I trained that fellow in order to get in one miss on you."[6]

Annie was shooting so well since returning from England that Frank did an unusual thing: he issued an open challenge to pit Annie against any gentleman shooter in Baltimore. Frank Starr, who owned a driving park, put down a hundred dollars for Fred Kell, a well-known Baltimore butcher who liked to shoot. But Kell met his match in Annie Oakley. " BEATEN BY A GIRL," the Baltimore *American* announced the next day. "Miss Oakley Outshoots Fred Kell—She Was Modest About It."[7]

Annie Oakley didn't win every match she ever entered, even if it sometimes seems that way. In fact, she lost at least two during 1888, one to her old friend Al Bandle of Cincinnati (ten to nine) and one to her new friend Phil Daly, Jr., of Long Branch, New Jersey (forty-three to forty-two). But even in defeat, Annie won admirers. A reporter from the Philadelphia *Commercial Gazette*, who watched Annie lose to Al Bandle, said her exhibition was "wonderful," and the applause she received, even in defeat, was "something to make her proud." "Her conduct, her coolness at the trap and her demeanor in general," he said, "is of a nature to make her friends."[8]

Needing more than shooting matches to keep Annie's name before the public, Frank turned again that spring to his old standby, the variety circuit. Manhattan had numerous theaters, and Frank, peddling Annie's popularity, undoubtedly had his pick. Considering the Butlers' concern with reputation, it's not surprising that Frank sought out the famous Tony Pastor, who ran the Fourteenth Street Theater, next door to Tammany Hall. Pastor always offered clean fare that catered to the family. He was an upstanding man, and his touring spring show would be perfect for the clean-cut Annie Oakley.

Tony Pastor, at fifty-one, was a short, stout man who'd been in show business since he was a boy, writing songs and singing comedy duets. Annie Oakley wasn't yet born when Pastor first appeared on the stage at Barnum's Museum, singing in blackface to the accompaniment of a tambourine. Pastor had opened a number of his own theaters in New York since then and had given many a celebrity his first, or best, opportunity on the stage, including some of the biggest stars of the day: Lillian Russell, Billy Emerson, Denman Thompson, Weber and Fields, Nat Goodwin, and Marie Lloyd.[9]

Annie Oakley was in good company when she opened with Tony Pastor on April 2 to a packed house at the South Broad Street Theatre in Philadelphia. She performed on the same bill with novelty acts like Little Tich, who stood about three feet tall and tickled the audience with his "big shoe dance." The O'Donnells danced a jig; Fannie and Beane and Charles Gilday introduced the Temperance Band and Miss Beane's original fan dance; Max Pettengill took the stage with his acting dog Jim; and Tony Pastor himself sang renditions of "Money the Days of Our Daddys" and "Rock-a-bye Baby."

Annie Oakley, advertised as "the wonder of both continents . . . the greatest rifle and wing shot in the world," concluded the show, a spot that probably had as much to do with her smoky guns as any other factor. The act was second nature to her by now. With her back to a target, sighting with a mirror, she broke balls swinging on a string, and with a Colt's repeater she broke more of them "as fast as they could be tossed into the air." "Miss Oakley," the papers said, "is a rattling shot at offhand and gives a spirited exhibition." And just as people always would, the papers found her a "pleasant-looking young woman" and becomingly modest.[10]

Annie performed with Pastor's company at the Criterion in Brooklyn, the Howard Atheneum in Boston, and Jacob & Proctor's in Hartford. She was playing in Syracuse, New York, on May 21, 1888, when Buffalo Bill's Wild West returned from its tour of England. Ten thousand people had waited on the docks near Erastina that Monday to greet the triumphant Cody. The colonel bowed, waved his hat, and told how Britons had kept him "jumping from his buckskins to a full-dress suit." He spoke in terms of the highest praise about the English people and about his horse Charlie, who had died on the voyage home and been buried at sea. But Annie Oakley seemed forgotten on the docks of Erastina. Probably still angry over the events in London, Cody even left her out of the pages of his updated autobiography, *Story of the Wild West and Camp-Fire Chats,* which was published that year.[11]

Annie didn't improve her relations with Cody when she left Tony Pastor's company that summer and signed up with a rival Wild West outfit. Details of the arrangement are sketchy, but it appears that Annie signed with the Comanche Bill Wild West for three hundred dollars a week, not knowing that it was a ragtag operation of a few unhappy Indians and dime-store cowboys. It was unusual for the professional Frank Butler to sign a contract in such haste with a show he apparently never had seen. Perhaps he was lured by the high salary or the good name of the backer, whom he did not identify, but who probably was Charles M. Southwell, the multimillionaire business manager at the Philadelphia Broad Street Opera House. The salary was not enough to calm Frank, however, when he saw at rehearsal that the cowboys could not even ride a horse.

"It won't do Missie," Frank said. "I can't afford to have you connected with a failure." He hurried to catch a ferry to Philadelphia, where he intended to cancel the contract. As he boarded the boat, he bought a newspaper and happened to read that another Wild West outfit, Pawnee Bill's Historical Wild West Exhibition and Indian Encampment, was broke and stranded in Pittsburgh. Pawnee Bill, whose real name was Gordon W. Lillie, had traveled for a time with Buffalo Bill's show, and Frank undoubtedly knew of him as an upstanding young man. Hoping to save Annie from embarrassment, Frank seized the moment. He talked Southwell into rescuing Pawnee Bill's Wild West from its debts and combining it with his own ragtag show. Lillie, who had had a tough year, readily agreed to the scheme. He had planned to take his show to an exhibition in Brussels, but it was canceled unexpectedly by the death of the German emperor, and Lillie had settled for a tour of the United States. He had played to modest crowds in St. Joseph, Missouri, Kansas City, and Indianapolis, before falling into debt.

Annie said Frank was so relieved when Southwell brought the Pawnee Bill show to Philadelphia and began rehearsals in earnest that "he forgot his dignity and kissed his wife." That small statement in her autobiography was the only reference that a prim Annie Oakley ever made to the physical intimacy she and Frank shared.[12]

Gordin Lillie hadn't been a showman for long. He was born in Bloomington, Illinois, where he received a high school education and worked for a time in his father's flour mill. When the family moved to Wellington, Kansas, he felt the call of the frontier and struck out on his own. He spent a season trapping, went on a roundup on the Skeleton River, and then accepted an appointment as secretary and teacher at the industrial school at the Pawnee Indian agency. He learned the Pawnee language, befriended the Indians, and become known as "the white chief of the Pawnees."[13]

Pawnee Bill's Wild West was in its first year when Annie Oakley joined, but already it was a respectable outfit of 165 horses, mules, and buffalo; 84 Indians; 50 cowboys and vaqueros; and 30 trappers, hunters, and scouts, all advertised as the "real article." Indians attacked a stagecoach as it wended its way into the center of the arena. A horsethief was lassoed by vigilantes, who hung him to a tree while the band played a dirge. Unbroken horses were broken to saddle, and a settler's cabin was burned. And just like old times, Annie Oakley tripped gracefully into the arena and smashed clay birds. Annie Oakley was back with the Wild West—where she seemed to belong.

"There is but one Annie Oakley," the Pawnee Bill ads read, "and she is with us."[14] Lillie advertised her heavily and made the most of her talent, even though his own wife, May Lillie, was a sharpshooter with the show as well. May was a graduate of Smith College and the daughter of a prominent Philadelphia physician. She seemed an unlikely candidate to become a sharpshooter, until Lillie brought her, as a young bride, to his Kansas ranch, where he and his cowboys taught her to shoot and ride sidesaddle. She took readily to the new lifestyle. She went on a hunt with the Pawnees in Indian Territory and killed eight prairie chickens and sixteen wild turkeys in one afternoon. The Indians were so impressed with her skill that they gave her a colt, which she named Hunter. May trained Hunter and rode him at Kansas fairs, where she was acclaimed "the most graceful lady rider in the state." When she learned to shoot from Hunter's back, Pawnee Bill put her in his show and billed her as "May Lillie, Princess of the Prairie" and "World's Champion Woman Rifle shot." [15]

May was a small, vivacious woman whose costume in the Wild West arena looked remarkably similar to the ones Annie Oakley wore. But despite that, and despite May's claim to the world's championship, Annie apparently got along well with her. They performed on the same bill for a month that summer, but there was no question who was the greater star. She was Annie Oakley, "fresh from her London triumph with Buffalo Bill." Annie received top billing, and she was the one Pawnee Bill turned to when he needed publicity. On the last Monday in July he drew twelve thousand people to the afternoon show by wagering two hundred dollars that Annie could kill forty of fifty pigeons with her little 20-bore guns. When she bagged forty-nine of the fifty birds, the papers raved that the feat was a first in the United States with such light-bore guns. [16]

Pawnee Bill tried other stunts to draw the crowds. He added a fireworks display to the show one night, and on another advertised the wedding of Wah-Ki-Kaw, a Kaw Indian chief, and Miss Annie Harris, a white woman, an interracial marriage that appalled the proper Annie Oakley. "An Indian had the nerve to become engaged to a non-descript," she recalled with contempt years later in her autobiography, "so the wedding was advertised." [17]

By mid-August Pawnee Bill's show had drawn a hundred fifty thousand people, and perhaps William F. Cody was beginning to reevaluate his loss of Annie Oakley. Certainly, she had proved herself a strong rival. It is not known when relations with Cody started to improve, but Annie certainly didn't hurt matters in early August when she quit the Pawnee Bill show, after only one month, to join Tony Pastor on a fall tour. Again, on a point of pride and money, Annie said Pawnee Bill tried to keep her, but Pastor objected, saying, "You can't keep Annie Oakley at any price." [18]

As things turned out, it was just as well. That August Pawnee Bill's show ran head-to-head in the South with Buffalo Bill's Wild West, and a bitter rivalry erupted. Lillie charged that Cody's advance men played dirty by pasting over his posters with their own. Lillie begged the public to ignore the mud throwing and judge his show on its merits. But the pleas weren't enough. By late October, Pawnee Bill was broke, and his show was attached by the sheriff in Easton, Maryland. Lillie didn't have enough money to pay his employees or his own hotel bill. The landlord seized his trunks, and May wired her parents for enough money to return to Philadelphia.[19]

Annie Oakley, meanwhile, was in Troy, New York, performing with Tony Pastor's company. The tour took her from Troy to Saratoga and on to Boston, Albany, Rochester, and Pittsburgh, where "the wonder of both continents" took time out from the stage to defeat trapshooter John Lovatt in a thirty-bird match. Ever conscious of keeping her hand in at the traps—and of making a little money on the side—Annie had secured permission to steal away from the show and compete in club shoots or private matches in whatever town they happened to be playing at the time. While the outside events may have angered Buffalo Bill in London, Pastor did not seem to mind. His company performed in the evenings, and the matches did not interfere.[20]

Before the end of autumn, Frank found a backer for the western drama he had advertised, and Annie Oakley prepared to embark on a new career, this time as an actress. The play, renamed *Deadwood Dick: or the Sunbeam of the Sierras*, opened to an unfavorable review at the New Standard Theatre in Philadelphia on Christmas Eve, 1888. Annie played "Sunbeam," a white girl who grew up among the Indians after she survived an attack on her family's covered wagon. She learned to shoot a gun and showed the audience what she could do by smashing glass balls "with unerring aim" and then running offstage, "leaving a houseful of smoke . . . and an astonished audience behind." Although publicity agent Den Howe had promised that Annie's play would be no blood-and-thunder melodrama, no fewer than twenty-five characters lost their lives during its three acts. It was in fact a typical western melodrama, promising "thrilling scenes, desperate situations and howling climaxes." The cast comprised a large band of cowboys and Indians, including chiefs Deep Water and Hunted Bear, and cowboys Pony Bob, Wichita Jim, Mexican Frank, and Cheyenne Charlie.[21]

Deadwood Dick, said the *North American,* was "as startling as anything that could be thought of outside the pages of a yellow-covered novel," a fact that thrilled the gallery gods, though not the newspaper critics. "The plot is unreasonable and the dialogue is remarkable for its bombastic crudity," said the Philadelphia *Press* of December 25. The leading man apparently had abandoned the company the night before the opening, forcing lines to be changed and the play to be cut at the last moment.

"I never quite understood just why the press abstained from vegetable throwing, but they threw not one carrot," Annie later wrote of her stage debut, though she personally received some favorable reviews. The Paterson, New Jersey, *Morning Call* said she had exhibited "marked dramatic ability and in several scenes rises far above the average." Though the *Morning Call* prophesied that the "little lady" had "a brilliant future before her," Annie's stage career lasted all of one month. The theater company fell apart in Chambersburg, Pennsylvania, late in January 1889, when assistant manager John Keenan suddenly disappeared with the show receipts. *Deadwood Dick* disbanded in turmoil, its actors penniless. According to the New York *Clipper* of February 2, 1889, Annie paid everyone's way into town, secured their baggage, and paid off all claims, then left for Philadelphia.

Interestingly, the *Clipper* listed C. M. Southwell and John Burke as managers of *Deadwood Dick*. What kind of arrangement was made is not known, but Burke's involvement undoubtedly was an effort to mend fences between Annie Oakley and William F. Cody. Something definitely was afoot, because only one month after the closing of *Deadwood Dick*, the Baltimore *Sun* announced that Annie Oakley had rejoined Buffalo Bill's Wild West and would be sailing for Paris with Cody's outfit in the spring.[22]

The events and circumstances of their reconciliation are lost to history. Perhaps Annie's stand with Pawnee Bill impressed upon Cody just what a formidable rival Annie was, and he wanted to have her on his side. More likely, Cody was thinking about his plans to return to Europe for an extensive tour of the Continent. Annie had been tremendously popular in England, and her absence from the show certainly would be noticed. According to Fern Campbell Swartwout, Salsbury made "every inducement" to persuade Annie and Frank to go abroad with the Wild West because he "knew the public would expect to see them."[23] It is possible that Annie demanded Lillian Smith's departure as part of her agreement to return to Cody's show. While there is no proof of this conjecture, it is important to note that Lillian left Buffalo Bill's Wild West the very year Annie rejoined.

If Annie and Frank held any grudge against Cody or his Wild West, they never said so publicly. In fact, they always spoke favorably of the show, even during the year they were separated from it. They viewed the Wild West as a great "bonanza" and probably rejoined eagerly. Certainly, they rejoined with their heads held high. After all, Annie Oakley had done quite well on her own. Why, the shooters of Newark recently had named their latest gun club after her. It was called the Annie Oakley Rifle Club of Newark. Members held their first annual ball and reception at Caledonian Park on Tuesday night, February 19, 1889. The guest of honor was Miss Annie Oakley herself, who made the trip up from Baltimore with her husband. A committee of admirers greeted the Butlers at the Newark train depot. One handed a bouquet of flowers to Annie and escorted her and Frank to the park in a carriage. When they arrived, they found every colored gas jet in the pavilion lighted and Nickols's orchestra ready to entertain. Annie, wearing a lavender silk dress and buff-colored felt hat, took part in the grand march and gave a "neat little speech." A dance program of thirty numbers, mostly waltzes and polkas, followed, and Annie became acquainted with members of the club, none of whom she had ever met before.

Another Annie Oakley Rifle Club formed, this one in Butte, Montana, and composed entirely of women. The Annie Oakley legend was taking root in America, just as it had in England. Word came that a sportsman had named his daughter after Annie, and that someone had written a letter to a local newspaper asking whether the town of Oakley, Ohio, was named after her. And in Jersey City, New Jersey, the Reverend Doctor Scudder used Annie as the text of one of his Sunday sermons. "If you will all aim as straight for Heaven as Annie Oakley does at the objects she shoots at," he said, "you can all be 'Little Sure Shots' and will be sure to get to Heaven." [24]

12.

A Postcard from Paris

Flags and bunting flapped in the wind as French president Sadi Carnot rode across the Champs Elysées, into the Avenue Montaigne, across the Pont d'Iéna, and to the doors of the iron-and-glass Central Dome. He stepped out of his carriage on a bright spring day in Paris to strains of "The Marseillaise," sung by a men's choir. Prime Minister Pierre Tirard followed and then members of the Cabinet and the French Senate and National Assembly, all on hand for the opening of the greatest world's fair of all time: the Paris Universal Exposition of 1889, celebrating the one-hundredth anniversary of the French Revolution.

So many visitors were in Paris that the city's population had swelled by two hundred thousand a day. All told, 32 million people would pay admission to the fair, including ninety thousand Americans, who arrived on the boat-trains from the port of Le Havre. They came into Paris at the rebuilt Saint-Lazare Station and ate their lunch at one of fifty restaurants and cafes that dotted the exposition grounds along the Seine. They toured the pavilions of many nations and talked excitedly about the most popular exhibit of all, that of fellow American Thomas A. Edison, who had brought his phonograph and recordings to Paris. Edison supplied headphones for the public, and people lined up early every morning for the chance to listen.

At night, they strolled under the new Eiffel Tower, which glowed in a flood of colored lights. Some marveled at the strange lattice-work and some ridiculed it, but no one disputed that the tower was the belle of the fair. Before summer's end, almost 2 million people would ride to the top, a trip that took only seven minutes in an American-made Otis elevator. Visitors explored the tower's three levels and paused to buy a souvenir or to eat in one of four restaurants, each offering a different cuisine. Distinguished visitors included Thomas Edison, King George of Greece, the shah of Persia, the khedive of Egypt, the bey of Djibouti, and Prince Edward and Princess Alexandra of England, whose signatures were said to have taken up a full page in the guest registry.[1]

Annie Oakley stepped into the elevator at the Eiffel Tower that summer, too, and rode to the top, where she gazed across the big city and the exhibition grounds below. She stopped at a souvenir stand and, thinking of old friends back home, bought a postcard, then mailed it in care of a sporting journal. One stamp would say hello to many friends. "Miss Annie Oakley has probably taken the longest sight of any in her life," the journal wrote upon the card's receipt, "as under date of August 16, top of 'tour Eiffel, Exposition Universelle, Paris,' she sends greetings to American shooters."[2]

Annie and Frank had sailed from New York in late April, docked at Le Havre, and set up camp with Buffalo Bill's Wild West at the Parc de Neuilly, just outside the Ternes gate. Buffalo Bill was getting into the habit of making long stands at big fairs. The crowds were huge and the receipts lucrative. The Wild West was a curiosity from the moment it began to disembark. Newspapermen had crowded the dock and scrambled aboard ship to get a look at the "strange and weird" Indians. They met Red Shirt, Eagle Man, Black Hawk, No Neck, and an Indian everyone called Napoleon because of his striking resemblance to the late emperor. Annie Oakley had "held quite a little court of her own" that day, but had stepped aside for the show's new French Canadians, Adriah Le Page and Goulet, who had been condemned to die in the Riel rebellion but had escaped to the United States. French newsmen crowded round them, elated to find someone with the Wild West who spoke French.[3]

The linguistic and cultural barrier became even more apparent when the Wild West staged its first dress rehearsal before several thousand prominent Parisians, including President and Mme. Carnot. Lacking any familiarity with American history, they were unable to fathom the meaning of the Wild West show. They sat aloof, not understanding what was going on. Applause was slim, and the show seemed headed for disaster when Annie bounded into the arena. "They sat like icebergs at first," she wrote. "There was no friendly welcome, just a 'you must show me' air." The only people ready to applaud were three or four "clackers" who stood at each corner of the reserved-seat section, ready to begin the applause at the appropriate moment. But Frank told them to sit down.

"I wanted honest applause or none at all," Annie wrote. The first crack of her gun sent the stiff, flying targets to pieces and brought ahs and then cries of bravo as her shots came faster and faster. Parisians didn't have to speak English or know American history to appreciate Annie Oakley's act. Good shooting was a universal language. As Annie tossed the last smoking gun on her table and bowed, the crowd roared and threw their handkerchiefs and sunshades into the arena. After that, Annie said, "The icebergs were ready to fight for me during my six months stay in Paris." [4] Nate Salsbury said that Annie had saved the show.

It was the happy ending to a story that had begun on an anxious note the day the Wild West docked in France. Annie had brought fifty pounds of her favorite English Schultze gunpowder with her but was told she could not land it because France had a monopoly on gunpowder. Annie was very disappointed. She didn't have time to experiment with a new brand. Frank would have to figure out new loads and proper packing. A mistake not only could throw Annie's shooting off, it could be dangerous—especially when instructions were written in French.

The way Annie Oakley saw it, there was only one thing to do: smuggle the powder in. She rounded up five hot-water bottles and four lady riders, whom she enlisted as co-conspirators. They poured the Schultze powder into the hot-water bottles, and then each woman put on a dress with a bustle, hiding the bottles within. Annie had never worn a bustle before, but on this occasion, she said, "I was glad to." She led the procession down the gangplank and safely on to French soil. "We sure did attract some attention when we went down the gang plank," Annie said, "for although the bustle originated in France it was going out about that time." Out-of-style as the bustle was, the scheme worked. Pragmatic and resolute as always, Annie just winked at the law and explained: "I was advertised very strongly and much was expected of me." She needed that Schultze powder to shoot well, and that was all that mattered. "It not only meant success for myself," she said, "but for the Wild West company." [5]

Annie's scheme was the beginning of another successful stand for Buffalo Bill's Wild West. Only Edison's phonograph and the Eiffel Tower itself were more popular. Distinguished Americans, in Paris for the fair, stopped by regularly. One day, Cody held a breakfast in honor

The Deadwood Coach and characters from the Wild West in Europe, 1889: Johnny Baker (second from left), John Burke (third from left), William F. Cody (fourth from left), Bronco Bill (standing, second from right), Buck Taylor, the original "King of the Cowboys" (standing, right), John Nelson (sitting atop coach). (Courtesy of the Denver Public Library, Western History Department)

of Russell Harrison, the son of the American president. They ate "genuine clam chowder, baked beans with a flavor of savory pork, corn bread, custard pie and ice cream," and Annie Oakley did her part by marking a nickel with a bullet, then giving it to Harrison as a token.[6]

At another breakfast, Annie met orator Chauncey M. Depew, ambassador Whitelaw Reid, and the great Thomas Edison. According to the *New York Times*, Annie walked up to Edison and asked him whether he thought he could invent an electric gun. She would like an electric gun, she explained, so she wouldn't have to deal with French gunpowder. "I have not come to that yet," Edison replied, "but it may come."[7] It probably was on this occasion that Annie asked Edison to sign her autograph book, which he did. His signature was one of hundreds she would collect. It was a curious hobby for a public celebrity, especially one whose name would become an American legend itself. If anything, Annie's hobby proved just how unpretentious she was.

The signatures in her book were impressive: Henri Journu, a great

European revolver expert and pigeon shot; Hilda de Clifford, considered one of the handsomest women of European nobility; and Captain C. E. Speedy, a British soldier who distinguished himself during the Soudan War by stealing into the enemy camp, recapturing the Union Jack, and returning it to his regiment. Annie collected the signatures of every member of the Chinese and Japanese embassies in London, as well as that of Lord Wantage, the head of the Wimbledon Camp; the king of Senegal; the king of Boudon; Prince Luitpold of Bavaria; and the duchess of Cumberland, sister of the prince of Wales.

Thomas Edison's signature was by far the most admired in Annie's book. It was said to "attract more attention than any king or prince," and even more than that of Mark Twain or Buffalo Bill Cody, who also signed Annie's book. Twain wrote: "You can do everything that can be done in the shooting line and then some"; Cody wrote: "To the loveliest and truest little woman, both in heart and aim in all the world." Annie had a way with people. When the Indian Rain-in-the-Face signed the book, he told her it was the only autograph he'd ever given without charging a dollar, a coup that Annie did not fail to mention. "The autograph album of Annie Oakley's is a rarity," the *American Field* said. "A noted collector offered her $500 for it, which she refused. He wanted her to name a price, which she declined to do as it was not for sale at any price."[8]

In Paris, Annie met President Carnot, who was so impressed with her shooting that he said, "When you feel like changing your nationality and profession there is a commission awaiting you in the French Army." The king of Senegal was thinking along the same lines. After witnessing Annie's exhibition, he offered Cody one hundred thousand francs to buy her. He wanted to take Annie home to West Africa to exterminate the wild tigers that frightened and killed his countrymen.[9] In Paris, as in London, Annie was an undoubted success.

And again, in Paris, as in London, Annie and Frank got to know the city's sportsmen and spent much time at their gun clubs. Frank took an interest in the differences between countries and shooters and occasionally wrote a newsy letter to the sporting journals back home. In one letter from Paris, dated November 6, 1889, he noted that Europeans were arming with the small-bore rifle and starting to use the new smokeless powder. Those were the kinds of topics that interested Frank Butler, a man whose life centered on powders and guns. He knew that a pound of French wood powder cost the equivalent of $3 and that the cheapest black powder available was $1.25 a pound. He'd worked with them all

Annie Oakley, ever the lady, poses in front of her tent on the showgrounds in Paris, 1889. (Courtesy of the Denver Public Library, Western History Department)

in France and like Annie always had definite opinions. "There is only one thing I can compare the French wood powder to; that is, the French match—both go off when good and ready," Frank wrote. "No matter how careful[ly] it is loaded, no two shells will go alike." Even as he wrote, Annie was "admiring and nursing" a black-and-blue mark on her cheek, the result of some unpredictable French powder she was using now that her Schultze had run out. The first French powder she'd tried, in fact, had burst one of her best guns.[10]

Frank noted in the same letter that Frenchmen were poor rifle shots, but very handy with pistols. There was so much interest in the sport, in fact, that Cody had added a new pistol act, Claude Daly, to the program, and American pistol shooter Ira Paine was making his eighth engagement in a Paris theater. Paine was known to pencil a line on a playing card, back up twenty feet, take a pistol, and pierce the line with a bullet.[11]

Annie and Frank, always eager to improve their act, sought out Paine that summer, and it wasn't long before reports filtered back to the United States that Annie Oakley had a new pistol stunt—putting a bullet through the ace of hearts. She probably had Ira Paine to thank for the stunt, which would become one of her best-known items. In fact, Annie not only pierced the ace of hearts head-on, she then turned the playing card sideways and split it down the edge with a bullet. One Paris correspondent who saw her perform the stunt was so impressed that he picked up the perforated cards and mailed them across the Atlantic for his editors to see. His report of July 19, 1889, is one of the earliest known mentions of Annie's card stunt, which was considered very difficult.[12]

According to one newspaper account, "all rifle shots agreed" that splitting a card edgewise was a feat requiring "greater skill than almost any other shown to an audience." A number of accounts over the next few years verify that Annie was doing quite a bit of exhibition work with pistols and revolvers. An 1890 edition of the London *Field* places her at a shooting match near Herne Bay, England, where she used a pistol of small bore "to split a card in two at a distance of about six paces" and to mark a coin that was thrown in the air. The *Field* said Annie succeeded in hitting the coin one time in four tries. Another 1890 report places her at a starling shoot in Ashford, England. "The feats she performed on the ground seem scarcely credible," said the *Kentish Express and Ashford News.* "Thus, if Mr. Butler held out in [his] hand a visiting card *edgeways* to her, at a distance of from ten to twenty paces, she invariably hit the *edge* of the card with a bullet from a pistol."[13]

The card stunt, which Annie performed at private exhibitions and in theaters, was so popular that it was said "to invariably bring down the house." Interestingly, no newspaper account in the thousands of accounts pasted in Annie Oakley's scrapbooks suggests that she did the card stunt in the Wild West arena, although it would become a popular part of her legend that she did.

When the Universal Exposition closed in the fall of 1889, Annie and Frank left Paris with the Wild West for a three-year tour of Europe. In her spare time, Annie tried her hand at the local gun clubs and became a tourist. She and Frank climbed to the top of Mount Vesuvius, visited the buried city of Pompeii, and spent an entire afternoon looking at the guns in the King's Armory in Dresden. When Annie swung an old thirty-five-pound shotgun to her shoulder and looked down the barrel, an armory guard rushed over, astounded. He couldn't believe that such a small woman could handle a gun like that. They talked for awhile, and as Annie left the armory, he gave her a box full of old bullets, which she would treasure for years.[14]

In Venice, Annie glided down the Grand Canal in a gondola and gazed at the dome of the church of Santa Maria della Salute, which rose above the low houses along the waterway. In Rome, she toured the Colosseum and witnessed the anniversary celebration of the coronation of Pope Leo XIII at the Vatican. The pope's hand was so heavy with jewels that Annie said "he seemed scarcely able to raise" it. Frank noticed the Vatican guards, who carried Remington rifles, and thought to himself that they looked out of place in the house of God.[15]

In Monte Cristo, Annie and Frank visited the Chateau d'If and chuckled to themselves as they watched an attendant sell "the original key" to Monte Cristo's cell to three different people. The Butlers were much too smart—and much too careful of their money—to fall for the sham.

In Munich, Annie marked a coin for Prince Luitpold of Bavaria, who visited the Wild West during a rehearsal. Annie was standing in the arena talking to Luitpold when Dynamite, the Wild West's most vicious bronco, broke away from cowboy Jim Mitchell and headed straight for them. Annie said Dynamite "made off like a kangaroo turning somersaults." The prince, thinking Dynamite was only a trick horse, stood there nonchalantly, smiling. Mitchell yelled "like a fiend for us to duck," Annie said, but the prince didn't move. Annie acted on impulse and with all her might shoved the prince to the ground just in time for the bucker to pass over him. "I suppose I am the only person alive that ever knocked a ruling sovereign down and got away with it," Annie said later. "Well sir! He was a good sportsman. He got up and enjoyed the rest of the show five times as much for his realization that he was seeing the real thing and not a parlor fake." The next morning, Luitpold's courier came to the Wild West camp, bearing a diamond bracelet for Annie Oakley and a cigarette holder for Jim Mitchell.[16]

Perhaps Annie wore her new bracelet to the Munich opera one evening, where she occupied the box of Count Wagner, the chief of the Wimbledon Camp and a native of Monaco. She was making new friends all across Europe. In Marseilles, she hurried down to the Custom House to pick up a box mailed to her by a friend in England. Inside were two dozen fresh eggs and a note telling her she should try the packing in her gun before throwing it away. The eggs were packed in Schultze powder.

"The duty on the eggs was about 40 cents, which I gladly paid," Annie wrote. Long out of Schultze powder, she hadn't won a single match since leaving Paris. But now, with her favorite Schultze powder in her gun, things turned around quickly in Marseilles. "I never shot better in my life than I did the next three days, either winning or dividing every event," she said. "It may be that I was in better form, but I am sure my Schultze load had a great deal to do with my good scores."[17] The Marseilles sportsmen were so impressed that they mounted three birds Annie had killed and gave her a gold medal. Annie and Frank reportedly shipped their winnings directly to their New York bank.

In Vienna, she and Frank toured the historic palace of Schönbrunn, where they met Francis Joseph I, emperor of Austria and Hungary. He was a hardworking man whose private life was overshadowed by his duties. Annie and Frank found him poring over a stack of papers on his desk. "He rose with a smile and greeted me with a handclasp," Annie said, "but his face looked tired and troubled." The emperor's life in the fortress-like palace made Annie Oakley pause for a moment and reflect on her own life: "I decided that being just plain little Annie Oakley with 10 minutes' work once or twice a day, was good enough for me," she said, "for I had at least my freedom."[18] It was curious that a woman so fêted viewed herself as only "plain little Annie Oakley." She seemed unimpressed by what really was celebrity status. Even at the height of her fame she never would lose that simple bearing and view of herself.

In Barcelona, Annie was shocked to hear some Spaniards standing outside the gate at the Wild West kitchen, fighting over the garbage. She hopped up on a box and looked over the fence—and never forgot what she saw. "Back from the rubble," she wrote in her autobiography, stood a woman with a tear-stained face. "Oh, I came too late and Carlos will starve," the woman was saying in Spanish. Annie Oakley motioned for the woman to be quiet and to come around the corner of the fence. Annie filled a basket with food for her and sent her on her way. Each day the woman came back, Annie said, "to slip out again with a bounteous basket under her shawl."[19]

The stand in Barcelona turned into a nightmare. The city was stricken with what became known as the Spanish flu, and members of the Wild West troupe, including Annie and Frank, suffered with diseases described variously as flu, smallpox, and typhoid. Orator Frank Richmond became ill and died in Barcelona on a day that Frank Butler called "one of the saddest" of his life. Though ill himself, Frank got out of bed and made arrangements to return Richmond's body to America.[20]

Christmas came, but the Wild West was under quarantine and still holed up in miserable Barcelona. According to Annie, Frank and Johnny Baker tried to cheer up the company by buying a Christmas turkey. They walked to a store and astounded the grocer by ordering a whole bird and not just a leg or a wing. The grocer thought no one had enough money for a whole bird. "The miracle of the loaves and fishes was repeated this Christmas day in the camp of Buffalo Bill," Annie wrote. Every sick man and every homesick cowboy was given a piece of the turkey. "What was left of that turkey," she wrote, "wouldn't have served a gnat for dessert."[21] In the narrow streets of Naples, Annie again saw filth and poverty and was horrified to learn that children were purposedly deformed to improve their chances as beggars. The troubles and the poverty she saw in Europe brought out Annie Oakley's charitable side. Later that year she gave what probably was her first free exhibition: notably, it was for children at the Vienna Orphan Asylum, an indication that Annie Oakley hadn't forgotten her own roots. She later gave ten dollars to an infirmary at Cardiff, Wales. Ten dollars may not seem like much, but Annie was never one to be extravagant. Ten dollars represented 10 percent of her weekly salary, so it was a tithe, and it must have seemed an appropriate sum, especially to a "saving woman."[22]

When the Wild West took up winter quarters at Benfield in Alsace-Lorraine, Annie and Frank left the Continent for England to see old friends. They were spending Christmas at the Royal Oak Hotel in Ashford, Kent, when Annie picked up a newspaper and read the most startling news story of her life: It said she had died of congestion of the lungs in Buenos Aires. The report, apparently first published in the French newspaper *Gaulois et Liberté* on December 29, 1890, was picked up by many other newspapers, and Annie's obituary was appearing all over Europe and America.

"Poor Anne Oakley Dies in a Far-Off Land—the Greatest of Female Shots," said the Cincinnati *Commercial* of January 2, 1891. Annie's mother cried for two days when she heard the news in North Star. And Buffalo Bill, who had returned to the United States for the winter, didn't know what to think. He sent three cables to Frank and anxiously awaited an answer. The response came back shortly: "Annie just finished a full

Christmas platter. No truth in report." A relieved Cody wrote back: "I am so glad our Annie ain't dead, ain't you?"[23]

Annie saw the humor in the situation, too. "I am, indeed, very grateful for your many kind words in my obituary," she wrote to one magazine. The eulogies had been glowing. The Cincinnati *Commercial* had called her a "vivacious" woman, "all nerve and energy." The New York *Daily Graphic* said she possessed such "extraordinary exactness of aim" that she never missed her target. The California *Breeder and Sportsman* said her death had caused "the deepest sorrow throughout the entire sporting circle." Annie Oakley, it said, was "bright, winsome, and refined," and best of all to Annie's ears, she had "proved herself a lady under all circumstances."[24]

Any amusement in the obituaries wore off, however, as Annie and Frank were kept busy for days answering hundreds of letters. Frank wrote to the *American Field, Shooting and Fishing,* the *Police Gazette,* the New York *Clipper,* the Baltimore *Sun,* and old friends back in the States. "I have answered more than a half thousand letters and telegrams," Frank told his friend Al Bandle. "How the report of her death gained circulation I do not know."[25] When the *American Field* received Frank's letter, it happily acknowledged that "Little Sure Shot was a very lively corpse in England" who was doing ten to fifteen miles a day in game shooting. Privately, however, Frank confided to Al Bandle that the news of her death had "affected Annie terribly," mostly because she was far away and unable to personally reassure her mother. Frank asked Bandle to make certain that the report was corrected in all the Cincinnati newspapers.

Very much alive, Annie rejoined the Wild West for a second tour of Europe in April 1891. The show opened in Stuttgart, Germany, and traveled to Karlsruhe, Mannheim, Mainz, Wiesbaden, Cologne, Dortmund, Duisburg, and Krefeld before moving to the border town of Aachen, where the Wild West set up camp on a strip of wasteland in the midst of three battalions of the kaiser's fifty-third infantry regiment. From the windows of their barracks, the soldiers looked down into the Wild West arena and watched the show for free. And when the Wild West packed up camp, the soldiers watched that, too. "We never moved without at least forty officers of the Prussian guard standing all about with notebooks taking down every detail of the performance," Annie recalled. "They made minute notes of how we pitched camp—the exact number of men needed, every man's position, how long it took, how we boarded the trains, and packed the horses, and broke camp; every living rope and bundle and kit was inspected and mapped." The Germans would use the information years later for troop advances during World War I. They took a special interest in the camp kitchen, Annie said, and thanks to Buffalo Bill, someday would serve meals "piping hot on the road to Brussels."[26]

It happened that Crown Prince Wilhelm, who years later would be blamed for starting World War I, visited the Wild West show five or six times during the European tour. During one of Annie's exhibitions, probably away from the Wild West arena during the fall of 1890 or the spring of 1891, Wilhelm watched her snip the end of a lighted cigarette that Frank held in his mouth. Probably wondering whether a trick was involved, or perhaps trying to show his bravery, Wilhelm asked Annie to do the stunt again while he held the cigarette. "She hesitated," the story later was told in the Philadelphia *Public Ledger.* "She never had missed, but it was taking risks with royalty." A slight deviation might have meant the wounding of the crown prince. Not wanting to take that chance, Annie put the cigarette in Wilhelm's hand. (Another version of the story said Wilhelm held the cigarette in his mouth, using a cigarette holder.) Annie shot the ashes off clean and, as people later would say, missed her chance to prevent World War I.[27]

Although the Wilhelm story cannot be verified by contemporary documents, it undoubtedly was true. Annie and Frank, who seldom lied about incidents in their career, told the story themselves during World War I, when their show career was long over and they certainly had nothing to gain from telling it. Furthermore, contemporary accounts do mention that Annie was performing the cigarette stunt during the Wild West's European tour. In one account, published in *Shooting and Fishing,* a man named Roy Rob said he witnessed the stunt. "Miss Annie Oakley gave a private exhibition for the benefit of a few friends, to-day," Rob wrote. With a .320 Winchester rifle, he said, Annie demolished a few sixpences and shilling pieces thrown in the air, and then "knocked the fire off a lighted cigarette while being smoked by an attendant at a distance of 30 feet."[28]

From Germany, the Wild West made stands in Belgium and Holland, then crossed the North Sea into England for a long tour of the British Isles. The show played Liverpool, Manchester, Sheffield, Bristol, Leicester, Birmingham, Brighton, and Portsmouth before crossing the border into Wales, and then Scotland, where it set up for the winter in the East-End Exhibition Building on Duke Street in Glasgow. Annie endeared herself there by donning the tartan outfit of the Scottish Highlands and posing for a picture.

"The proud heart of the nation swells with patriotic pride," one reporter wrote upon seeing her. Also enamored was a Glasgow publication called the *Eastern Bells,* which declared in its December issue that Miss Oakley was a living illustration that "a woman, independent of her physique, can accomplish whatever she persistently and earnestly sets her mind to overtake." Annie's legend was growing all across Europe. In November, the Edinburgh *Evening Dispatch* had called her "the best feminine shot in the world," a statement that was becoming more and more common. In July, the Manchester *Courier* had counted a total of forty-one prizes that Annie had earned in matches and tournaments up to that time and declared that she was "absolutely without a rival as a professional" in her line, and that included the infamous Doc Carver. Annie wasn't called simply Annie Oakley anymore; she was Annie Oakley, "the famous shot." [29]

When the Wild West rolled over the Cheviot Hills and Pennines, across the Avon and into London, Britons remembered her. They came to see her again at Earl's Court, five years now since that first magical year. Playing host now to the International Horticultural Exhibition, Earl's Court was a fairyland of gardens and fountains, gravel walks and flowers. "The Yankeeries" of 1887 had become "The Floweries" and "The Bloomeries" of 1892.

Buffalo Bill, now forty-six years old, was a trifle grayer, and Annie Oakley, now thirty-one, was showing signs of her first wrinkles after constant exposure to "rain and shine." But still, the papers said, Buffalo Bill's "eye is as clear and his aim as true as ever," and Annie Oakley "trips into the circle with her usual grace, and shoots with her usual skill." Her manner was as "bright and merry" as ever. [30]

Buck Taylor had left the Wild West to start his own show, and, of course, Frank Richmond was dead. But the old guide John Nelson still was around; Johnny Baker still was performing his headstand as part of his act; and Major Burke was showing off another band of Indians. His latest group, straight from the American reservations, included Short Bull and Kicking Bear, the Ghost Dance preacher.

Nate Salsbury was as business-minded as ever. Worried by an accusation that the Wild West was mistreating its Indians, he had spent the winter of 1890–91 expanding the show in case Indians no longer could be hired. In one of the most successful innovations in the history of the show, Salsbury enlisted groups of military horsemen from various nations and called them the Congress of Rough Riders of the World. He hired cuirassiers from Germany, lancers from England, dragoons from France, cavalrymen from America, Cossacks from Russia, and gauchos from Argentina. Such a display of horsemanship was no small attraction in the horse-and-buggy days, and again, London opened its arms to the Wild West.

Annie's days passed much as they had five years before. She frequented the London Gun Club, offered shooting lessons to the ladies, and mixed with society. One day she was fêted by Annie Oppenheim at 30 Redcliffe Square in Kensington. The house was crowded with celebrated people, good music, and gay dresses. Annie Oakley, uncharacteristically lavish, was "elegantly attired" in a pearl gray dress with salmon pink broché, high sleeves, and a large, white hat of Brussels lace trimmed with white ostrich feathers.[31]

Other days, Annie was out riding her new bicycle, which she had ordered in Glasgow. Bicycles, or "wheels" as they were called, were a major fad of the 1890s. Annie's wheel was a thirty-five-pound ladies "Premier" with solid tires and upright handlebars. "I am equally as fond of it as my horse," she said. She thought bicycling was a healthy, pleasant exercise, though she wanted no part of racing cycles, with their drop handlebars. She thought the bent-over sitting position was unladylike. "If I thought that I looked like some of those curled up young men whom I often meet on my trips, I should discontinue cycling at once," she said. Sitting properly upright, Annie took her wheel on shopping trips and leisurely rides around London. The new cycling magazines called her "the little Cycling Sure Shot," took her aside for interviews and learned that she had hoped to give a shooting exhibition aboard her wheel in the Wild West arena. "It was my intention to have done so," she said, "in fact, I practiced every day." But the ground in the arena was too soft to pedal a bicycle, so Annie dropped the idea and stuck with her old act, which no one seemed to mind. "Miss Annie Oakley's shooting is more wonderful than of yore, because, I suppose, practice makes perfect," said the London Figaro.[32]

Annie was described as a "magnetic lady," who received "as noisy a welcome as one could wish for." As of yore, she was "swift of foot and true of eye," a "clever little lady" who "kisses her hand to the audience" before "dashing off" and disappearing from "the gaze of her many admirers." As one newspaper summed it up, "everything goes 'with a bang'—literally enough."[33]

The Moonshine ran a full-page cartoon depicting Annie Oakley, "The

Buffalo Gal of Buffalo Bill's Wild West," surrounded by a host of famous admirers. Among them were the fictitious Indian chiefs, Hearthstone and Tummyache, who christened Annie Kickwingti Tararaboomdeay or "Little Take the Cake." The fictitious character Ally Sloper fell in love and wrote that it was "perfect joy to die at Annie's hands. Love's bullets pierced me through; my wound is mortal."[34]

Annie Oakley was smitten, too—with England. "There is no place like England," she told a reporter after returning from the long tour on the Continent. "It was as if we had come home." If it wasn't "for my dear old mother, who is now lonely at home in the States," she said, "I should live here always," a statement that, fortunately for Annie's apple-pie reputation, never was circulated widely in the United States.[35]

In a bit of irony for a woman who would become a symbol of the boisterous American West, Annie Oakley was comfortably at home with the aristocrats of Europe. So proper herself, she liked their decorum. "There is no pompous pretense of superiority about them," she said. She found them "affable" and "not a bit stuck-up," and noted that the ladies even wore "sensible dresses." "At all events, they treated me delightfully," she said. "I suppose it was because a crack shot in petticoats was a novelty and a curiosity to them."[36]

But surely, it was more than that. Annie's natural intelligence and good taste invariably won her friends and admirers wherever she went and undoubtedly helped to secure her place in the upper circles of British society. Appropriately, her thirtieth birthday had come, not along the Mississippi or the Missouri rivers, but along the Elbe and the Rhine. Annie Oakley had come of age in Europe. Her travels had been a lesson in culture, geography, and politics, a lesson that gave a much wider view of the world than that which passed by the crossroads at North Star. Though Annie still referred to herself as "just plain little Annie Oakley," she was no longer any such thing. After three and a half years abroad, her natural polish shone all the brighter.

She came home with the Wild West aboard the steamship *Mohawk*, which tied up at a wharf along the Hudson River on October 27, 1892. The first person to run down the gangplank, said the New York *Recorder*, was Miss Annie Oakley. She was followed by the old regulars, Johnny Baker, Jule Keen, and Major John M. Burke, "the patriot, with a corner of his red, white and blue handkerchief peeping out of his coat pocket." The Wild West had come home.

13.

A Press Sweetheart

Annie Oakley returned to the United States a star. Within a week of her arrival home on October 27, 1892, she was interviewed by the New York *World*, the Newark *Sunday Call*, and *Shooting and Fishing* magazine. She gave interviews gladly, knowing that it paid to keep her name before the public. "I guess the press has made me famous," she once said. "But you know, some really peculiar things have been said."[1] She laughed now about the reports of her death that had circulated while she was in England and joked that Frank had been rather hurt to read about her engagement to an English nobleman. Despite the errors, the press had been good to her—so good, in fact, that an uncomplimentary account was all but unheard of during her show career. Not surprisingly, she and Frank got along well with the newspapermen and made friends with some of the writers on the sporting journals. That first week back in New York they paid a social call to the New York *Clipper* and invited the trapshooting editor of *Forest and Stream* to dinner at the Continental Hotel in Newark, where they were staying.

As she often would do, Annie pulled her guns out of a trunk to show to him, including her favorite Lancaster shotgun, which she had been using for five years now. It was "still in prime condition," he said, "although the stock, with innumerable scars, looked as though it had passed 'through the wars.'" On occasion, the Butlers became nostalgic, and talked about the old days when inviting an editor to dinner would have been unthinkable. Why, it wasn't so long ago, Frank said, that he remembered seeing the first newspaper notice ever written about Annie

Oakley. "We were down in Jersey, and, to tell the truth, the Butler treasury was not in bond-buying condition," Frank said. He only had about three dollars in his pocket and invested it all in copies of the journal that had treated Annie so kindly. It took him awhile to save enough money to buy stamps, but when he did he "scattered those papers all over the land," hoping they would bring further engagements. Frank always was a good manager. It was about the same time that he saw Annie's first lithograph plastered on a wall. He was so excited that he dropped off a streetcar to admire it. But then, Frank said, "being short of change, I had to walk three miles or so back to town." [2]

Frank smiled now when he thought about how things had changed. Gone were the inexpensive boardinghouses and the scrimping to buy pretty ribbons for Annie's hair. The Butlers made good money now, $100 a week, according to a reporter for the *World* who said he had seen a copy of the Wild West weekly wage roll. Annie's salary, he said, was five times what the cowboys made and was the highest of any on the list. By the turn of the century, she would make $150 a week including expenses, a sum that Annie said "was not as big as most folks think." But to be sure, $150 a week was a fortune in a day when the average worker in the United States made $483 a year. [3] The Butlers saved their money and would retire, as one newspaperman put it, "with a wealth of this world's goods."

The important role that money played in their lives cannot be overstated. Annie's conversation was laced with references to money, and there can be no doubt that she was very careful with it. She could tell you down to the penny, for example, how much she paid for a copy of the New York *Clipper* while she was in Europe. Press agent Dexter Fellows said Annie was so miserly that she siphoned off lemonade from Buffalo Bill's private pitcher and carried it back to her own tent. Fellows's memoirs, published a decade after Annie's death, are biting on the subject of Annie Oakley and money. In the memoirs, Fellows compared Annie's ways to the term *Annie Oakley*, which came to stand for free tickets to theatrical and sporting events. "The further connotation of getting something for nothing also applied to Annie's code of living," he wrote. Fellows said he and Annie once played penny-ante poker and that she lost about eighty cents. "For weeks she complained about her 'heavy losses,' and I could never coax her into a game again." Fellows also said that, unlike other performers, Annie never splurged on a hotel room when the show waited over in a Sunday town for the Monday performance. [4]

Frank was money-minded, too. He kept track of the stock market and invested their savings in U.S. gold bonds, Continental Tobacco, Dupont, and other preferred stocks. Just how businesslike the Butlers were has long been overlooked by historians. More than once Annie spoke of her skill "merely as a matter of dollars and cents," and said she had "no love of exhibition work" and did it only "as a matter of business." As early as 1887 she told how she turned down an engagement at the famous Crystal Palace in London because "the Palace Company could only pay a ridiculously small sum, so that I could not think of engaging." [5]

Annie was so careful with money that legend says the Wild West Indians sometimes gave her their money for safekeeping. There is no proof of this, although Annie's niece Fern Campbell Swartwout, who cannot always be trusted on details of Annie's show life, did tell such a story. According to her, a Pawnee named Long John gave his money to Annie to watch. However, one day Long John was gambling and kept coming to Annie's tent to replenish his losses. Annie told John to quit gambling, but he would not listen. "John bring back heap money," he said. But, of course, a shame-faced John did not bring back more money. "I can remember hearing my aunt say to John, 'Heap much money, John?' And he would laugh, and say, 'John not fool any more.'" [6]

Of course, Annie Oakley had learned the value of a dollar years ago when she milked cows at the Darke County poor farm and watched her mother trying to make a living off the little farm at the North Star crossroads. Those times had left an indelible impression on Annie Oakley. "Yes, I've made a good deal of money in my time," she would say, "but I never believe in wasting a dollar of it. I believe that God gives everybody a talent, and if she develops it and makes money it is not right to squander that money in selfish, extravagant living, but she must try to do good with it . . . I believe in simple living." [7] For the most part she did indeed live simply, and as she grew older, more charitably, though always aware of the state of her bank account.

With their savings, the Butlers in the winter of 1892–93 began looking around northern New Jersey for a house to buy. Annie and Frank were free until the spring and had time to shop. Annie made plans to visit her mother in Ohio, and took time out to visit friends in Pompton, New Jersey, where she became the talk of the town when she took to riding and shooting from her bicycle within view of the neighbors. The Sussex *Register* said it wasn't unusual to see her pedaling through a field, smashing balls and nipping tin pans as she went. One newspaper

Annie Oakley shooting from her "wheel," 1894. She designed the riding costume herself, hooking the skirt to her leggings so it wouldn't ride up. (Courtesy of the Garst Museum, Greenville, Ohio)

said she was "weaning the village children from their love of school," and rumors spread to Kansas City that Annie was riding her bicycle all the way to Chicago, giving exhibitions along the way.[8]

Although there was no truth to that rumor, Annie did hope to try her new bicycle stunt that spring when Buffalo Bill's Wild West opened at the Chicago Columbian Exposition, held to celebrate the four-hundredth anniversary of the landing of Columbus.

The great world's fair opened on a rainy Monday, May 1, 1893, on a bleak South Side beach that had been transformed into a six-hundred-acre park of classical white buildings and beautiful fountains. The huge Manufacturers Building, said to be the largest in the world, loomed over the grounds. It was so big that one reporter decided that the Capitol in Washington, if set down on its floor, "would be something like a peppermint drop on a frosted cake." The Hall of Mines, the Hall of Agriculture, the Arts Palace, and the Woman's Building (designed by a woman, Sophia G. Hayden) all were part of a beautiful new city, "The White City," on the shore of Lake Michigan.

As journalist Amy Leslie saw it, "there was only the mighty stretch toward heaven of glistening domes, marble arms and gigantic eagles wings." Amy perched in the Manufacturers Building on opening day and watched President Grover Cleveland throw a golden switch that turned water into the tremendous fountains. Members of Cleveland's Cabinet, Chicago Mayor Carter H. Harrison, Buffalo Bill Cody, and a multitude of people from around the world looked on. There was a Chinese in a quilted skirt and silk jacket, an Egyptian in a bright red costume with gold embroidery, and a Korean wearing a broad-brimmed hat with a small, high crown. "It was," said a reporter from the Chicago *Inter Ocean,* "the passing by of people from all corners of the earth."[9]

The only blot on the White City was "a streak of black," otherwise known as the Midway Plaisance, a conglomeration of restaurants, carnival booths, and rides that stretched for a mile along the west side of Stony Island Avenue, just outside the fair gates. At its worst, midway gambling wheels were manipulated by magnets and nudity shows were faked with mirrors. And the three hundred "so-called restaurants" were so bad that the Chicago *Herald* decided they were "the indigestion union of the entire country." But visitors ate there anyway, then headed down the midway to play "pitch and toss," take a ride in a gigantic new Ferris wheel, or sail along in a "clothesline chariot," which ran for seventy-five feet along a cable stretched eight feet above the ground.

"The man in search of pleasure climbed a platform, took hold of the handles and went sailing through the air like a cash box in one of the big stores." Down at the south end of the midway, where the sidewalks began to lead out into bare patches of prairie, "a man with leather lungs" was herding people into the roller cars of a switchback railway. The train rolled at about a hundred miles an hour, turning sharp curves as it went. A ride cost only five cents "for three minutes of breathless pleasure." One could trade for knickknacks in a Chinese market, see a dwarf elephant at the Hagenbeck animal show, ride a camel on Cairo Street, or peek into a bamboo hut in the Java Village. But the most popular attraction on the midway was Fahreda Mahzar, a belly dancer better known as "Little Egypt, the Darling of the Nile." This wicked show brought revivalist Dwight Moody and gospel composer Ira David Sankey to the midway, where they set up a tent and held revival meetings.[10]

Just across Stony Island Avenue, Buffalo Bill's Wild West and Congress of Rough Riders of the World had set up camp on thirteen acres at Sixty-third Street. Though never considered wicked or fake, the Wild West was deemed too undignified for the White City, and fair officials had refused to let it set up within the gates. Undaunted, Cody had gone across the street to Jackson Park, where the Wild West opened five days before the fair, on April 26.

The rain was coming down in blinding sheets as Buffalo Bill, mounted on a splendid horse, rode into the arena that day. Thousands of spectators huddled under the canvas-covered grandstands and stayed dry, but Buffalo Bill himself was dripping wet. Thunder rolled and lightning flashed, but Cody didn't seem to mind. He lifted his soggy sombrero to the crowd, shook the water out of his long locks, and bowed right and left. Buffalo Bill gave such a wonderful exhibition of shooting, the Chicago *Herald* said, that the "bits of glass in the air were falling as fast as the rain."[11]

Within a month the Wild West had become as popular as the White City itself, and no visit to the fair was considered complete without a trip across Stony Island Avenue to the Wild West amphitheater. As the Chicago *Telegram* put it, the Wild West was a "world beater, the best attraction in the city." The Chicago World's Fair brought the Wild West to the height of its fame, and with it Annie Oakley, who fast was becoming one of the best-known women in America. Annie played to thousands of people every day that season as the Wild West broke attendance and income records. On Sunday, May 28, 22,464 people watched the

Annie Oakley practicing on the showgrounds, 1892. (Courtesy of the Salsbury Collection, Denver Public Library, Western History Department)

show, and on Sunday, October 8, the Wild West took in $19,000 in just two performances. By the time the fair ended, Buffalo Bill's Wild West had posted not only its most prosperous year, but what would be called the most prosperous year in the history of outdoor entertainment. It showed to 6 million people and cleared a cool million dollars.[12]

It was during the Chicago World's Fair that Amy Leslie, "drenched and gasping," flew into Annie Oakley's tent one rainy day for an interview. She found Annie entertaining Nate Salsbury, John Burke, and "two or three lovely ladies from New York." They all enjoyed "ices and malting jelly cake" while the wind rocked the lamps, tumbled over a stack of guns, and howled defiance.[13] They told stories of other storms and became better acquainted.

Like Annie, Amy Leslie was small, though plump. She was thirty-seven at this time, an Iowan by birth who had studied vocal music at the Chicago Conservatory and achieved considerable fame as a light opera soprano. Amy had toured with a number of companies until her son died of diphtheria while she was preparing for the lead role in a production of *Castles in the Air*. Grief-stricken, she quit the cast, never to return to the stage. She settled in Chicago with her mother, obtained a divorce, and decided to seek a career in journalism. In 1890, she wrote a review of *Castles in the Air*, sold it to the Chicago *Daily News*, and was hired as drama critic, a position she held for the next forty years.[14]

Always good-natured, Amy Leslie developed an intimacy with many of the great stage performers she wrote about, Annie Oakley included. Though the two women couldn't have been more different, Amy Leslie and Annie Oakley became friends in a professional way, and for the next several years, Amy would drop into Annie's tent or dressing room any time the Wild West was in Chicago. As a city woman who loved the night life and the theatrical world, Amy Leslie found Annie Oakley to be "a plain, kindly little woman" who talked "with broad, clear gentleness" of the farmlands where she had grown up. Amy Leslie found Annie to live "one of the most retired, modest, commonplace sorts of life"— that is, when she wasn't hunting or setting target and trap records.[15]

How different Annie Oakley must have seemed from the other stars whom Amy Leslie came to know. Though Annie was as famous as Lillian Russell, Lillie Langtry, and even the great Sarah Bernhardt, her life was very different. Amy Leslie wrote of them all, but Annie Oakley stood apart. Far from Annie's simple Oxford cotton dresses, Sarah Bernhardt was inclined "to filmy gowns, half lace, half vapory silk," which kept her "in a seductive shiver." The closest Bernhardt got to the wilds that Annie Oakley loved were the costly furs she wore, "sometimes with hideous little heads snarling from the edges." Lillian Russell was a professional beauty, a stunning woman compared to Annie Oakley. For more than thirty years Russell starred in one operetta or musical show after another, emblazoned always "as one of the most beautiful women in the world." While Amy Leslie found Lillian, like Annie, "simple as a schoolgirl," Annie Oakley never would be "watched and petted" in the same way as Lillian Russell. And besides that, the proper Annie would have frowned on Lillian's four marriages. And then there was Lillie Langtry, "witty and wise," always "scoffing and mocking and philosophizing, or betting or flirting"—how different from the down-to-earth and sincere Annie Oakley. Lillie Langtry was "rich, well-born, and of exquisite refinement." She loved roses and had hundreds of them sent over every day from her famous rose nursery at Kentford. Annie Oakley never would be so extravagant.[16]

Although Annie Oakley was every bit as famous as Langtry, Russell, and Bernhardt she really was not a part of the "legitimate" stage. Annie Oakley belonged to the circus world and the show lot, and as such, she was better loved by the American people.[17] But fame, Annie Oakley insisted, was good for only a few things; it brought many engagements and an excellent salary. Even during the great Chicago World's Fair, when Annie's name was on thousands of lips, she seemed to care not a whit for fame. "Truly I long for the day when my work with the rifle and gun will be over with, and when I can take to the field and stream as often as true inclination may lead me there," she said. Annie Oakley loved the out-of-doors more than all else, and that would never change, no matter how famous and how rich she became. "I guess I could never settle down to city life and be happy about it," she said.[18] Amy Leslie marveled at Annie's simplicity and that of Frank Butler, whom she described as "exactly the sort of man that Annie is a woman—plain, kindly, homelike and genuine." Amy found the Butlers unpretentious and their character above reproach. "There is not a nicer wife or woman in the land than Annie Oakley," she wrote. "When she was in Europe royalty courted her and she accepted it as she would the complacent attentions of a village quilting party." When Annie offered Amy a drink of wine from the cask in her tent, Amy noticed that Annie didn't take a drink herself. "She herself never touches stimulants," Amy wrote, "naturally from her occupation this might be inferred, for, though great shots can be pretty well shot themselves, they do not shoot well under the influence of anything unsteadying."[19]

Amid all the hoopla in Chicago, Annie Oakley quietly was tendered a reception in her honor on June 28 at the Ohio State Building inside the White City. Ohio governor William McKinley and Congressman Anderson were there. They complimented Annie for her skill with "shooting irons" and "voiced their admiration of her as a daughter of Ohio," a fact that Anderson had been surprised to learn. But *Forest and Stream* wasn't surprised by Anderson's ignorance; although Annie Oakley was known "in all corners of Europe and America," it said, "in her own native State of Ohio she is most nearly without honor."[20]

But that was beginning to change, at least in Greenville, and certainly among the sportsmen of Cincinnati. Before the World's Fair ended, the Greenville *Sunday Courier* was reprinting articles about Annie, running her portrait, and proudly proclaiming her "The Darke County Girl," the county's most famous daughter. The respected *American Field* was attaching the word "great" to her name and saying that she had had "greater honors conferred on her than any other American woman."

She was "modest and deserving," the *Field* said, "loved most by those who know her best." Even the U.S. Army was beginning to recognize Annie Oakley as an authority on shooting. That fall the army sent a handful of sharpshooters to the World's Fair to take a few pointers from her. In Union City, Indiana, a newspaperman compared her to Joan of Arc, and in New York City a newspaperwoman looked on Annie's shooting costume with envy. It "made my befrilled gown blush and I sighed for dress reform."[21]

14.

At Home in Nutley

Nutley, New Jersey, was a pretty little town. It sat in a green valley along the Passaic River, only thirteen miles from New York City. Residents worked in the mills along the river or the quarries down in Belleville or Avondale. They played baseball on the diamonds along Passaic Avenue and danced on the open-air floor just back from Centre Street. In winter, they skated on the cotton mill ponds or raced their bobsleds down Povershon Hill.

So close to Manhattan, Nutley was home to a number of writers and artists who built their glass-enclosed studios among the trees overlooking the Passaic's Third River, which wound through the heart of town. The artist Frank Fowler, who painted the ceiling frescoes on the old Waldorf-Astoria ballroom, was one of the first to build a studio/home in the little enclave everyone called the Enclosure. In time, it would be occupied by a succession of artists, including Frederick Dana Marsh, known for his paintings of industrial scenes, and Guy Pene du Bois, a satirical painter and newspaper art critic.[1] Over the years, Nutley would be home to a long line of luminaries, but perhaps the best remembered was an artist of a different sort—the sharpshooter, Annie Oakley.

She and Frank had been looking for a home in northern New Jersey ever since they had returned from Europe. There were rumors that they'd purchased a house and six acres near Hollywood Park in Long Branch, but for reasons unknown, decided instead to have a house built in Nutley. They bought a lot from a Mr. J. Fisher Satterthwaite and began building the house of their dreams in the fall of 1892. According to

128

Mrs. William Longfelder, an acquaintance, Annie decided to settle in Nutley after "she happened to be passing through" and was impressed by the town's beauty. Or perhaps, Annie and Frank had discovered Nutley on their way to Eaton Stone's place north of town. Stone, at seventy-six, was an old circus man who was known as the first person ever to turn a somersault on a bareback horse. His eight-sided barn out on Kingsland Street was a favorite place for circus people to train in the winter. Surely, Annie and Frank knew of it. Or perhaps, as another story went, Frank discovered Nutley when he got off a train at the wrong stop.[2]

Though it seems ironic that Annie Oakley of the Wild West would build a house in New Jersey, the decision was logical. The key undoubtedly lay with Buffalo Bill's Wild West, which was planning to open another long stand just across the bay in South Brooklyn. And, most important, there were hints that Cody was considering setting the show up there permanently.[3] Annie and Frank could spend the remainder of their Wild West career commuting to New York: lots of Nutley residents did.

After a decade of traveling, the thought of settling down in their own home must have been appealing. Nutley was a perfect spot; it was close to the city, but it felt like the country. And so it was that during a cold stretch in December, shortly before Christmas, 1893, Annie Oakley and Frank Butler moved into their new house at 304 Grant Avenue. It was a roomy house, said to have cost as much as nine thousand dollars. It had three stories, a porch across the front, a railed balcony, and a turret at the side. Legend would say that Annie built the house without closets because she was so used to living out of a trunk. But the legend most certainly is not true. Annie Oakley, traveler though she was, was much too practical to build a house without closets. The legend may have grown out of a statement that Annie built the house "without thought to closets."[4]

It didn't take long for the Butlers to make friends in Nutley, among whom was Henry Cuyler Bunner, thirty-nine, editor of the satirical magazine *Puck*. Bunner had a wide circle of sophisticated friends, some of whom joked about his rural way of life and his menagerie of house pets, kept by his children. The story was told how the usually tranquil Annie Oakley was visiting at Bunner's house one day and grew fiery when she saw some boys mistreating one of Bunner's pet pigs.[5]

At her own house, built to her specifications, Annie unpacked a mounted blue rock pigeon she had killed in England and put it on the mantel. Frank also was making a home. He joined the Nutley Rod and Gun Club and volunteered to act as referee at an upcoming shooting match against the Yanticaw Club.[6]

Less than a week after moving in, the Butlers had dinner guests, an event that was duly noted in the social columns of the local newspapers. Invited were J. M. Brown, manager of the Atlantic Transport Company of New York; Louis E. Cooke of the Barnum & Bailey show; and a Mr. and Mrs. Cannon of Newark. Mr. Cannon was a noted one-armed sportsman. Also invited was Captain Wiltshire of the steamship *Mohawk*, which had carried the Wild West home from Europe the year before.[7] The Butlers made friends wherever they went. And now, with a home of their own, they opened their door unhesitatingly. In a public letter unusual for someone so famous, Annie Oakley showed a sentimental side and proved just how much of a kinship she felt with fellow sportsmen. "I beg of all friends and sportsmen not to pass by without stopping," she wrote to *Forest and Stream* that Christmas Eve. "They will find the latch string on the outside. No matter if they shoot a $30 or a $300 gun their welcome will be just the same." She intended, she said, to set aside a "sportsmen's room" in her new house and asked hunters to contribute mounted birds, animal heads, or skins to her collection, preferably specimens they had killed themselves. Annie promised to put the giver's name on each specimen. Her letter "created a furor, all the American sportsmen papers taking it up," *Forest and Stream* reported. "There isn't a shooter in America who wouldn't fight for her."[8]

One shooter in particular, a Mr. Gloan of Cincinnati, was so touched by Annie's letter that he decided to make certain she received a proper house-warming. He asked the sportsmen of America to donate a dollar each to buy Annie a proper gift, which they did, a solid silver table service. The gift was not out of place in Annie's new home. She had crystal aplenty and what Amy Leslie described as "a store of household linen which is almost fabulous considering how unpretentious the Nutley home and how great its furnishing in beautiful fabrics and needlecraft." Annie Oakley, of course, had done the sewing herself.[9]

Annie hired a maid to clean house and cook while she spent time with her horses in the stable out back. Life in Nutley could not have been better. Even Annie's sportsmen's room was taking shape. From Kansas City, noted pigeon shot J. A. R. Elliott sent an albino quail mounted in a glass case, and a Mr. Bill Fields sent an "enormous owl, nicely mounted."[10]

That March, Annie and Frank were invited to participate in the biggest social event of the year, the Nutley Amateur Circus, a charity event for the Red Cross Society; proceeds would buy hospital supplies and endow a bed at St. Barnabas's Hospital in Newark.[11] Nutley enlisted Henry Bunner as publicity agent, and he soon was circulating press releases to all the big papers in New York. A dozen Nutley artists hand painted souvenir programs, and businessmen donated lumber, built tiered seats, and strung electric lights in Eaton Stone's old barn. Someone gave the building a new coat of whitewash, and someone else talked the Erie Railroad into running a special train to within fifty yards of the door. Nutley was alive with the amateur circus. Even ordinary townspeople got in on the show; across the porches of their homes, they strung square, white banners with a red cross in the center.

It was a social event so full of a good cause and big names that the New York newspapers could not ignore it. They all ran stories, which Annie and Frank clipped and pasted in their scrapbooks. Among the lot was a story by a reporter from the New York *Sun* who took the Erie Railroad out to Nutley to look around the Sunday before the circus. It had been a picturesque ride along the Passaic from Paterson down to Newark. As the train made its way through the suburbs out to Nutley, it passed assorted lines of red and green horsecars and stopped on the far corner of every block. Quaint, well-to-do Nutley seemed an unlikely place for a showtown, but a showtown it was in Eaton Stone's barn that Sunday.

Bareback riders were in the ring taking last-minute instructions from old Stone himself, who surprised the man from the *Sun* by prancing around the arena on a horse "with remarkable vigor." A trick pony was learning to stand on a narrow pedestal, and from outside came the sharp crack of a pistol, evidence that Annie Oakley was nearby "getting her touch on the trigger." The reporter found Annie out back smashing clay targets, one after the other. Beside her stood Frank Butler, "acting the part of a trap to spring the clay pigeons into the air." When Annie had finished shooting, the reporter walked up to her and asked what she thought were the qualifications of a dead shot. "I suppose it's a gift, though practice helps," she told him. "Still, I've gone for months without touching a gun, and then stepped into the ring without preliminary practice and made as good a score as I ever did.

"It's a matter of feeling," she said. "The marksman who hesitates is lost. Just take it for granted you are going to hit and fire away before you have time to doubt the certainty of success."[12]

As they talked, someone urged Annie to show the reporter how she could pick up a hat while riding a speeding horse. Annie accepted the "bantering challenge" and mounted her horse, sitting astride. She urged the animal into a gallop and circled the ring. Just before she came to the hat, she swung over, "holding on, heaven and her muscles only know how," and made a sweeping reach with her arm. She regained her seat, "waving the hat triumphantly aloft."

Annie Oakley's performance alone, said the Newark *Daily Advertiser,* would be worth the trip to the Nutley circus on Tuesday evening, March 27, 1894. Tickets, at one dollar apiece, had sold out in advance, and even the performers paid to get in. The only "deadheads" who didn't pay were the reporters—and Clara Barton of the Red Cross Society.

The crowds began to stream into Eaton Stone's barn early that Tuesday evening, and by eight o'clock, six hundred people had crowded in, filling every seat. "Everybody who is anybody out in the many suburbs of Newark was on hand," the New York *Press* said. Wall Street brokers worked as ushers, and pretty girls sold peanuts wrapped in a ten-cent bag with a red cross printed on it. Incandescent lamps shone, flags fluttered from the rafters, and whitewash brushed off on everyone's clothes. That didn't seem to matter, though, as Barnum's old Robinson band struck up a circus tune and eight riders dashed into the ring on fiery steeds.

Al Stirratt leaped a hurdle on his pony, E. L. Field came on with a bear and a monkey, and Professor Donovan boxed with Alpheus Geer. Charles Smith, an electrician posing as a tramp, drew a big laugh when he plodded into the arena on the back of a fat horse named "Little Surefoot," which everyone recognized as Molly, the delivery horse from the hat factory. Then Henry Bunner stood up and read a poem he had written about the "Greatest rider ever known: This, ladies and gentlemen, is Eaton Stone."

A performer who needed no introduction, said *Harper's Weekly,* was Miss Annie Oakley. She was no amateur, of course, but no one at the amateur circus seemed to mind as she rode into the arena, standing on the back of a horse. The applause of recognition was instant. And then, in a stunt she'd never before done in public, Annie smashed glass balls while the horse circled the arena, she standing up all the while. She made it look so easy that the New York *Sun* decided that Annie Oakley broke glass balls with a gun as calmly as other people broke hardboiled eggs with a knife. By common consent, the New York *Herald* voted Annie's act "the most satisfactory of the evening." [13]

While Annie and Frank were in Nutley raising money for the Red Cross, Nate Salsbury was in San Francisco trying to stir up new attractions for Buffalo Bill's Wild West. He'd been seen at the Midwinter Fair, where the San Francisco *Examiner* said he had made an offer to buy the Colorado Gold Mine and transport it back to South Brooklyn, where the Wild West was preparing to open a new season at Ambrose Park. Nothing apparently came of the deal, but the Wild West opened "with a hurrah" anyway on Saturday, May 12, 1894, and "A Very Fine Sight It All Was, Too," declared a headline in the New York *World*.

Ambrose Park, which had been an old cinder dump before the Wild West moved in, had been transformed into a twenty-four-acre tent city of colored flags and flowers. A twenty-foot-high panorama of the Big Horn Mountains with wooded hillsides and snow-capped peaks jutted above a corrugated steel fence encircling the lot. Inside was the largest arena in the Wild West's history, measuring 450 feet long by 312 feet wide and surrounded on three sides by a huge, canvas-covered grandstand.

Although the show didn't begin until three in the afternoon, ten thousand people were on the grounds by one o'clock. They walked down the avenues of the Wild West village and inspected the tents of the Indians, the Mexicans, and the armies of the nations. Beds of scarlet geraniums bloomed around every doorstep and a lattice of vines and roses stood here and there, planted by the German soldiers, who were judged by the New York *Sun* to be the best housekeepers on the Wild West lot. The floors of their tents were so well scrubbed and the beds so neatly made that they "would make the reputation of a chambermaid." [14]

The tents of Buffalo Bill, Nate Salsbury, and Annie Oakley stood near the main gate, each identified by a wooden nameplate hanging over the entrance. [15] Nearby was a log cabin, erected as press headquarters for John Burke. Reporters dubbed it "scoop shanty" and looked around at the bows and arrows, Indian bead work, and photographs of the Wild West that decorated the walls. Major Burke, as usual, collared a few reporters and took them down to the mess tent to taste camp fare, which he was pleased to call hard tack, bacon, and melted snow water. "But to those who never bivouacked," said a reporter from the New York *World*, camp fare tasted an awful lot like cold chicken and champagne.

By showtime, the stands were full of New Yorkers, who sat munching peanuts, drinking pink lemonade or beer, and smoking cigars and cigarettes. As the crowds waited for the show to begin, the vendors did their work.

"Every one allowed to smoke," one vendor yelled.

"Have some popcorn, honey-coated, 'fore the show starts," another shouted.

Men carrying flat wire baskets filled with glasses walked back and forth in the aisles. "Orange Jooce! Sweet 'n' cool! Orange Jooce!" they yelled. Others swung foaming glasses of lager, and a "dreadful youth with a dreadful voice" never stopped shouting, "Programmes! Programmes!"

Those who bought a programme for ten cents read about the Pony Express, the Deadwood coach, and the American bison. They stared at photographs of Buffalo Bill, Johnny Baker, and Annie Oakley, then took a bite of popcorn and a sip of lemonade. Annie Oakley's legend was born in that moment. It took hold as the breeze, salty and light, blew in

Indians and Annie Oakley pose in the Wild West mountains. (Courtesy of the Western History Collections, University of Oklahoma)

from the bay, flapping the colored flags atop the grandstands and billowing the canvas mountains in the distance. Two or three white clouds sailed over and the bank of human faces stretched away to pink indistinctness. "Brooklyn," one reporter wrote, "lay breathless just outside."

Suddenly, at the far end of the arena a wooden gate swung open, and the Indian warriors of a time now past swooped out. They seemed to spring out of the ground, a phantom horde of spears, bonnets, war plumes, and feathers, a dark mass of men and animals. "As they came dashing the course they grew vivid in color-flying groups . . . riding like the wind and giving voice like demons . . . it was as if barbarism had come to us with its teeth drawn." [16]

The "grand entree" was more thrilling now than it had been years ago at Erastina, what with the addition of the soldiers of many nations. They swept out from behind the gate, troop after troop, a kaleidoscope of color and motion: Mexicans in mushroom hats and leather trousers with lariats at their saddlebows; cowboys mounted on ponies and swinging their hats; Arabs, in burnouses and turbans; real Riffians, swarthy and fierce, and Cossacks on gaunt horses, wild and fleet. The show was color and contrast and motion. If Colonel Cody "had raked the earth for a picture," said the New York *World*, "he could not have got together the primitive colors more successfully." To the *American Mercury*, Buffalo Bill's Wild West was "the greatest show ever put together," and no one should miss seeing it. [17]

Since Ambrose Park sat on the shore of New York's Upper Bay, easily reachable by the Thirty-ninth Street ferry, a ride straight to the Wild West gate cost only a nickel. Or one could take an excursion steamer, ride the elevated railway, hop the Third Avenue trolley, or board a streetcar over the Brooklyn Bridge. The Wild West was the "most get-at-able" place in Brooklyn, the papers declared, and a thousand Wild West posters plastered on a thousand walls in New York agreed. The most famous poster showed Buffalo Bill, hat in hand, flying over New York Harbor on his horse. "All Roads Lead to Buffalo Bill's Wild West," it declared, as indeed they did.

Adding to the glamor was an enormous new electric light system that enabled the show to play at night. The lights were so powerful they could illuminate boats in the harbor and were visible from beyond the Statue of Liberty. They were a friendly sight, greeting the ferries as they pulled up to the Wild West dock. Hundreds of incandescent lamps were fastened to the poles in and around the Wild West grandstand, and two movable search lights illuminated the targets for the sharpshooters. [18]

The setup, by the Edison Electric Illuminating Company of Brooklyn, was said to be the most complete private plant in the country, and engineer Sylvester McCarroll bragged that it consumed only two and one half tons of coal every twenty-four hours.[19] Every evening before the show began, Mr. M. B. Bailey and his assistant, a Mr. Heermann, climbed to a little iron room atop the grandstand, where they operated the movable search lights. They grabbed the enormous lights by their frames and focused one on the gate from which the action would spring and the other on a square peephole in the huge mountain scenery. Seconds before 8:15, Buffalo Bill's head appeared in the hole, a hand came out, and a sombrero waved. Bailey caught the signal and shouted to Heermann: "Catch that band of Indians," and the big, white circle of light focused on the thundering ponies and their riders as they swept from behind the gate. Catching the Indians was easy compared to catching Annie Oakley's act, when Bailey and Heermann had to illuminate targets flying in every direction. "She may be an expert shot to hit them on the wing, but so is Mr. Bailey, for he must find and follow each of the clay pigeons and glass balls with his single ray of light before she can get a shot at them," the *Brooklyn Standard* reported.

In private, Annie spent her time swimming in the bay, writing letters, taking walks, riding her horse, and pedaling her bicycle to Nutley occasionally to check on the Grant Avenue house, which she and the money-minded Frank had leased for the summer. In a delightful, though probably exaggerated, account, she outlined her daily schedule for the New York *Recorder* that summer. She said she began her day with a cold sponge bath, then took breakfast, "never omitting fruit," and spent a half hour over the morning newspaper. She took a morning walk, "always at a brisk pace," and sometimes rode her wheel, sitting "very straight." She took a light lunch, devoted a few hours to letter writing and at about four in the afternoon was "jolly ready" for a horseback ride or another walk. She liked to fence in the evening and worked out with a pair of light dumbbells, never weighing "more than three pounds." "On one pretext or another, I get all the outdoor exercise possible," she said, and encouraged other women to do likewise, though she was quick to add that she didn't want "women to go in for sport so that they neglect their homes." Annie was proud of her athleticism and noted that she could run one hundred yards in just thirteen seconds. "Pretty good for a woman, isn't it?" she said.[20]

She got her best exercise in the Wild West arena, where she lifted her loaded seven-pound shotguns to her shoulder about 150 times a day. That worked out, she calculated, to more than one thousand pounds lifted every day. She told the *Recorder* that she completed her day with a warm bath and then headed off to bed. "I generally sleep so sound that only the breakfast bell awakens me," she said. "Tell the young to try this, and if they don't find it beneficial I am mistaken, and I don't think I am." [21]

Annie Oakley lived a life of leisure that summer compared to the sixty-five thousand sewing girls who worked long hours across the bay for five dollars a week. With a salary now of at least a hundred a week and her room and board paid, Annie Oakley was in a class with few Americans. She didn't even have to cook her own breakfast; it waited for her every morning at the sound of the breakfast bell in the big Wild West cook tent. Annie's every need was cared for. One June day when she needed a piece of tape, she ran over to see Ma Whittaker, camp nurse and mother hen. A reporter from the New York *Commercial* happened to be in "Marm's" tent when "a pretty, smiling little woman came across the path." "Say, Mamma, have you got a little piece of red tape—about a yard will do," the little woman inquired. Ma got up, found the tape, and introduced the newcomer as Miss Annie Oakley. "This is the girl that can shoot a fly a mile off," Marm told the reporter. Annie just smiled and said, "Oh, I shoot a little. Marm is always saying something nice." [22]

September came to Ambrose Park, and with it, some of the best publicity the Wild West ever received. It began with a trolley ride to West Orange, New Jersey, where Buffalo Bill and fifteen of his Wild West Indians strutted for a brief moment before Thomas A. Edison's new battery-driven movie camera, the kinetograph. It sat inside in a large frame building, totally covered with black tar paper. The whole shanty revolved on a pivot so it always could face the sun. Inside was a single room with a small stage at one end, also draped in black and open to the sun. It was the first motion picture studio, affectionately referred to as the Black Maria.

Buffalo Bill and his Indians—and later, Annie Oakley—were among a long line of celebrities and everyday people whom Edison enticed in 1893 and 1894 to appear before his crude movie camera. Among the earliest of these stars had been boxer "Gentleman Jim" Corbett, strong man Eugene Sandow, and the dancer Carmencita. Buffalo Bill joined the list of luminaries when he stepped into the glare of the Black Maria and discharged his Winchester sixteen times at imaginary objects. And then the Indians trooped out into the sunshine, their bodies "fairly ablaze" with the colors they had painted themselves. Parts His Hair looked like a "zebra suffering from erysipelas." Holy Bear's breast looked like a "wonderful sunset scene," and Charging Crow's cheeks were so red they looked "as hot as one of Ella Wheeler Wilcox's poems of passion."

When Annie Oakley paraded before the kinetograph later that fall, Edison was immensely pleased, the New York *Recorder* said, because his machine proved delicate enough to reproduce the smoke from Annie's guns and the shattering image of the breaking balls. What became of that historic footage is not known, though it probably was shown in one of the kinetoscope parlors that opened in New York as early as April 14, 1894. The first parlor was such a hit that crowds waited in long lines to see the pictures that lived and moved for ninety seconds. Soon there were parlors in Chicago, Baltimore, Atlantic City, and San Francisco. People put a nickel in the box, peeped through a binocular-like slit in the top and watched Edison's subjects in action. Ironically, the movie industry that Edison's kinetoscope spawned eventually would lead to the demise of the great outdoor Wild West shows, whose stars had been among its earliest subjects.[23]

That times were changing became apparent as the season closed at Ambrose Park on October 6. Even the effervescent Major Burke admitted that the season had not been as successful as hoped. He blamed the weather and the financial depression of 1893, which had cut into the Wild West's gate receipts at a time when expenses to run the show were as high as ever. The electric light plant alone was said to have cost more than $30,000, and the elaborate posters, some lithographed in fourteen colors, were rumored to cost $5,000 a week to keep up. Simply feeding the outfit of almost 750 people was a tremendous expense. The New York *Tribune* reported daily operating expenses of $1,100 a day, and the New York *Journal* agreed that Cody and Salsbury had sunk "a fortune in the enterprise."[24]

With profits down, Cody discarded any plans he may have had for setting up permanently in South Brooklyn and instead struck a deal with James A. Bailey, the circus man, to take the Wild West on the road. The arrangement would change the Wild West forever and virtually end the show's tradition of playing long stands in one spot. To make matters worse, Nate Salsbury became ill. He went home, never to travel with the Wild West again. Annie and Frank, who knew that Salsbury would be sorely missed, "had the feeling that something dreadful had happened." And indeed it had. The change in fortunes was abrupt. While only a year earlier Cody had enjoyed the greatest season in outdoor show business, by mid-July of 1894 he was complaining that he was in the tightest squeeze of his life.[25]

The signs of ending and change were all around as the Cowboy Band marched down the main street of the Wild West village and, as it always did at the end of a season, halted in front of Buffalo Bill's tent to play "Auld Lang Syne." The grandstands were deserted now, the Indian tepees had been struck, and the shutters on scoop shanty banged dismally in the wind. "Sadness seemed to pervade the place," wrote a reporter from the *New York Times*. "Each banner fluttered with indignation and if there were not tears in the eyes of the fierce-looking bison . . . then the distance was deceptive."[26]

15.

Village on Wheels

To increase profits after the disappointing stand in South Brooklyn, Buffalo Bill's Wild West went on the road. Cody contracted with James A. Bailey, the circus man, who agreed to provide transportation and local expenses in exchange for a share of the profits. The deal put Bailey in charge of routing the three largest shows on the road—Buffalo Bill, Barnum & Bailey, and Ringling Brothers—and it was his intention to route them so they didn't compete with one another. Not surprisingly, the schedule that Bailey devised for the Wild West was as grueling as that of any circus. Beginning in 1895, Buffalo Bill's Wild West would play one-night stands in hundreds of big and small towns across the country, tapping all the business it could, then moving on to the next town along the railroad line.

In 1895, the Wild West would play 131 towns; in 1896, 132 towns. Their names read like a road map of America—Cumberland, Parkersburg, Kokomo, and Springfield, Saginaw, Ann Arbor, and Kalamazoo. The Wild West wound north to Duluth, south to Louisville, and west to Sioux Falls. In 1896, the show traveled ten thousand miles on a score of railroads with names as familiar as the states they crossed—the Baltimore & Ohio, the Wabash, the Illinois Central, and the Atchison, Topeka & Santa Fe. The Ohio Central took the show to Toledo, and the Michigan Central took it to Detroit. It rode the Erie to Mansfield, caught the Baltimore & Ohio in Columbus, and the Northern Pacific in Duluth. The Wild West train comprised fifty-two cars in all, ten more than Barnum and fourteen more than Ringling, making it the biggest of the big three.[1]

While Annie Oakley slept, the show train sped along. It was in the wee hours one stuffy summer night when the long show train blew its whistle and pulled onto a side track near the depot in Detroit. A reporter, who'd been waiting patiently for its arrival, jumped up, grabbed his notebook, and went looking for a story. He walked hurriedly, past a string of dingy white stock cars with the large letters "Buffalo Bill's Wild West" painted on the side. Horses neighed, tossed their heads, and tried to poke their noses out between the slats. A long line of flatcars followed. They were loaded with wagons of canvas, musicians' chariots, and the familiar old Deadwood stagecoach. The Wild West's hired hands, dozing in crowded sleeping cars, brought up the rear. The windows were rolled down, and here the reporter caught a glimpse of a naked elbow with a snoring head resting in its angle, and there, a head backed up against a pair of feet.

When the train whistle blew again, the army of men, looking grouchy and tired, rolled from their bunks and tumbled out onto the platform, hoisting up their trousers and rubbing their eyes. One fellow jumped to the ground with his boots in his hand, sat on the bottom step of the car and brushed the cinders from between his toes. The men growled and swore and passed around tobacco and squirted or spat until they were better humored.[2]

Annie Oakley and Frank Butler traveled in the second section of the train, which arrived at the depot not long after the first. Their accommodations were much more comfortable than those of Buffalo Bill's hired hands. They had their own stateroom, as did Cody, built into one end of a coach. Inside was a bed, a dresser, and two comfortable chairs. Annie and Frank even had running water. Annie kept attractive curtains at the windows and made sure they matched the bedspread and dresser covers.[3]

While Annie dozed in her stateroom that summer night, workmen pulled gangplanks out from under the stock cars, opened the side doors, and let out the horses, who tried to nibble the sparse grass that grew along the siding. Men hauled the wagons from the flatcars, hitched up the draft horses, and hurried to the showgrounds. Annie would follow later by catching a cab or, as press agent Dexter Fellows insisted, by hitching a ride on a wagon to save money.[4]

By the time Annie arrived on the grounds, the hired hands already had marked off the limits of the arena with little flags on iron rods. They pounded in stakes, fastened poles with guy ropes, and put up the great canvas grandstand, a feat that required 22,750 yards of canvas, 1,104 stakes, and twenty miles of rope. The tent was so big that one news-paper said "a person sitting at one end of it would need a spyglass . . . to distinguish a friend at the other end."[5]

The crew erected the Wild West barber shop, the repair shop, black-smith shop, and laundry. There was a wardrobe tent, a tent for the elec-tric light plant, and two tents for the horses, draft and show. The Wild West was a self-sufficient operation, a virtual village on wheels. Even the glass balls Annie shot were molded on the lot.

It took only an hour for the workmen to do their jobs, and they began going in relays to the cook's tent, already up and giving out the aroma of coffee and frying meats. They took seats along blue benches and put their elbows on tables covered with red cloths. They ate a steaming breakfast of wheatcakes and potatoes, steak, bacon, chops, tea, and cof-fee. Aproned waiters, carrying platters of beef, hastily tread "the floor of uneven earth," while through an open flap at the side of the tent came the demands of the cooks, bent over four giant kettles and a cooking range as big as a hayrick. "That range is the first thing off the train al-ways," said Dexter Fellows. "They get the fire into it as soon as we get into town, and inside of 20 minutes breakfast is ready for serving."[6]

With the village up and breakfast done, the performers gathered for the daily street parade, which was almost as popular as the show itself. In Decatur, Illinois, administrators let children out of school at ten in the morning so they could see the parade on Tuesday, May 26, 1896. It happened that way in Columbus, Indiana, too, and later in Atchison, Kansas, where even the strict Catholics at St. Benedict's College let the students come down from their campus hill to see the parade. In Em-poria, Kansas, editor William Allen White anchored a spot on the curb and listened to the old-timers discussing the big crowds. Why, they seemed greater than those present the day Ulysses S. Grant had given a speech in Emporia eighteen years before. "Buffalo Bill is a bigger man than Old Grant if the crowd is a right measure by which to judge," White wrote in the *Gazette*.[7]

Country and city folks alike stood at the curb in Ottumwa, Iowa, on Friday afternoon, August 26, 1898. "From early morning crowds began coming into the city from every direction—by train and wagon," said the *Daily Courier*. Incoming trains carried extra coaches and were "laden to the steps with people from neighboring towns." In Owens-boro, Kentucky, the *Messenger* estimated that five thousand strangers were in town on May 15, 1896, swelling the city's population to the largest in its history. "Every country road was lined with country people coming to see the show," the *Messenger* said. "Every wagon yard, livery stable and other available hitching place was crowded," and the line of parade was "jammed almost to suffocation." People who could afford them rented horses and carriages to avoid the crush on the sidewalks. Others rode bicycles, and still others found seats on house tops and in the second- and third-floor windows along Main Street and Third.

"Here comes the parade," the St. Paul *Dispatch* wrote on September 16, 1896. "There is music, and then the clattering hoofs of a hundred ponies." The Indians advanced in double columns, their blankets pulled up beneath their chins. The fleeting figures of the "red devils" reminded one of "poor Custer," of Boone and Bridger and Carson. The frontier may have been newly dead, but the Wild West brought it alive.

So many people were on the streets in Creston, Iowa, when the Wild West parade marched by on August 25, 1898, that downtown hotels and restaurants were "taxed to the utmost to feed the multitude," said the Creston *Daily Advertiser*. Several church societies cashed in on the day by serving meals and lunches and "all did a thriving business."

In Council Bluffs, Iowa, "the whole city seemed to have turned its face toward the grounds," reported the *Daily Nonpareil* on October 8, 1896. The motor company pressed thirteen extra cars into service, but still they couldn't carry the crowds. Among the multitudes were the pickpockets, who did their work despite two Pinkerton detectives from New York who traveled with the Wild West show.[8] Stories of unlucky victims were common. In Ottawa, Illinois, a Mrs. Hampson was relieved of her pocketbook while she stood in front of Riale's grocery. "She immediately fainted," the *Daily Journal* of June 16, 1896, said, "and the thief made good his escape." In Owensboro, James Matthews was robbed of $27.22 while trying to get to the Wild West ticket wagon, and Albert Guenther was relieved of $4.75 while he rode a streetcar to the afternoon show.

In Findlay, Ohio, the *Republican* urged people to lock their doors and windows while they were at the showgrounds, and in Burlington, Iowa, thirty suspicious-looking strangers were detained in "the cooler" until the Wild West left town. That was usually only one day, unless the show was stopping over on a Sunday, when it did not play. Sundays were a day of rest. Annie occasionally went hunting or fishing or rested in a hammock by her tent. Many performers did their laundry on Sundays, though Fern Campbell Swartwout said that Annie sometimes hired a woman in the community to do hers.[9]

Annie Oakley relaxes outside her tent. Inside, a favorite portrait of herself on horseback, drawn by the Hardy sisters, stands on the floor. Annie loved flower gardens and probably planted this one herself. (From Cooper, *Annie Oakley, Woman at Arms*)

Then it was back on the road again. Life was continuous motion: rolling in at dawn, setting up, parading, performing at two and again at eight, then tearing down, catching the train, and starting all over the next day. By 1898, Annie Oakley had run across fields from Bangor to Macon, thrown kisses from Green Bay to Chattanooga, and shattered clay pigeons, two times a day, six days a week, from Norfolk to Omaha. "I have often been asked how many shells I have fired," she wrote. "If I had time to go through my scrapbooks, I might get a rough idea. I really think I have fired more shots than anyone else. I know one year I used 40,000 shot shells; also several thousand ball cartridges."[10] Did she never tire of shooting, a reporter asked her. "I won't say 'never;' but—well—hardly ever. Shooting, you see, has become to me a second nature in a way. Sometimes—very seldom—my eyes ache a little. While shooting, I scarce realise that I have a gun in my hands. I look straight at the object to be fired at, and the moment the butt of the gun touches my shoulder I fire. A moment's hesitation invariably means a miss."[11]

By the turn of the century, Americans everywhere had seen Buffalo Bill's Wild West, and Annie Oakley as a part of it. Annie's legend had taken root during the long runs in London, Chicago, and New York; and now it spread and grew in the last years of the century as the Wild West played every principal town from Boston to Denver. Annie's name appeared over and over again in hundreds of advertisements and newspapers stories in hundreds of different towns. And this in a time before radio, television, and movies, a time when people remembered what they saw and read and talked about it long afterward. They remembered well the little woman in the short shirts who blew them kisses and then smashed clay balls with an ease that belied her sex. They remembered and they marveled, and the name Annie Oakley become a household word.

But for Annie Oakley herself life on the road was far from glamorous. A rainstorm could turn the arena to mud and mire the show down for hours, as it did one day in Wheeling, West Virginia. The mud was so thick that even a liberal dosing of straw and sawdust did nothing to contain it. Wild West patrons sank almost to their knees while trying to make it to the arena, and hundreds of pairs of men's and women's overshoes could be seen sticking in the mud all around. And "dresses were lifted," reported the Wheeling *Intelligencer,* "as women never dreamed of lifting them before." When Johnny Baker stood on his head to shoot "he was in great danger of sinking out of sight," and one of the Arab riders slipped and "took an involuntary head-to-foot bath in a pool of mud and slimy water," much to the merriment of the nine thousand people in the stands. Frank Butler said it once rained so hard that a clay pigeon floated out of a trap, and Fern Campbell Swartwout told how, to avoid the mud, Annie sometimes had to stand on a bale of hay to dress. Annie had a pair of high rubber boots she wore for muddy occasions, like one in Hartford, Connecticut, when the arena was "a sea of soft mud-puddin'," three to five inches deep. To evade it, said the Hartford *Times,* was impossible, and Annie Oakley "came near falling a dozen times."[12]

A few days earlier in Stamford, Connecticut, the earth was so soft from a long rain that the heavy Wild West wagons sank to their bodies in mud. It was only by attaching twelve to twenty horses on each wagon

Annie Oakley, c. 1896. (Courtesy of the Denver Public Library, Western History Department)

that they would move at all, said the Stamford *Telegram*. But no matter how hard the horses pulled, the heavy electric light wagon refused to budge. Without lights, Cody was forced to cancel the evening performance, disappointing thousands of people.[13]

In Beloit, Wisconsin, a heavy rain weakened the old wooden bridge over Turtle Creek, and the first wagon across caused the bridge to settle, making it unsafe. The show wagons tried to ford the stream just below the bridge but became stuck in the soft sand. "They turned the tongue around and tried to pull it out the other way it came in but it was impossible and they were compelled to unload the wagon where it stood," the Beloit *Daily Free Press* said.

In Muskegon, Michigan, the show was about to begin when a wind storm blew up suddenly. "The wind blew a terrible gale and everything went before it," said the Muskegon *Daily Chronicle*. Refreshment stands blew down, and wooden shelves were caught by the wind and carried through the air. "Pink lemonade that a minute before had been five cents a glass was for a few minutes as free as water." Spectators took refuge in a nearby cornfield while the Wild West crews tried to save the big canvas tent. Its entrance "was swaying dangerously in the wind and the sides were flapping like flags in a stiff breeze."

In Trinidad, Colorado, the Wild West ran into a snowstorm and by the time the show was over, the big canvas tent had accumulated six inches of snow. The tent sagged badly under the weight, and the canvasmen got busy trying to repair it. The damage was so severe that they still were working on it ten days later when the show reached Topeka, Kansas.

The weather was only one hazard on the road. In New Brighton, Pennsylvania, Sleeping Car No. 56 caught fire when a five-gallon can of gasoline for the stove exploded. The flames enveloped the bedding and car woodwork and burned two men. In the Detroit railyards, Switch Engine No. 1286 ran into the first section of the show train. It crushed the caboose and pushed it into a sleeping car, burying Wild West hired hands in an ocean of broken glass, seats, and floor splinters. "All of the 78 men in the sleeper were more or less injured and shaken up, but only 10 were taken to the hospitals," reported the Detroit *Free Press*. One man was killed.[14]

The grueling life could wear a man down. By June 1897 Buffalo Bill was talking about retiring. "There is no question that Buffalo Bill is tired of the show business," the Worcester, Massachusetts, *Telegram* reported. "It is generally talked that he will retire in 1900, and at times he becomes decidedly disgusted with it all." He was so disgusted in Manchester, New Hampshire, that he was short with a reporter, who inquired how he was doing. "You see what I am doing," Cody snapped. "I am sitting here nursing a felon and swearing at the weather. We have been travelling around in just this kind of luck for two weeks and it's knocking us out of three or four thousand dollars every day." Cody even was growing tired of his long hair. "I do hate long hair," he said one day to a reporter from the New York *Sun*, who stood watching him twisting his locks, now silver-gray, into a little knot behind his head. "But people have come to identify me with long hair, so I won't cut it. Long hair is business and not art with me." [15]

Annie Oakley complained now and then, too. "Women have frequently said to me that I earned my money easily," she once said, "but they only saw the easiest part of my work. They do not think of the times when we would be obliged to 'show' in mud ankle deep, and then go to our train drenched to the skin in the storms we encountered. Of course I became accustomed to that sort of thing. One gets used to almost anything in the 'show' business." [16]

And besides, life on the road had its virtues. Annie and Frank sometimes snuck away to go fishing or hunting, as they did near Sheldon, Iowa, on a September day in 1896. Johnny Baker and band leader William Sweeney went with them, and between them they shot six prairie chickens and one rabbit. The next day, near Sioux Falls, South Dakota, they came back with one prairie chicken, one jack rabbit, and a duck. [17]

Life on the road also made it easy to see old friends. In Philadelphia, May Lillie came around to see Annie, and in Lincoln, Illinois, Captain Bogardus, now sixty-two, stopped by with his son Ed to say hello. Doc Carver was playing Sioux Falls on the same day the Wild West was in town, but no one said whether he stopped by to pay his respects. Carver, still billed as "the most famous shot in the world," was appearing at the Tri-State Fair along with two diving horses, the trick bicyclist Nicolet, and two elks that ran a harness race. [18]

In Kansas City, Buffalo Bill stayed at the Coates House Hotel, where a number of his old friends came by to visit. One of them, M. R. Russell, had kept a saloon in Salina, Kansas, back in 1867 when Cody was shooting buffalo for the Kansas Pacific Railroad. "Bill made barrels of money in those days but he spent it as he made it," Russell told the

Kansas City *Star*. "Many a time Bill has slept on a billiard table with me. Isn't that so Bill?" Bill remembered it all, the *Star* said, "and began talking of old times. He looked out the hotel window and said with a broad sweep of his hand: 'I used to know every hill and gully and ravine around here, and all your Kaws and your Blues and your creeks. I've ridden . . . over every bit of this ground where Kansas City is built.'"[19]

Annie Oakley's fondest memories lay back in Ohio, where the Wild West played in Piqua on July Fourth, 1896. For Annie, that day brought a most special visitor: her mother. Piqua was only thirty miles from North Star, and Susan Shaw had ridden over with Annie's brother, her sisters, and a number of nephews and nieces, including little Fern. It was the first time they ever had seen Annie perform, and "everyone," it was said, "joined with Annie in trying to make things pleasant" for her relatives. Judging from the papers, everyone seemed to be pleased. "Anna [*sic*] Oakley performed some wonderful feats of marksmanship, which elicited much applause from the 20,000 spectators present," one newspaper reported. "She is a Darke County girl, and her many friends here feel very proud of her."[20]

Two of Annie's oldest friends, Nancy Ann and Crawford Edington, showed up at the Wild West lot a few days later in Bluffton, Indiana. The Edingtons had managed the poor farm where Annie had stayed as a girl. They must have thought all along that the industrious little Annie Moses would make something of herself.[21]

A stop in Chicago reunited William Sweeney, M. B. Bailey, and Jule Keen with their wives, who had come to the train station to see them. Buffalo Bill's wife did not travel with the show, either. She stayed back at the ranch in North Platte. How different it was for Annie and Frank. One seldom traveled without the other. They were good friends as well as husband and wife. They worked together and spent their leisure together. Theirs was a lifetime commitment. They never were heard to argue, and if they did, they kept it to themselves. In public, they were a devoted couple, and Frank especially seemed the adoring, ever-loving husband. He called Annie Missie; and she called him Jimmie, a name that, according to Fern Campbell Swartwout, was coined one day when Annie was ill. Frank came into her room and began to do funny stunts to make her laugh. "Now Jimmie, the squirrel does tricks," Annie had said, and from that day on she had called him Jimmie when she wanted to be funny. The name caught on and would be used by friends and relatives in later years. Jimmie wrote poems for Missie and protected her from the crush of gunmen who wanted to challenge her. She darned his socks and cooked his dinner in the wintertime.[22]

"To Missie," Frank once wrote at the top of a poem he had typed for her. It went like this:

> Trials keep you weary
> Troubles gather thick around
> Don't you fret, my dearie,
> We are still on top of ground
> Tears will turn to treasures, dearie,
> Hope is never lost;
> Life's a joy and a pleasure, dearie,
> No matter what it cost.
> Trials keep you weary,
> Troubles hard to bear,
> Love like ours, dearie,
> Make the burdens light as air,
> What if the storm assails us, dearie,
> It passes in awhile,
> You and I together, dearie,
> Will face the gale and smile

At the bottom, in ink, he signed the poem "Jimmie" and pasted it in their scrapbooks. Frank was a sensitive man. Over the years he would paste many poems in the scrapbooks, including one that probably was an allegory of his and Annie's young love.[23]

> Jim was a squirrel that lived in a park.
> He washed his face with his tail, and went for a lark.
> He met a Miss Chipmunk, another kind of a squirrel.
> Says Jim, "She will do for my very best girl."
>
> So he cocked his left ear, and winked his right eye.
> Miss Chipmunk looked bashful, but made no reply.
> But Jim was a squirrel that never would tarry.
> So he made his best bow, and asked her to marry.
>
> Miss Chipmunk smiled sweetly, saying, "Between me and you,
> This is very sudden, but I don't care if I do."
> Then they were happy as squirrels could be.
> And lived in a hole in the big Elm Tree.
>
> They jumped and they played every day of their life.
> For she loved her Jim, and Jim loved his wife.

Anyone who ever met the Butlers, never doubted it.

Despite its difficulties, life on the road wore well with Annie Oakley. She seemed as youthful as ever, though in truth she was pushing forty. Amy Leslie found her as "petite and chic and peerless" as ever when she sought Annie out during a Wild West performance at the Chicago Coliseum in August 1897.[24] Amy found Annie sitting in one of the coliseum's tiny, curtained dressing rooms. "Nearly fourteen years, you know, now, rain or shine, snow or heat, twice a day in all sorts of weather," Annie said. She was "darning rather prodigious holes in a pair of Mr. Butler's hose," Amy wrote, "and was as intent upon having every pretty stitch as neat as a pigeon-shot from her pet gun." Amy found Annie's "dainty womanliness and simplicity" refreshing. As Annie darned and stitched, "she forgot she was Annie Oakley and became simple Mrs. Butler of Nutley," Amy wrote. As she worked, Annie related how "last week in Cincinnati, I waded knee deep in water and shot with a pouring rain in my face. Had to wear rubber boots and a leather dress. It used to be fun, but I don't believe I care so much for it nowadays."

"Did you like the white target as well as my old-time black?" Annie suddenly inquired, looking up from her darning. "I did not, to tell the truth," she went on, "and I cannot understand Col. Cody using the milk-white balls instead of cream, brown or russet, but Johnnie [Baker] is past all reckoning and all interference. I do not think indoor daylight or electricity at night plays well with the dazzling white target, but then I never shot anything but the chutes, so I cannot very well dictate."[25]

That was Annie Oakley, darning a pair of socks rather than throwing them away, musing on the difficulties of her life, but only for a moment, and then switching instantly to the immediate—the best color for glass balls, a subject on which, it is important to note, she had a very definite opinion. From her words it also can be surmised that she on occasion used Johnny Baker as a go-between with Cody. Amy Leslie apparently overlooked that and what it might have said about the behind-the-scenes politics at the Wild West. How many other times, perhaps, had Annie and Frank tried to interfere or do things their own way? There is no way to know, but it is doubtful that Annie was as uncomplicated as writers like Amy Leslie chose to portray her. Still, Amy was on target with the outer woman. Annie was as dainty and womanly as Amy said she was, a stickler for perfection, living her life from day to day, never seeming to dwell on the past or long for the future. "Is not my work fascinating?" Annie repeated a question another day. "Oh, I don't know. It is hard work like everything else. Of course, I am used to it."[26]

If Annie had a dream, she never talked about it. She seemed content to go where life led, doing her job, and stealing to the fields and forests when she could. Buffalo Bill, on the other hand, seemed a man almost obsessed with the future. He talked about the Big Horn Valley in Wyoming, where he hoped to retire. He already had irrigated three hundred thousand acres of land and invested much money. In time, he would found the town of Cody and its newspaper, the *Enterprise*. "I do not want to die a showman," he said to Amy Leslie that August in Chicago. "I am a showman by accident . . . I grow very tired of this sort of sham-hero worship sometimes. The children's affection only is welcome." [27] Annie Oakley, too, had thought of retiring. "I have thought several times I would not go with the show another year, but I always do," she said in 1899. And go with it she would, right into the new century. [28]

16.

The Old Home Folks

To recuperate from the long season on the road, Annie and Frank often vacationed in the South during the fall and winter. A vacation usually meant one thing—finding the birds. There was nothing in the world that Annie Oakley loved more. Over the years, she and Frank went after the quail in the Blue Ridge Mountains of Virginia, near the Hot Springs of Arkansas, and in the old haunts of Davy Crockett near Crowson, Tennessee.

In Hot Springs, Annie and Frank hunted with local sportsman John J. Sumpter, Jr., and his wife. By the time the foursome came home that evening with sixty-three birds in their bag, John Sumpter had bagged a few stories to tell his friends: They wouldn't believe the kind of shooting he had seen from Annie Oakley. "Why, she kills quail while you are getting your gun to the shoulder," he said. "Twice I shot her bird after she had killed it—couldn't get there quick enough." Sumpter had kept score and knew that Annie had killed sixteen more birds than anyone else on the trip.[1]

She found good hunting another autumn in Crowson, Tennessee. She spent several days in the field, including time with a Tennessee hunter named Joe Eakin, who was a local legend. He held a record of six dozen quail in one day. But even Joe Eakin had to fight for his birds against Annie Oakley. "Miss Annie's so quick with her gun," he said, "if you want to get a shot at a bird you must shoot mighty quick or wait till she misses, and that may keep you waiting some time."[2]

In Virginia, Annie and Frank hunted one year with a Professor J. C. Schuyler, who brought along his Gordon setter, Pash. Pash scampered

153

on ahead as the trio rode to a favorite hunting spot. By the time they dismounted, Pash already had found the birds. He stopped, motionless, and pointed. "As pretty as a picture," Annie said, and the professor stepped forward, rustling some leaves and sending the birds skyward. Annie and Frank fired instantly, killing three birds before Schuyler had gotten one shot off. "Professor," Annie said to him, "You must not let me rob you of your sport." Annie Oakley was fast, and she was good no matter where she was shooting, in the arena, at the traps, or in the field. Once again, her private life proved that the public woman in the Wild West arena was, indeed, the crack shot she claimed to be. In the Blue Ridge Mountains that day, Annie killed three times as many birds as Frank, twice as many as Schuyler—and bagged eighteen in a row the next day.[3] As in the old days in the Darke County woodlands, the great number of birds she killed never seemed to bother her. Though by today's standards her attitude may seem callous, game was abundant then and hunting was an accepted part of American life. Conservation was an issue of the future.

Despite Annie's sterling reputation in the field, there always were skeptics. In Tennessee, a Mr. Walter Swain had listened to them during an exhibition Annie had given. The skeptics were ready to wager fifty dollars that the objects Annie shot at were fake. But they changed their tune, Swain said, when Annie shot a meadowlark on the wing right before their eyes, then broke a brick tossed in the air, and with a second shot demolished one of the pieces before it touched the ground. The skeptics became believers, Swain said, "and wisely kept quiet concerning the fifty dollars."[4]

Of all Annie's vacations, her fondest was a two-week stay on a country estate in Shropshire, England, back in the fall of 1887. She'd spent twelve to fifteen hours a day rambling over the five-thousand-acre estate along the Severn. She'd come home exhausted to a comfortable lodge, enjoyed a delicious dinner, and then settled down in an easy chair around an open fire to discuss the day's sport. It was to bed at 9:30 and up again at the first streak of dawn. That was the kind of life Annie Oakley loved: tramping through the woods with her dogs and familiar shotgun at her side, the crunch of leaves underfoot, the flutter of wings, and the smell of burnt gunpowder. She preferred the woods to the parlor, her warm mittens to evening gloves. She always had and she always would. "Any woman who does not thoroughly enjoy tramping across the country on a clear frosty morning with a good gun and a pair of dogs does not know how to enjoy life," she once said. "God intended women to be outside as well as men, and they do not know what they are missing when they stay cooped up in the house enjoying themselves with a novel."[5]

Though many people thought of Annie Oakley only as an exhibition shooter, nothing could have been further from the truth. In her heart, she was a sportsman. She talked of the hunt as a noble and natural pursuit, healthy and pleasurable. Exhibition shooting was a job that paid the bills. "[I] only engage in it," she said, "for the money there is in the practice."[6]

Besides hunting vacations, Annie and Frank often went back to Darke County between engagements over the years. Annie's mother still lived on the family farm, and her sisters Hulda and Emily lived in the county. It was in the off-season that Annie came to know her nieces and nephews and took a special liking to Hulda's daughter, Fern, who would give a rare view of the Butlers' personal life in her biography, *Missie*.

Even as a child, Fern recognized that winter was a special time for her famous aunt and uncle. They relaxed at the farm and took inventory. Annie made new costumes or mended old ones, then hung them on the clothesline to air. She brushed them, sponged them down, pressed them, and put them in her traveling trunk, wrapped in tissue paper so they wouldn't wrinkle. The technique worked so well that Fern said people often marveled at the good condition of Annie's costumes, even after long months on the road. Years of traveling had taught Frank how to pack, as well. Always in charge of the guns, he wrapped them in cotton bed blankets, never allowing two to touch. His method worked so well and he took such good care of them, Fern said, that even guns they had used for years looked like new.[7]

Frank wrote poems for Fern and her friends, and Annie amused them with little pranks. The Butlers were fun to have around. One day Annie took a sheet of paper, tore off little pieces, wet them, and pasted them on her eyelids, forehead, chin, and ears. "Then she began to make funny noises and wiggle her face," Fern recalled. "We all just loved such pranks and never thought we could do them as well as she could do them."

Though Fern idolized Annie, she found her aunt to be exacting and hard to please, especially when it came to sewing, and admitted that some members of the family "seemed to think she was simply cranky or queer and did not seem to be able to tolerate her exactness." Rush Blakeley, Annie's nephew by marriage, told how Annie, wearing white gloves and getting ready to go out, was apt to run a finger over a window ledge to check for dust.[8]

Despite Annie's quirks, she was a loyal friend. As a child, Fern struck up a friendship with her by showing Annie a new sewing basket she had been given. "I am sure nothing ever pleased her more," Fern wrote, "and she told me of how hard it had been for her to get even a little thread to sew with when she was a little girl."

Annie was there another day when Fern was sewing a dress for a doll. Trouble erupted when Fern mistakenly cut into some material that her mother was using to make a dress for Annie. Because the pattern called for all the material, the dress couldn't be finished, and Hulda was angry. She wanted to punish young Fern, but Aunt Annie came to the rescue. "My aunt picked me up and kissed me and said mother could have the old dress to make over for me. . . . She also said when I grew up I could make her a dress to pay for the material I had spoiled, which I did and many more. Aunt Annie was my staunch friend ever after."[9] The ever frugal Aunt Annie often would send old or little-used dresses home to Ohio so Fern could cut them up and make new clothes.

Annie and Frank themselves came back to Ohio whenever they could. They sometimes stayed at the Hotel Turpen in Greenville before heading up to North Star. They knew W. A. Browne, editor of the Greenville *Daily Advocate,* and had given at least one shooting exhibition at the Greenville Gun Club grounds. Annie was an honorary member of the club. Sometimes, she and Frank hunted up in the old stomping grounds around North Star. Frank was popular with the local farmers, who were drawn to his Irish humor and enjoyed the stories he liked to tell. Though he'd always been a city slicker, nattily dressed right down to his polished shoes, Frank grew fond of the country life and its people. One day while drinking a glass of buttermilk, which he loved, he held it in the air and declared that a pig in Ohio was better off than a gentleman in New York.[10]

Frank was always good for a humorous line and a good story, like the one he told about a mutt who followed the Wild West show one summer. Every day the dog buried a bone under the ammunition wagon and went back to dig it up the next day, not realizing the show had moved during the night. The dog never seemed to catch on, as Frank told the story, and by fall "he was burying the bones three times as deep as he was tall." Frank laughed at that, and said, "If that fool dog was a bird dog he would be smart enough to find out his mistake."[11]

Of course, Frank was partial to bird dogs. He was a hunter with many tales to tell of dogs, hunts, and travels. Frank and Annie, as one newspaper described them, were "charming conversationalists." They always were kindly received in Greenville, though Frank had to laugh at how the home folks persisted in telling tall tales of Annie's prowess with the gun. To listen to them, he said, you'd think she never missed a shot.[12]

Frank was never one to put Annie down, but he delighted in telling stories about her, sometimes at her expense. For example, there was the one about the postal clerk in New York. Annie had hurried up to the counter one day and asked the clerk to cash a money order for her.

"Where did you get this?" the clerk demanded.

"Why! It's mine, that's my name," Annie responded.

"I beg your pardon," the clerk said, "but I know Annie Oakley and have seen her shoot fifty times. She is a much smaller woman than you. Identify yourself and I'll pay it."

"Good," Annie said. "Hold the letter up, and I'll put a bullet through the stamp." The clerk paid the order at once, Frank said, and muttered something to himself about what a difference the style of dress made in a woman's appearance.[13]

Frank had another story, which the Newark *Evening News* said he told "with much glee, as a good joke on his wife." The story was set in Arkansas, where he and Annie were spending a few days with friends in the Hot Springs. A tramp who said he was starving, lame, and tired, came to the door. Annie took pity on him and persuaded her friends to feed him and put him up in the barn for a few days.

"On the morning of the fourth day, when she carried his breakfast to the barn, she was surprised to learn that her protege had mounted her $500 bicycle and peddled off some hours before," Frank said. "Mrs. Butler took the trail at once, but the police got there first, and before night had the tramp locked up in jail for being drunk." But the joke was on Annie. The tramp had sold her wheel for one dollar and she had to spend five dollars to buy it back.[14]

Then there was the story about another tramp who came to the door at the Nutley house one day. He begged for food, and Annie pointed to the woodpile.

"Chop wood and you get a breakfast," she said.

"Nix," came the tramp's reply. "I'll get breakfast without chopping wood."

"How will you manage it?" Annie asked.

"I'll come in and take it," he said and started toward the door.

"Halt!" commanded Annie Oakley, and the tramp found himself

157

looking into the muzzle of a .44-caliber revolver, behind which glistened a pair of cool, determined eyes.

"Right about face—double quick—march," Annie ordered, and the tramp obeyed. As he reached the gate, two reports rang out and the tramp's hat was pierced by two bullets from Annie's revolver. The noise brought Frank to the scene just as the tramp plunged into the woods opposite the house.

"What's your hurry?" Frank shouted, but the tramp was too pressed for time to answer questions. Frank went into the house and found Annie sitting on the floor laughing heartily.

"I couldn't help it," she said. "It was such a bad hat and such a good shot that I had to do it, and I thought it would give him a scare." [15]

True or not, the story told worlds about the Butlers and their attitude toward life. They believed in hard work and in what they thought was right. And Annie Oakley, fiercely proud and independent, could take care of herself. Besides that, the story had a good punch line for a man who loved to tell a story.

"He was as Irish as you make it," Annie's niece Irene Patterson Black said of Frank. "He could hold the paper upside down and read you a story." Irene said that Frank would come into a room full of people "and with just the straightest face tell some kind of story and have everyone of them really believing it, even if he'd just made it all up. That used to kind of make Aunt Ann mad." [16]

Annie's first professional performance before the old home folks came on a rainy summer day in 1900 when the Wild West played Greenville for the first time. Greenville had changed since the days when little Annie Moses sold bundles of quail at the Katzenberger grocery. Broadway was being paved that summer, and residents were talking about the new Greenville Home Telephone Company, incorporated that June. Greenville had a sewage system and an electric light and power company now. And in just two years, it would be given the status of a city. [17]

The air was damp that Wednesday afternoon, July 25, 1900, as Annie Oakley tripped into the Greenville arena. It had rained all night and part of the morning, but still an estimated ten thousand people filled the stands. Annie's mother and sisters, Hulda and Emily, were there, and according to the papers, they wore Quaker garb. (Annie's father and family were Quakers.)

If Annie was nervous, no one mentioned it, and she ran through her performance as she had countless others, never seeming to clutch. But this performance before the old home folks was different from any she would ever give. In the middle of her act, a Mr. C. M. Anderson and Will F. Baker of Greenville interrupted her and called her over to a platform where they stood. Baker carried a present under his arm, and Anderson turned to Annie to make the presentation. "This is your first professional appearance before a Darke County audience," he said, "and a few of your many friends . . . desire to honor you." With that, he handed Annie a solid silver loving cup, inlaid with gold, and inscribed: "To Miss Anna [sic] Oakley, From Old Friends in Greenville, O., July 25, 1900."

"You will accept it," Anderson continued, "not for its intrinsic worth, but as a testimonial of the appreciation of your old home friends. Not only do they sound your praises for accuracy of your shot, but as well for the accuracy of your unsullied life.

"The best wishes of the donors accompany you wherever fate and your profession may lead you. Always remember, they regard you as a daughter of this dear old county."

Annie was overcome by emotion. "Thank you, and God bless you all," was all she could say. Her throat was clogged and tears ran down her cheeks. When editor W. A. Browne of the Greenville *Daily Advocate* talked to Annie later that evening, she still was very emotional. "I have received and won many medals from many sources, all of which I prize very highly," she told him, "but this cup takes the foreground. I prize it more highly than anything ever presented to me."[18]

That was saying a lot for a woman who had received dozens of gifts, including a gold medal from the London Gun Club and a silver tea service from all the sportsmen in America. Annie had so many medals and badges that a reporter once remarked that if she attempted to wear them all she would "surely collapse beneath their weight." She had rings, bracelets, pins, and necklaces, and before her career was over, a total of twenty-seven gold medals. There was one from the *Police Gazette,* another from gunmaker Charles Lancaster, and one from the shooting grounds in Milan, Italy.[19]

She must have held that cup by its handles, turned it around, and read again and again the inscription: "From Old Friends in Greenville, O." The words touched Annie Oakley. She had lived a bohemian life, probably feeling at times as though she had no home. She had spent countless nights in unfamiliar cities and strange hotels. Even the house at Nutley was boarded up or rented during the show season. Her roots were deep in the Darke County forests, but her life was on the road.

A Wild West poster depicting the highlights of Annie Oakley's life: Annie shooting in the field, in the Wild West arena, and at the Nutley Amateur Circus. At the top is the silver loving cup given to her by "old home friends" in Greenville, Ohio. (Courtesy of the Circus World Museum, Baraboo, Wis.)

The homeless little girl who had run away from the Wolfe farm so long ago now was embraced by her entire hometown.

The silver loving cup that meant so much to Annie Oakley soon was immortalized on a famous Wild West poster that depicted the highlights of Annie's career. A picture of the loving cup was inscribed at the very top of the poster, just above a large portrait of a very serious-looking and bemedaled Annie Oakley. There was her starched white collar, her curly brown hair on her shoulder, and the silver star on her sombrero. Surrounding Annie were the images of her life. There she was standing on a horse at the Nutley Amateur Circus, and there she was shooting doubles from her wheel. There she was smashing clay pigeons in a Colorado blizzard, leaping her gun table, sighting backwards through a mirror, and hunting quail in the field. "Annie Oakley, the Peerless Wing and Rifle Shot," the poster said. There never would be another like her.

17.

End of the Road

Annie Oakley entered the new century as one of the old-timers, just like the Wild West show itself. Though the Deadwood coach still rocked in the arena, Buffalo Bill talked now about the new electric cars that brought the crowds to the gate. The show itself had changed. The bill now advertised Teddy Roosevelt's charge up San Juan Hill, the storming of the walls of Tien-Tsin, and the casting of the lifeline to a distressed vessel at sea. The Cowboy Band played "Ship Ahoy" and "Rocked in the Cradle of the Deep," and the passing of the West did indeed seem final.[1] Even the press agents had a new line: Buffalo Bill's Wild West was "history in concrete form," they said, a last chance to view an era now passing.

The season of 1901 got off to an ominous start when One Bear's tepee caught fire and burned down early on an April evening in Washington, D.C. Another day, a cannon discharged prematurely while artilleryman James Myrely was using the wooden rammer. The blast tore off his right hand and sent splinters up his arm. Doctors had to amputate. In Chicago, Annie fell as she was sprinting across the arena, causing "audible 'Ohs'" from the audience. But when everyone saw that she was all right, the "ohs" turned into "heavy laughs."[2]

In Wheeling, West Virginia, the brakes on the wagon carrying the electric light plant went out on a downgrade over a bridge. By the time the wagon cleared the bridge and tried to turn into Ohio Street, it was traveling at a 2:40 clip. It couldn't negotiate the turn. Horses, wagon, and driver were thrown into a heap acros Penn Street. The driver was all

Annie, c. 1900. Johnny Baker's daughters, Gladys and Della, are pictured in her brooch. (Courtesy of the Garst Museum, Greenville, Ohio)

right, but the wagon was badly damaged and the electric dynamo disarranged. The chief electrician couldn't find parts to fix it in Wheeling and set out for Pittsburgh. Without the dynamo, Buffalo Bill had to cancel the night performance.[3]

Another accident occurred just outside Altoona, Pennsylvania, when the second section of the show train ran into the first section in a heavy fog. Frank Fisher, a canvasman, was struck by a piece of flying timber and suffered a bad cut over his left eye. Four horses were hurt, and four cars and a caboose were wrecked.[4] Danger lurked always as the show train sped through the night.

It had been a weary year, and Annie and Frank looked forward to the last show dates of the season, Monday, October 28, in Charlotte, North Carolina, and Tuesday, October 29, in Danville, Virginia. The Cowboy Band would play "Auld Lang Syne" there and the Wild West would ship most of its 540 horses to winter pasture in Coatsville, New Jersey. The stands were crowded that Monday night in Latta Park in Charlotte, as Annie leaped her gun table, kissed her hand to the crowd, ran the length of the arena, and gave that funny little kick, just as she had done for seventeen years. No one could have guessed that the performance was the last Annie Oakley ever would give as a member of Buffalo Bill's Wild West. After the show, Frank probably grabbed a lantern and they walked to their train coach, just as they always did. They settled down in their stateroom for the night, eager to reach Danville and for a long season to end.

At three in the morning, as Annie and Frank slept, their section of the train was rolling along through the cornfields just north of the little town of Linwood, not yet halfway to Danville. Suddenly, as the engine came out of a deep cut on a curve, the bright headlights of another train appeared out of the darkness ahead. Emergency brakes screeched, but there wasn't time to stop. Engineers, brakemen, and firemen jumped into the fields just before the engines collided head-on. Five stock cars on the twenty-one car show train shattered and fell into a ditch. On the other train, a tender and a boxcar filled with fertilizer were demolished.

The scene, as reported by the Charlotte *News*, was grim.[5] "Beneath this pile of wrecked timber and heavy rolling stock was a perfect mass of horse flesh. A portion of the bodies of the animals were scattered here and there and inside the cars the poor beasts were wedged in like so many sardines." For more than an hour, the faint groans of dying animals were heard beneath the pile of debris. Not a single horse that was in the first five cars was saved.

The people on the train were more fortunate. Only four, reported the Charlotte *Observer*, were hurt: trainmaster H. A. Williams, engineer A. T. Rollins, fireman L. L. Cranford, and brakeman Malone.[6] A greater disaster was averted, the papers said, because both trains had slowed to about eight miles an hour before the impact. It soon was ascertained that a freight train, southbound No. 75, had slammed into the show train on a high fill in a cornfield near the banks of Swearing Creek. "Both engines were badly smashed and all the cars of both trains violently jolted," the *Observer* said. The blame was laid on freight engineer T. F. Lynch of the Southern Railway, who was said to have misread his orders. He was supposed to wait on a side track until all sections of the show train had passed. However, Lynch apparently overlooked the fact that the show train ran in two sections (some accounts say three sections). Or it is possible that Lynch miscounted how many sections had passed before he pulled out of the siding and onto the main track.

News of the wreck spread quickly, and thousands of people from nearby Salisbury and Lexington came out to get a look at it, making "a harvest day for the toll bridge over the Yadkin," the *Observer* said. Though the tracks had been cleared by midafternoon, there still was much to see. Turks, Indians, "and all sorts of foreigners" were "jabbering away in the most excited manner" as they looked over the bodies of dead horses, which lay in heaps among the wreckage. Salisbury veterinarian D. H. Manogue faced one of the busiest days of his life. He worked to save the injured horses, but many had to be shot. Their bodies were sold for fifty cents apiece to H. T. Hatton of Salisbury, who planned to ship them to Baltimore for the value of their hides and bones.

It was a busy day for the railroad men, too. They took the damaged engines to Spencer for repairs and sent a fresh engine out to pull in the rear section of the show train, which had not been damaged. They pulled the cars into the station at Linwood, where cowboys corraled the buffalo in a nearby field and loaded the remaining horses on cattlecars bound for the big stockyards at Spencer. The Indians and South American gauchos milled about the station and soon attracted a large crowd of curious people.

According to the newspapers, no member of the Wild West show was hurt. "The employees of the show train were thrown out of their berths but none were injured," the *Observer* said. "All the members of the Wild West show escaped injury," it repeated in another story. When a reporter spoke with Johnny Baker and William F. Cody, they talked about dead horses and damages, which were expected to run between fifty and sixty thousand dollars. Interestingly, no one mentioned Annie Oakley—even though the train wreck that dark Tuesday, October 29, 1901, eventually would be blamed for injuring her so severely that her hair turned white seventeen hours afterward.

The story is one of those ingrained pieces of the Annie Oakley legend that has never been challenged—even though it certainly is not true. The facts are that Annie Oakley's thick brown hair did turn white suddenly and that she and Frank insisted forever afterward that it happened because of the train wreck. However, accounts strongly suggest that the Butlers, although usually truthful, in this case lied about the whole thing. No one in North Carolina mentioned anything about Annie being injured in the train wreck, though biographers have painted a picture of a limp and injured Annie being carried from the wreckage in Frank's arms—a touching scene, but purely fictional. If Annie really had been injured it seems very odd that the newspapers, who talked to Buffalo Bill and Johnny Baker, did not mention it. In an interview seven years later, Annie was quoted as saying that her "right hip was torn away" and that for almost a year after the operation she couldn't use a rifle or a shotgun. That wasn't true, either.[7] If she had been so badly injured—or taken to a hospital for an operation—someone would have noticed. Furthermore, only the engine, tender, and stock cars were reported damaged. Annie's coach, like Buffalo Bill's, was farther back in the line of cars and apparently was unscathed.

An account in the *American Field*, written just one week after the wreck, said Annie received two slight injuries, one on the hand and one on the back. "Happily," the *Field* said, "these injuries are not regarded as serious." Frank told the *American Field* that his watch had been smashed and that Annie "was badly shaken up, and her back was strained."[8] If Annie's hip had been torn away, her loving husband and manager would have mentioned it. Curiously, he also did not mention anything about white hair, an inexplicable omission if, in fact, Annie's hair had turned white immediately after the wreck.

Further proof that Annie was doing just fine came on December 17, 1901, almost two months later, when she appeared in a shooting match at Lake Denmark, New Jersey. Contrary to legend that says she couldn't pick up a gun, the *American Field* said she hit twenty-three of twenty-five live pigeons that day, while competing on a team with J. T. Morley. They defeated G. H. Cook and Annie's old friend Frank Class. "Miss Oakley's shooting was the feature of the day," a notice in the *Field* said.

"She had quite recovered from the effects of the shaking up she had in the railroad accident she figured in two months ago."[9]

Surely, if Annie's beautiful, long brown hair had been white, someone at the match would have remarked on the change. But no one did. No one mentioned Annie's hair at all, in fact, until January 16, 1902, when she appeared at another shooting match, this one at Interstate Park in Queens, Long Island. Suddenly, her hair was a topic of discussion. The New York *Sun* was the first to notice the change, which was impossible to miss. Annie's dark brown hair was white, and not just streaked with white—it was totally white, save for a few strands here and there. The transformation was incredible. The ever-youthful Annie Oakley suddenly didn't look twenty-five anymore. If anything, she looked older than her forty-one years. What had happened?

The question would be repeated again and again for years, and for years Annie and Frank gave the same answer—it was that awful train wreck in North Carolina. "The shock which she received at that time was so great to her nervous system that her hair turned gray in eighteen hours," reported the *Sun* (the number of hours it took sometimes varied).[10]

The story of the train wreck was a logical way to explain Annie's newly white hair, but judging from the time element alone, the story couldn't be true. The transformation must have occurred sometime between the match at Lake Denmark on December 17, 1901, and the match in Long Island on January 16, 1902. If it didn't happen in the train wreck, as Annie and Frank said, then when did it happen, and what caused it? The only clue is a newspaper clipping, written by Amy Leslie and pasted in Annie's scrapbooks. Here is what it said:

Annie Oakley, the imperishable Annie, is still suffering from her remarkable experience in the baths of a celebrated health resort. . . . The first day the attendant forgot Little Sure Shot and went away, leaving her in a fierce, hot bath usually limited to sixty seconds, for forty scalding minutes, and when released Annie's bonny, imperishable brown hair had turned white clear to her crown, her face and hands were speckled with dark brown patches and one side of her back was blistered. She was in a dead faint and restoration was a question for an hour or so.[11]

The incident probably occurred in the Arkansas Hot Springs that Annie so much liked to visit. Two newspaper accounts of the incident, both undated, were pasted in the scrapbooks. On one of the clippings,

Popular portrait of Annie Oakley, "Little Sure Shot." (Courtesy of the Western History Collections, University of Oklahoma)

someone took a fountain pen and scratched out the part about Annie's hair turning white to the crown. Could Annie have scratched that line out just as she had scratched out the name Moses in the family Bible? What did she have to cover up, and why would she and Frank take the trouble to lie about the incident for years?

The answer is simple to anyone who understands Annie Oakley. The little woman with the Quaker upbringing was as modest as she was prim and proper. She probably was scantily clothed when the incident occurred, and that probably embarrassed her, so that she didn't want to talk about it. In any case, a lady's bath was not a proper topic of discussion. Amy Leslie was a woman and a friend. Annie probably told the true story to her, never dreaming it would end up in the Chicago *Daily News.*

The shock of the hot springs brought an end to Annie Oakley's career with Buffalo Bill's Wild West. How could bonny, brown-haired Annie Oakley, whose image depended so much on her youth and vigor, trip gaily into the arena with hair not just streaked with gray like Buffalo Bill's, but totally white? Annie's long hair, which she liked to toss over her shoulder to get a clear shot, was an important part of her stage image. The day it turned white was the day she decided to quit the Wild West, which had not performed since the train wreck.

There had been no word in Charlotte or Linwood, or even at Lake Denmark, that Annie was planning to retire. She was tired, she told the press, but she planned to take a rest, not quit. The subject of Annie's retirement was not raised until after that fateful day in the hot springs. Annie first mentioned it to the New York *Sun* that January on Long Island. "Miss Oakley," the *Sun* said, "stated that she would never go in the Wild West business again." [12]

Frank made the formal announcement in a letter to Bill McClure, Cody's aide-de-camp. It was not an easy decision. "It is like giving up a big fortune to leave the dear old wild west," Frank wrote, "but a better position influences us and we must go." Of course, it wasn't really the new position but circumstances that had brought about the change. Frank would carry the load now. He had been offered a job with the Union Metallic Cartridge Company of Bridgeport, Connecticut. [13]

18.

The Western Girl

Just one year after leaving Buffalo Bill's Wild West, Annie Oakley embarked on another career, as an actress. Her name had become so synonymous by now with the Old West that Langdon McCormick had written a play especially for her, called— what else?—*The Western Girl*. It was set in Fiddletown, Colorado, "in the early days, when every man went armed and the law was little respected." The Rocky Mountains towered as a stage backdrop and the old Leadville coach stood off to the side.

Of course, Annie Oakley had never been a Colorado pioneer and she'd only seen the Rockies from a distance, but Americans would not remember that. She was six-guns and a ten-gallon hat, as western as Buffalo Bill himself. Her western image had become so well established by the turn of the century that it lives still in American folklore. But long before Broadway, movies, and television capitalized on Annie's western image, she did so herself.

In *The Western Girl* she played Nancy Barry, the good daughter of a bad bandit. Her sister was blind and the man she loved was stalwart and true, a U.S. cavalryman, Lieutenant Robert Hawley. Two soldiers, one miner, a Mexican dancer, and, of course, a cowboy rounded out the cast. "To rescue all of them at sundry times," the critics explained, was Nance's mission. She lassoed the villainess and pulled her by the neck over a yawning chasm in the mountains. The villainess fell screaming to her death in the torrent below, but the blind sister was saved, much to the delight of the audience, whom the Rochester *Union and Advertiser* said "goes wild over the incident." And then, with her trusty gun and

Poster from *The Western Girl*, 1902, in which Annie Oakley starred as Nance Barry; here, she lassoes the villainess and pulls her by the neck over a yawning chasm. (Courtesy of the Garst Museum, Greenville, Ohio)

her good horse Bess, Nancy Barry saved Lieutenant Hawley from the half-breed Lafonde. Nance wore the white hat, saved the nice people, and nipped evil in the bud. What better role for the good girl, Annie Oakley?

With an irony befitting a "western girl" from New Jersey, the play opened in Elizabeth in November 1902, then moved on to Paterson and Atlantic City. It was a play made to order for the sharpshooter everyone remembered from Buffalo Bill's Wild West. Annie still wore her short skirts, her leggings, and her sombrero—with the addition of a curly brown wig to cover her now-white hair. She shot a bottle out of her drunk father's hand, blasted her way out of a room where she was imprisoned, smashed twenty glass balls to pieces without a miss, and altogether lived up to her Wild West reputation. "Miss Oakley is clever in her role, and supported by a first-class company," said the Wilkes-Barre *Record*.[1] The play was dashing, sparkling, and sensational—pure melodrama, which appealed to the crowds of the day.

ANNIE OAKLEY

Though she'd only been on the stage twice before in her life—both times in western roles—Annie Oakley showed promise as an actress. The English certainly had liked her when, between seasons with the Wild West, she had starred in the play *Miss Rora* in 1895. Annie had played Aurora Blackburn, a little girl reared by two miners "in the vicinity of Arizona" after her father was murdered by Indians. They taught her to ride a horse and to shoot a gun, and before long Aurora was the best shot in camp. The role, said the South Wales *Argus*, fit Annie Oakley "like the proverbial glove." The role had afforded ample opportunity for Annie to show off her shooting. In the first act alone, she smashed six composition balls suspended in the air, extinguished the lights of a couple of candles, split a photograph of herself placed edgewise, smashed a ball as it was being swung around from a long rod, and then pulverized a dozen more composition balls thrown in the air in quick succession. She rode her Arabian horse Gypsy right up on the stage, and in the last act, Gypsy carried Annie over a fence in the center of the stage. Horse and rider were pursuing a pack of foxhounds, which Annie had brought with her from the States. The Gloucester *Chronicle* had said she had a "capricious and frolicsome style" and was "the heart and soul of the whole piece." The Nottingham *Evening News* had found her "sprightly and winsome" with "a natural grace, dash, and vivacity." "The best compliment we can pay her," the Pontypridd *Chronicle* had said, "is that she is as great a success on the stage as she was at the Wild West Show."[2]

The American press was kind to *The Western Girl*. Only one paper was truly critical, and even that criticism was tempered with praise. It came from the Rochester, New York, *Democrat and Chronicle*, whose reviewer found *The Western Girl* "rather a disappointment," and Annie Oakley "a star who can't act"—at least, if one compared her to real actresses like Sarah Bernhardt or Maude Adams. But when compared with other public figures, such as baseball players and bicycle riders who had gone on the stage, Annie shone. "She comes nearer to acting than any of the rest of them," the reviewer said, with the one exception of Jim Corbett, the boxer. Her manner was "self-possessed" but "unassuming." She wasn't awkward or "afraid of the sound of her own voice." She read her lines "intelligently" and her enunciation was "clear, distinct and agreeable." "Her inexperience seldom, and then but slightly, damages the scenes in which she figures," the critic said, "and when she is called upon to do things with her rifle she is 'all there' and entirely mistress of the situation." He decided that Annie had a "good notion of facial expression," and that during scenes of quiet comedy and sentiment she "acted very decently." Certainly, he concluded, *The Western Girl* was in no danger of falling flat because of any awkwardness or ineptitude of its star.[3]

In Camden, New Jersey, Annie received six curtain calls on Christmas Day, 1902. "Time has indeed dealt lightly with Annie Oakley," a Camden newspaper said. "Her hand is as steady and her aim is as unerring as in the good old days when she was given the name 'Little Sure Shot.'" Of course, her hair was no longer brown, but no one knew that, thanks to her curly brown wig.

She also had gained a considerable amount of weight since leaving the regimen of the Wild West, and she looked startlingly plump in photos from *The Western Girl.* Her appearance that year shocked her sister Hulda and even her old friend, W. A. Browne, editor of the Greenville *Advocate,* who saw her when she visited Greenville that year. Annie had "the appearance of a woman sixty years of age" if one judged by her hair alone, he said. And more, "the lack of exercise has caused Mrs. Butler to take on considerable extra averdupois [*sic*]." Frank said Annie weighed 138 pounds, 8 more than she'd ever weighed in her life.[4]

While Annie played in *The Western Girl* that Christmas, Buffalo Bill, gray and tired, was in London to begin another long tour. And over in Long Branch, New Jersey, Nate Salsbury had died that very Christmas Eve. While Annie played Camden, Salsbury was buried in Woodlawn Cemetery in New York.

The Western Girl closed in March 1903, and Annie spent a leisurely summer. She visited her mother in Greenville, stayed a few days at the Avon Inn in Atlantic City, and competed in a shooting tournament in Wilkes-Barre, Pennsylvania. That August, she went to Atlantic Highlands, New Jersey, to spend some time at the seashore. *The Western Girl* had done so well that she talked about starring in a new play by Langdon McCormick and perhaps touring Australia with Frank.

But any plans Annie had, and any potential for a long-lived acting career, were cut short by a scurrilous newspaper story that appeared in the Chicago *Examiner* and *American* on August 11, 1903, two days before Annie's forty-third birthday. The story changed the course of Annie Oakley's life and would consume her thoughts for the next five years.

"ANNIE OAKLEY ASKS COURT FOR MERCY—Famous Woman Crack Shot . . . Steals to Secure Cocaine," screamed the headline that Tuesday morning. "Annie Oakley . . . lies to-day in a cell at the Harrison Street

Station, under a bridewell sentence for stealing the trousers of a negro in order to get money with which to buy cocaine," the story read. The imposter, it was later learned, was Maude Fontenella, who once had performed in a burlesque Wild West show as "Any Oakley."[5]

"I plead guilty, your honor, but I hope you will have pity upon me," Fontenella begged under Annie's name. "An uncontrollable appetite for drugs has brought me here. I began the use of it years ago to steady me under the strain of the life I was leading and now it has lost me everything. Please give me a chance to pull myself together."

The reporter who filed the false story, Ernest Stout, later swore that a police inspector had verified that the woman was the real Annie Oakley. "The striking beauty of the woman whom the crowds at the World's Fair admired is now entirely gone," the reporter wrote. "Although she is but twenty-eight years old, she looks almost forty. Hers, in fact, is one of the extreme cases which have come up in the Harrison Street Police Court.

"To-day she will be taken to the bridewell to serve out a sentence of 45 days and costs. 'A good long stay in the bridewell will do you good,' the court said."

The story was sent out over the Publishers Press telegraph wire and picked up by newspapers all around the country. Some papers that did not get it off the wire clipped it from other newspapers and ran it word for word in their own. "Annie Oakley, Famous Rifle Shot is Destitute," said the headline in the *Times* of Rochester, New York, a city where Annie Oakley had played in *The Western Girl* only seven months before. "Annie Oakley in Prison, Famous Rifle Shot of Buffalo Bill's Show a Cocaine Victim," said the headline in the Philadelphia *Press*, a paper published only one hundred miles from Annie's home in Nutley.

Friends nationwide read the stories, but they didn't believe them. Anyone who knew the straitlaced Annie Oakley knew they couldn't have been true. Indignant, they clipped the stories and mailed them to Annie at the Grant Avenue house in Nutley. The more stories Annie received in the mail and the more of them she read, the angrier she became. This was far worse than reading her own obituary, as she had done back in 1891. She dashed off letters to the newspapers, only this time her letters had nothing nice to say.

"Dear Sir," she wrote to the Brooklyn *Standard Union* on August 12, 1903. "Woman posing as Annie Oakley in Chicago is a fraud . . . and I have not been to Chicago since last winter. If you will take the trouble to inquire at Nutley, N.J. (my home), you will find I own property enough to live on. Now that you have done me an injustice in publishing that article, I hope you will contradict it."

"Sir," she wrote to the Philadelphia *Press* on August 13 from Atlantic Highlands, "Woman posing as Annie Oakley in Chicago is fraud. I am spending summer here. Contradict at once. Some one will pay for this dreadful mistake."

And the press did contradict "that article." The Publishers Press sent out a retraction the very next day, and newspapers that had run the story apologized. Friends sent their sympathy, and sportsmen declared their support. But Annie Oakley would not be consoled. Amy Leslie shook her head and wrote a column saying that this kind of thing happened often to celebrities. But that did not console Annie, either. The New York *Daily News* wrote an editorial apology and sent ten copies of it to Annie along with a personal letter. But that wasn't enough. Annie Oakley was devastated.[6] "That terrible piece . . . nearly killed me," she said. "The only thing that kept me alive was the desire to purge my character."[7]

She would not rest until that day came. Annie Oakley set out to clear her name in what was called at the time the largest libel suit ever initiated. Initially, she brought twenty-five lawsuits demanding damages of $25,000 each against twenty-five newspapers that had printed the story of the destitute woman in the Chicago jail. Those suits alone sought a total of $625,000. Before she was through, Annie Oakley would sue fifty-five newspapers and win or settle out of court with all but one of them. "The only thing left for a person who is slandered in the press in the north is to sue for money," she told the Piqua, Ohio, *Leader-Dispatch*. "In the south they do differently and simply kill the man who slanders the good name of a woman. When the article was published my husband and I talked it over and he said, 'Well, I am able to earn our living if necessary and we will spend what we have to get you justice.'"[8]

If anything ever proved Annie Oakley's determination, her concern for her reputation, and her fierce pride it was the lawsuits she brought against the very press that had spoken so kindly of her throughout her long career. All seemed forgotten as she pursued the newspapers without mercy. What deep scar caused her to be so upset? There is no way to know, but one can surmise that a reaction so strong and so emotional must have gone to Annie's core. Could it have been rooted in that long-ago time when Annie Moses was sent to the poor farm and abused by a family whose name she never told? Annie Oakley had risen above her beginnings, but perhaps out of them, in some way to compensate, came the fierce pride that surfaced again and again in her life, most pointedly in the libel suits she brought in 1903. The prideful side of Annie Oakley had always been there. How else was she able to ignore those country-club ladies who had snickered at her when she stood at the traps in the early days? Hadn't she shown Lillian Smith a thing or two? She melted when the London editor J. J. Walsh gave her what she said was the biggest compliment of her life, that he had found her to be quite a lady.

Reputation mattered more than anything else to Annie Oakley, more even than money. But money she understood, so she determined to hit the newspaper culprits in their pockets. Of all of them, she most despised William Randolph Hearst. She became so obsessed that she clipped anti-Hearst articles and pasted them in her scrapbooks. After all, it was Hearst's Chicago *Examiner and American* that had first run the despicable story that distressed Annie Oakley's sensibilities as nothing else ever had.

To defend himself against Annie's libel suits, Hearst hired a detective and sent him to Greenville to try to dig up dirt about her life. When Annie heard about it, she was indignant. They "tried their best to discover that my life was not what a good woman's should be," she said. "But they couldn't find out anything like that for there was nothing of that sort to discover." And, indeed, there was not. The people in Greenville were indignant, too, and reportedly refused to let the Hearst detective stay in town overnight. "Not believed here," one Greenville newspaper wrote after reading the Hearst story. It simply was "too absurd for belief. A base libel against Darke County's famous woman shot."[9]

Amy Leslie didn't believe the story, either, and dashed off a letter to Annie, urging her to "make those people pay you big money." "Sue those people for fifty thousand dollars *right away*," she wrote. "That is small enough sum to demand after they have heaped every disgrace on you. . . . Get some good New Jersey lawyer who has no newspaper ax to grind and go at it as if you meant to shoot to kill." Amy said she and a Mr. Cook for Barnum & Bailey's show had told the *American* that the story was a lie, but the newspaper had gone right ahead anyway. "Now you soak them good and hard," Amy urged. "Every decent paper will applaud you."[10]

The nice little woman whom Amy had known in Chicago did just that, proving once and for all just how stubborn she could be. Annie put aside her acting and her shooting and pursued the newspapers relentlessly: among them, the St. Louis *Star*, the Jacksonville *Metropolis*, the Hoboken *Observer*, the Scranton *Truth*, the Bridgeport *Telegram-Union*, the New Orleans *Times-Democrat,* the Charleston *News and Courier,* the Brooklyn *Citizen,* and, of course, the Chicago *Examiner* and the Chicago *American.*

The trials began in March 1904. Courtrooms filled as Annie traveled from city to city over the next few years to testify in her own behalf. Americans were eager to get a look at the famous sharpshooter they had seen at a distance in the Wild West arena. And when they saw her up close, they were surprised, just as almost everyone who ever met her had been. The girl they remembered as "bounding over a barrier with brown curls flaming from beneath the broad rimmed sombrero" now wore "diamond ear-rings" and had "a wealth of beautiful tinted gray hair." She reminded one, not of a deadly crack shot, but of "a kindly school teacher." She wore a black dress, touched with red velvet at the collar and white at the cuffs. Over her face was a black veil, which she lifted when she took the stand. "She acted the cultured lady in every respect," the papers said. Her voice was "well modulated and low" and her features were "refined and almost classical."

As she began to tell her life's story, the courtroom grew hushed. Everyone present, including the twelve men on the jury and even the judge, appeared greatly interested in what she had to say. She told the crowded courtroom that she had married Frank Butler in 1882 and had taken the name Annie Oakley that year.[11] She gave her occupation as "shooting expert and actress." Her age, she said, was thirty-eight, though it really was forty-four.

"About her there is nothing that would in the least indicate that she has been for 17 years before the public," said the *Florida Times-Union* on January 17, 1905. "There is nothing of the flash and glitter that so often characterize the professional actress or circus performer." Annie exuded an air of "perfect refinement" and "polished courtesy." "It is easy to understand," the *Times-Union* said, "why she was so popular socially in many of the most exclusive circles."

People remembered that Annie had met the prince of Wales, who now was King Edward VII. What had he said about her shooting, they wanted to know, and the courtroom grew quiet as Annie repeated the famous words she had had engraved on her medal from the London Gun Club: "I know of no one more worthy of it." At that, one reporter said, "Annie Oakley dropped her eyes to the floor and blushed like a small school girl who had been complimented by her teacher."[12]

Every word Annie spoke, the papers said, "made an excellent impression on the jurors," and it wasn't surprising that the verdicts began coming in her favor, though the awards weren't as high as she had sought. She was awarded damages of $2,000 from the Jacksonville *Metropolis*, $900 from the Scranton *Truth*, $7,500 from the New Orleans *Times-Democrat*, and $3,000 from the Hoboken *Observer*. The biggest verdict came, as Annie would have liked, from Hearst's Chicago papers. She received $27,500 from "Gloomy Bill," who had gotten into more trouble during the trial by printing in his newspapers several facts that had been excluded from the testimony. The judge berated Hearst for trying to prejudice the jury.[13]

When she wasn't on the witness stand, Annie sat at her counsel's bench, her hand to her ear, leaning over slightly in her chair, listening to all the proceedings with the utmost attention. On the stand, she sat patiently while defense attorneys pressed her for details and pleaded with the jury that the newspapers had published the article in good faith and had intended no malice. Annie Oakley, they said, was a stage name for Annie Butler, and certainly Mrs. Butler of Nutley, New Jersey, had not been defamed. They had not written about her, but about Annie Oakley, "who appears in the circus ring in short skirts, buckskin leggings and cowboy hat."

In Scranton, Pennsylvania, the defense attorney repeated the name, "Annie Oakley," looked at Annie and said: "You do not claim to have an absolute right to that name do you?"

"I do not believe it is customary for people to steal other people's names," Annie replied.

"You're the woman who used to shoot out here and run along and turn head over heels, allowing your skirts to fall, and you wore buckskin leggings," he continued.

"I beg your pardon, you're wrong," Annie snapped. "I never wore buckskin leggins, neither did I allow my skirts to fall."

"Didn't you turn hand-springs?" he pressed.

"I am the lady who shot, but I didn't turn hand-springs," Annie said.[14]

In her quiet way, Annie could be as cutting as any lawyer she faced. When one lawyer asked for her definition of an education, she replied: "My idea of an education, is that it is a very good thing when backed by common sense, and a very bad thing in the head of a cheap lawyer."[15]

She had had her fill of lawyers who disparaged her livelihood and her motives. In Scranton, a Colonel Fitzsimmons had had the courtroom in stitches when he declared that Buffalo Bill fooled the public by painting up "some of the hangers-on" and putting them in the arena as real Indians. "You and I go to the show and pay our money," Fitzsimmons said, "and it is often that we see Indians from Tipperary, Zulus from Cardiff and Arabs from Vermont." He looked at Annie Oakley then and accused her of bringing a lawsuit as a way to get free publicity. "The newspapers have made her," he said. "It is they that have made her known from one end of the world to the other. They are the means of her greatness, and it now ill becomes her to strike back at the very thing that has given her the position she now holds. . . . The trouble that has come to this woman is simply the result of greatness. She is know the world over and anything that concerns her is a matter for publication." [16]

It was a clever speech and there was some truth in it; the press had been good to Annie Oakley and had certainly furthered her reputation over the years. But Colonel Fitzsimmons had Annie Oakley figured all wrong. She hadn't brought the lawsuits for publicity or even for money. What she wanted was simple: she wanted her good name cleared.

"I was with her part of the time she was prosecuting her cases, and I know the trials were hard for her to endure," Fern Campbell Swartwout wrote. "She would often fast and pray for days before a trial date. She said her mind was clearer when she got on the witness stand." [17]

As hard as the trials were, Annie vowed to keep on. "There were months when I prayed to God every day to only spare my reason so as to let me clear myself of this," she said, "and I will do it. It has aged me many years and caused me much expense, but I intend to keep on until the end." [18] And she did, although it would take until 1910 for all the lawsuits and appeals to conclude. Fern Campbell Swartwout said the Butlers collected $800,000 from their lawsuits, but according to Frank, who refused to say how much they did collect, that figure was much too high. "The general impression is that she made a lot of money out of these suits," as much as a quarter of a million dollars, he told *Forest and Stream*. "I only wish this was true. If it was, every dollar above her expenses and above the amount she might have earned during those six years would have been spent on a charity that would be a monument to the name of Annie Oakley; but any one who has had any lawsuits knows they cost money, and wherever it was possible to do so, she had the best attorneys. They come high, but are the cheapest in the end." [19]

Judging from known awards, the $27,500 Annie got from Hearst was unusually high. There was at least one other big award—$20,000 from the St. Louis *Star*—but many others were much lower. Figures under $5,000 were common. For example, Colonel Fitzsimmons got the paper in Scranton off the hook for $900. Though simple arithmetic shows that even an average award of $5,000 a case would have given Annie and

Frank more than a quarter of a million dollars, the business-minded Butlers obviously subtracted lawyers' fees, traveling expenses, and lost income from the total.

"I want to say right here, that when she entered these suits, it was not money but vindication she was after," Frank told *Forest and Stream*.[20] And Annie Oakley did win her vindication, though it came at the expense of a press that had treated her so well over the years. But even now the adoring newspapermen—including those who had been burned so badly—seemed to forgive her. A few years after the lawsuits, the Hoboken *Observer* wrote a complimentary story about Annie Oakley and took the time to send it to her along with a little note: "Dear Mrs. Butler," the note read. "Although you dug into us for three thousand 'Iron Men' at a time when three thousand was a large sum with us—you see we still love you."[21]

19.

At the Traps

While Annie prosecuted the lawsuits, Frank worked as a representative for the Union Metallic Cartridge Company. He traveled the country, promoting UMC products to American trapshooters, whose numbers had been growing as states imposed game limits and restrictions on the hunting season. The number of trap-shooters grew from an estimated one hundred thousand in 1906 to six hundred thousand in 1916. That year, the *New York Times* estimated that 36 million clay pigeons would be "killed" at a cost of $270,000 in targets and $12 million in shells.[1]

Gun and cartridge manufacturers like UMC wanted to get in on the boom. They hired well-known shooters like Rollo Heikes, Tom Marshall, and W. H. Heer to give free shooting exhibitions at American gun clubs, which had grown in number to an estimated five thousand by 1916. There even was a club exclusively for women, formed in 1913 by Miss Harriet D. Hammond of Wilmington, Delaware. Frank Butler wasn't considered as good a shot as a Rollo Heikes or a Tom Marshall, but he'd spent a lifetime around guns and was well known in shooting circles. He picked a good company to work for. Union Metallic of Bridgeport, Connecticut, was a successful firm founded in 1867 by Marcellus Hartley. In 1912, it would merge with the Remington Arms Company.[2]

As manager of the UMC eastern squad, Frank traveled from one gun club to another, setting up the company's new canvas tent, unfolding chairs, and putting up a table laid out with UMC advertising. Frank always had had a good head for business. At the New Jersey State

Championships in Freehold, he distributed Annie Oakley pins, which were so popular he could hardly meet the demand. He went about his business in a quiet, unassuming way. He was a respected and popular manager, full of common sense and a keen wit. "Butler's bird busters," he called his squad. But according to *Forest and Stream,* there was nothing of the "brass band annex" about Frank Butler, and he always was "strictly on the job."[3]

Frank's life became so full of gun clubs and shooting that he attended two hundred matches in the year 1906 alone. One blustery spring day he was a guest at the Northside Rod and Gun Club in Paterson, New Jersey. He went out and won three events that day, proving, as one paper put it, that "there are two shooters in the family." The wind had blown stiff across the fields, but inside the clubhouse it was warm. There was hot coffee to drink, and frankfurters to eat. Frank enjoyed the camaraderie of the clubs, though on occasion he and Annie would complain about clubhouses that had the bar attached to the lobby. The respectable Butlers, ever aware of their reputations, didn't want to risk the smell of smoke and whiskey and would have preferred a separate room for the bar.[4]

Before the lawsuits consumed her, Annie had been doing a great deal of serious trap work, too. In the winter and spring of 1902, she shot matches in Philadelphia, Altoona, Lebanon, and Cresson, Pennsylvania; Newark, Franklin, Lake Denmark, Rutherford, Freehold, and Oradell, New Jersey; Baltimore, Maryland; and Queens, New York. She won a fifty-dollar gold watch in Queens and split the hundred dollars in prize money with her partner, Steve Van Allen, at Lake Denmark. She made a straight score of twenty-one at the gun club in Franklin, fifteen straight at the gun club in Cresson; and ten straight at the Keystone Club in Philadelphia.[5]

In April 1902, she entered the biggest tournament of all, the tenth annual Grand American Handicap. Held at Blue River Park in Kansas City, it was the last to use live pigeons. In the field of 493 shooters, Annie was a familiar face. She had competed in the Grand American at Elkwood Park, New Jersey, in 1895, and at Interstate Park in Queens, New York, in 1900.[6] This year, she was one of only three women competing. The others were Mrs. S. S. Johnston of Minneapolis, who said she followed the game purely for sport, and, of all people, Miss Lillian F. Smith, who told the Kansas City *Star* that she had taken up shotgun shooting only two years before. Lillian was a vaudeville performer now, and it sounded as if she hadn't changed. She was going by the name Wenona, which she had taken during the Pan American Exposition in Buffalo the year before. She said she'd been adopted into the Sioux tribe, but the *Star* wasn't fooled. "Her make-up was so good," the newspaper said, "that it deceived most people, and a number of the society women of Buffalo entertained her, thinking she was an Indian princess." If Annie and Lillian had words, no one mentioned it. That there was an article on the women at all showed how unusual they were at the big trapshooting event. The shooters were principally businessmen, a well-groomed and prosperous group with plenty of means to enjoy the sport. They began arriving in Kansas City on a Sunday and took rooms in the leading hotels, the Midland, the Coates House, and the Baltimore.

On Monday, they took the Metropolitan Street Car trolleys out to Blue River Park, where the preliminary events got under way the first thing that morning. The day had dawned ideal for wingshooting: the sky was clear, the air bracing. The birds would be quick to wing and fast to flight. Thousands of birds were caged in a half dozen coups by the shooting grounds. The Interstate Association had purchased them for $1.50 a dozen from Kansas and Missouri farmers. After the day's shoot, a dealer would gather up the dead birds, take them downtown by the wagonload, and sell them to hotels, where they'd be turned into pigeon pie. Others would be sorted by age and color, packed in barrels, and shipped to markets all over the United States.

Beyond the pigeon coops stood the shooting ground and the traps, the little iron boxes from which the birds would fly. Annie stood twenty-seven yards from the traps, a distance considered stiff for a woman. The better a shooter was, the farther away he was made to stand. There was confidence in the way Annie stepped to the mark. She grasped her shotgun firmly, swung it quickly from right to left, then dropped the butt well below her armpit.

"Pull!" she cried. The trap was sprung, the pigeon rose, and Annie's gun responded with one report or two, depending on the need. It was a "dead bird," or if she missed, a "lost bird." She dropped her used shells in a box and moved on to the next station along the runway. Her form at the traps was considered perfect. Standing sidewise, she leaned forward, one foot a little behind the other. "See the grace of it?" she said.[7] But how, admirers wanted to know, did she aim to kill the flying bird? "I can truthfully say that I have tried for years to frame a reply to that seemingly simple question," Annie said, "but have not been able to settle upon a fully satisfactory answer yet. With all my experience and after consulting the best shots of America and Europe, I can find no better answer than to say: You must shoot until you overcome confusion at quickly sighting on a moving object." Strive to take deliberate aim, she advised. Make the proper allowance ahead, above, or below the bird, according to which direction it was going, then press the trigger. It was as "simple" as that.[8]

Annie said she had received thousands of letters and inquiries about guns and shooting over the years. One person even wanted to know whether she shot with one eye or both eyes open. "I always adhere to both eyes," she answered, "believing that, if a person can see with one eye, he can see better with two. But I don't mean to say that there are no good shots who shut one eye."[9] Annie tried to answer the many questions people asked her in a little booklet she wrote, probably in 1899, called *Annie Oakley, A Brief Sketch of Her Career and Notes on Shooting.* She offered the booklet to anyone who wrote to her and who enclosed two cents for return postage.

In its pages Annie told about her guns. "As to my own collection of firearms, I have many shotguns, most of them hammerless," she wrote. "They weigh about six pounds." She had so many guns that she once said they could "line this tent on all four sides if they were stacked as closely as I could stack them." Many had been given to her by gun companies, not only as tokens of esteem, but undoubtedly as advertising tools. The guns she used in her exhibitions were all made to order, she said, and the others were just for ornament.[10]

Annie not only had many guns, she had many makes of guns. Various accounts, usually written by sporting magazines, show that her shotguns included Lancaster, Cashmore, Francotte, Parker, Purday, Spencer, Scott, L. C. Smith, Ithaca, Cranston, and P. Webley & Sons. Her rifles included Winchester, Stevens, Marlin, Lancaster, Holland, and Remington. Her pistols and revolvers were Smith & Wesson, Stevens, Colt, and Renette.

"Which gun do you prefer?" Jacob Pentz of *Shooting and Fishing* once asked her. "I have but little choice, if the gun is of fine quality," Annie answered. "There is Purday; there is Grant; there is Lancaster; there is Francotte. Each makes a good enough weapon for anybody. I use the two you see almost constantly (Lancaster and Francotte), and I cannot say that one is better than the other. I have also a Premier Scott which I think a good deal of."[11] When it came to the make of a gun, Annie was adamant about only one thing: quality. "Nobody should trust their lives behind a cheap gun," she told *Gameland* in March 1893. Although many accounts suggest that the Lancaster guns were Annie's favorites, she never endorsed one make of gun over another and, in fact, said such an endorsement would have been foolish. "Guns, rifles and pistols are of many styles, and to declare that any one make is superior to all others would show a very narrow mind and limited knowledge of firearms," she wrote in 1899. "The fancy of the shooter, his or her physique, and the kind of game to be hunted, should govern the choice of intelligent shooters." [12]

Although Annie Oakley was not among the big money winners at the 1902 Grand American Handicap, her reputation in the elite trapshooting world already was long established. [13] It was Annie Oakley's work at the traps that proved so decisively that the woman in the Wild West arena had been all she claimed to be. Annie Oakley was so highly respected in the trapshooting fraternity that her name would go down as one of the all-time greats of the sport. "I take my hat off to no one when it comes to shooting," she once said. And rightly so. When the Amateur Trapshooting Association founded its Hall of Fame, Annie Oakley's name would be among those at the top of the list. [14]

Annie Oakley proved her proficiency at the shooting line once and for all in the summer of 1906 when, with the bulk of her litigation behind, she joined Frank on the road with the UMC squad. She showed up in Dubois, Pennsylvania, one April wearing a "neat fitting checkered habit," a natty straw sailor hat, and a gray veil, which hid her gray hair. She looked, said the Dubois *Morning Journal,* "just as young as when we first saw her many years ago with Col. William F. Cody's wild west show."

With the grace of old, Annie inaugurated her exhibition with gun work that "excited the wonderment of all." She easily broke small wooden balls thrown in the air and shattered the larger pieces before they reached the ground. She hit brass disks, pennies, "pee wee" marbles, and .22 cartridges "all so small that the eye could hardly follow their flight." The only evidence of their being hit, the *Journal* said, was "a whizz, puff of white dust, or explosion." The ladies applauded when Annie shot the ashes off Frank's cigarette. Then, "in rapid order," she clipped four pieces of ordinary school chalk that Frank held between his fingers. Holding the gun at her hip, she "rolled a tin can away from her with rapid shots." She "scrambled" eggs thrown inwards from a distance of fifty yards and "smashed" tomatoes while holding her gun upside down. "It was," said the *Morning Journal,* "the most remarkable exhibition ever witnessed in Dubois." [15]

In Rumford, Maine, Annie showed how a can of water blew up when she shot it with a 38-55 soft-point bullet, and in Lewiston she entertained a crowd of three hundred people for over an hour, "performing feat after feat with a rapidity and variety that held undivided attention." "Every shot there was something that dropped," said a paper in Escanaba, Michigan. In Collinsville, New Jersey, Annie fired at a potato on a stick, chipping off piece after piece in ten shots, and in Morristown she did an old favorite—splitting two playing cards in two. They were held up to form a cross the the edge of one literally bisecting the edge of the other. "In one shot," said the *Daily Record,* "she hit the center of the cross and split each of the cards into two pieces." [16]

By June 1907, Annie's life was as full of shooting as it ever had been. That month she appeared during Ladies Day at the Trenton Shooting Association tournament, and in August at the Fourteenth Annual Target and Live Bird Tournament "down by the sea" at Betteron, Maryland. Her picture appeared on UMC advertisements for sure-fire blank cartridges and even for a time on advertisements for a dandruff treatment.

It was during their years with UMC that Frank and Annie became fast friends with the actor Fred Stone, a man with a temperament much like their own. Fred Stone was a pleasant family man who didn't drink or swear. Like the Butlers, he saw himself as a "rolling stone," whom the show business had taken all over the country. He'd traveled with the Berry and Sealers Wagon Circus as a boy and in 1895, as a young man of twenty-two, had gone on the Chicago stage with his partner Dave Montgomery. As the blackface comedians Montgomery and Stone, they got their big break seven years later when Stone landed a part as the scarecrow in *The Wizard of Oz,* and Montgomery was cast as the Tin Woodman. *The Wizard* was a tremendous hit, and for the next four years Fred Stone played opposite the little Kansas girl Dorothy (Anna Laughlin), doing his contortionist and acrobatic dances in theater after theater.

During *The Wizard,* Fred met the woman of his dreams, Allene Crater, who was cast in the role of the Lunatic Lady. They married and had three daughters, Dorothy, Carol, and Paula. They bought a place in Amityville, New York, along the wilds of Narriskatuck Creek on Long Island. Fred had horses and dogs on his place, and friends liked to tease him about his "Western ranch." [17] By 1907, when Montgomery and Stone were starring in a new play called *The Red Mill,* Fred occasionally

Annie Oakley hunting quail in Pinehurst, N.C., February 8, 1908. The signature is Annie's. (Courtesy of the Buffalo Bill Historical Center, Cody, Wyo.)

was taking the time out to go hunting with Frank Butler. They never told the circumstances of their meeting, but it probably was through show business. The Butlers made a trapshooting enthusiast of Fred Stone.

"Wherever the company went on the road, I joined the local gun club," Stone wrote in his autobiography. "I got more pleasure out of breaking 100 straight in a 100-target match at the Chicago Gun Club than I did out of all our Chicago *Red Mill* notices." Stone was so enthusiastic about the sport that he installed three expert traps on his ranch and learned to do trick shooting at the instruction of a very qualified teacher—Annie Oakley. Annie and Frank spent many long weekends at Stone's place in Amityville.

They were there one day when Fred, who was a baseball fan, came home with his team in tow. When the team decided to stay for lunch, Annie joined Allene and Fred's mother in the kitchen. While the women cooked, Fred gave a shooting exhibition on the lawn. The familiar pop of the shotgun attracted Annie's attention, and she came outside to see what was going on. "Can I have the gun for a minute?" she asked Fred, and he handed her his automatic shotgun. Frank threw up five targets in a bunch, and Annie, her hair shining white in the afternoon sun, gunned all five before they hit the ground.

"Thanks, Fred," she said, and went back into the house.

Mason Peters, a newspaper man in the group, couldn't believe what he'd seen. He mopped his head, turned to Stone and said, "My God, Fred, was that your mother?" Fred Stone loved to tell that story about Annie Oakley. "It was always amusing to watch people who were meeting her for the first time," he said. "They expected to see a big, masculine, blustering sort of person, and the tiny woman with the quiet voice took them by surprise. . . . There was never a sweeter, gentler, more lovable woman than Annie Oakley." [18]

Fred Stone also counted among his friends the already famous Will Rogers. Rogers and Stone had a lot in common; both were outdoorsmen and both were absorbed in their profession. Rogers taught Fred to do rope tricks, and Fred taught Rogers some dance routines. Will Rogers and his family lived nearby in Amityville, and they spent much time together. Fred told how his daughters and Rogers's three children learned to ride on the same old cowpony named Dopey. Through Fred Stone, Annie Oakley and Frank Butler came to know Will Rogers. [19]

Life was pleasant and easy around Stone's place, and Annie and Frank spent many happy days there. One day Annie set a record at Fred's traps by hitting 1,016 brass disks without a miss. It took three hours. She hadn't had time to do that kind of shooting since back in the 1880s when she was trying to make a name for herself. On August 18, 1908, Annie decided to try her hand at 500 targets in a row. She carried a whole case of shells out to Fred Stone's traps and began shooting. She used her regular load of three drams of New Schultze powder and one and a half ounces of No. 7½ chilled shot. She made a fantastic score—483 of 500, or 96.6 percent. [20]

Only fifteen minutes after she'd finished shooting, a telegram arrived from Piqua, Ohio. Annie's celebration ceased then and there: Her mother had died. Annie left that afternoon for Ohio. [21]

20.

The Final Stand

They buried Susan Shaw in the little Yorkshire cemetery, just down the road from North Star. Only a week
after Susan's death, news came that Tony Pastor had suffered a paralytic
stroke and died. James A. Bailey had died in 1906, and Nate Salsbury
was dead as well. Annie's friend Henry Bunner had passed away a decade ago, at just forty years of age. And dead these long years, too, was
Annie's oldest friend, G. A. Katzenberger, who had died in Greenville
in 1895. Members of the Greenville Gun Club had mourned his death;
he had been one of its most enthusiastic and popular members.[1]

Even the house in Nutley was gone. With Frank on the road so much
and Annie so preoccupied with her lawsuits, the Butlers sold the house
in 1904 and moved to an apartment at 180th Street and Fort Washington
Avenue in New York City. Their apartment overlooked fashionable
Riverside Drive and the beautiful bluffs along the Hudson. But the
Butlers didn't settle in there. They moved again, this time to 22 Eppirt
Street in East Orange, New Jersey, where they were still living.[2]

Life was changing, there could be no doubt. Annie and Frank could
make the train run from New York to Chicago now in only eighteen
hours, thanks to fast trains introduced in June 1905. The year before,
the Wright Brothers had made their first flight at Kitty Hawk, and in
1903 a Packard automobile had been driven from San Francisco to New
York in only fifty-two days. In 1909, Henry Ford introduced his Model
T, and by 1911 millions of Americans were bumping and rolling around
the country in the horseless carriage.

As the new century marked its first decade, Annie Oakley turned fifty years old. She was the old-timer now, her name harkening back to the frontier and the roaming bison. But even after a decade out of the spotlight, and though most Americans probably had no idea where she was living or what she was doing, her popularity endured. That was evident at the annual Sportsman Show in Madison Square Garden on March 2, 1911. When it was announced that Annie Oakley was to shoot, the mass of spectators got up out of their seats and crowded to the upper end of the Garden to see her. And just as everyone remembered, "no object, however small," escaped her aim.[3]

Annie said she had received many offers to reenter show business, and there was evidence that she was beginning to think seriously about it. Any one of the eighteen Wild West shows on the road in 1910 would have loved to list her on their bill, white hair and all. Even as an old-timer, Annie Oakley would draw crowds.[4]

Perhaps to test the water, she paid a visit to Buffalo Bill's show in Madison Square Garden in May 1910. The show had merged with Pawnee Bill's Historic Wild West and Great Far East, and the "Two Bills Show," as it was called, was the largest on the road. William F. Cody, a showman still, greeted Annie with the same kindness he had shown for so many years, and for two weeks she was a welcome guest at his show. She must have felt at home, and for old times' sake, she rode out into the tanbark arena with "the boys."[5]

The visit ran deeper than the purely personal, and word slipped out that Buffalo Bill had asked Annie to rejoin his troupe. Surprisingly, she turned him down.[6] Perhaps the keen businessman Frank Butler had shied away from a deal with Cody because the old showman had announced publicly that he was about to retire. Or perhaps the Two Bills Show had not offered the Butlers enough money. Whatever the reason, business apparently came before loyalty, and Annie looked around for a better offer. It wasn't long in coming. Just a year later Annie Oakley was on the road again, this time with the Young Buffalo Wild West.

The Young Buffalo show was cut from the same mold as Buffalo Bill's Wild West, but they were not associated in any way. Young Buffalo advertised the holdup of the stagecoach, the riding of the Pony Express, the hanging of a horsethief, and a "Fight at the Water Hole," in which Indians illustrated their "crafty warfare" by attacking a band of cowboys. Ambrose Means was the star cowboy. He roped a buffalo with a lariat and threw the animal down singlehanded. Montana Jack and Fred Burns rode with the show as champion ropers. Buffalo Vernon engaged in a "hand and horn contest with a Texas steer," and Prairie Rose was introduced as "beyond cavil the greatest and most intrepid female rider of the known world." Young Buffalo himself was Mr. Joe R. Smith, a young man with a black moustache and goatee, and a head of long, black hair.

The show, which toured on its own yellow and red train, was owned by Vernon C. Seavers, a theater and amusement park owner in Peoria, Illinois. How much Seavers paid to get Annie Oakley, no one said, but it must have been a good salary, for Annie didn't come cheap. According to *Billboard,* she had been "the best paid arenic star" for a quarter century. She had "accumulated a big share of this world's goods" and didn't need a job, *Billboard* said. But "the lure of the sawdust ring claimed her again for its own, and she finally consented to join the Young Buffalo Show." Frank, as always, accompanied her as manager.[7]

With Annie on the bill, the Young Buffalo Wild West advertised the "most noted quartette of sharpshooters ever on a single program." Besides Annie Oakley, "the peerless wing and rifle shot of the world," Young Buffalo had the one and only Captain Adam Bogardus, who was back in the show business, too, though he was seventy-eight years old. Annie and the captain shot alongside "the noted marksmen" Curtis Liston and Captain O. G. Stevens.[8]

The "most noted quartette" performed seventeenth on the program, right before the roping and riding "of the wildest and most untamable horses procurable anywhere." Rough-and-ready cowboys and cowgirls "right from the plains" danced a quadrille on horseback, and the Cossacks performed "remarkable and fancy trick equestrianism." It was just like old times, and Annie Oakley was at home again, though on the road. The show took her to Rockville, Terre Haute, Indianapolis, and Richmond, Indiana. In mid-May she was in Dayton, Ohio; by June she was in Yonkers, New York; and by July she was in Montreal. Twenty-six years had passed since Annie had played Canada with Buffalo Bill and made friends with old Sitting Bull. But Little Sure Shot was as big a star and as fine a shot as she ever had been.

"Miss Annie Oakley carried the honors of the afternoon," said the London, Ontario, *Free Press.* "Miss Oakley's performance was marvelous," said the Nashville *Tennessean.* "She makes a phenomenal display," said the Hartford *Post.* "Annie Oakley looks as though she had discovered the secret that Ponce De Leon sought so long in vain," *Billboard* wrote that year. "She is as bright and alert, as when I saw her a slip of a girl with long braids 25 years ago when I was a kid." If Annie had a complaint, the *Billboard* said, it was that many people prefaced an introduction to her by saying, "Why, I thought Annie Oakley had died several years ago."[9] Far from it. When the Young Buffalo show pulled into Hopkinsville, Kentucky, on November 1, 1911, for the last stand of the season, Annie had traveled 8,226 miles in twenty-seven weeks—and she had not missed one performance.

Annie Oakley stayed with the Young Buffalo show for the next two years, 1912 and 1913, weathering the show's merger in 1912 with the Colonal Fred Cummins Wild West and Indian Congress. The combined show now had Prince Oskazuma the fire eater, Little Dot Greer the snake enchantress, Mrs. Windecker the mindreader, some oriental and Singhalese dancers, clowns, Arabs, and six elephants, but it still was mostly Wild West. A Sioux Indian chief shot a bow and arrow, and Billy Waites performed with his Australian bullwhip. With the long, sharp lashes, he snuffed a cigar, cut off the end of a piece of paper, and jerked a handkerchief out of someone's pocket. Ray Thompson's troupe of high school horses did the "turkey trot" and the "grizzly bear" dance. Young Buffalo himself "pranced about on a fiery horse," and Vernon C. Seavers, Jr., eight years old, was "the youngest cowboy in the world."[10]

As the Utica, New York, *Press* put it: Young Buffalo "had the '49'ers chuck wagon, the holdup of the overland mail and—Annie Oakley." Even at fifty-two years old, she still was the star of any Wild West show. She was "better even than the boomerang hurling and the bull whips of the Australians," said the Rochester *Herald* of August 1, 1912. Annie's shooting "was the feature of the entire exhibition." With the sun shining directly in her face, she broke clay pigeons, glass balls, and eggs with unerring aim. "The elephants were great, and the clowns did their best to make Young Buffalo's Wild West show," one newspaper said, "but it remained for the veteran Annie Oakley, best female shot in the world, to make the show a success. Of all the stunts presented there was none which gained greater applause in the crowded tents than that of the 'young woman' . . . who smashed with her eyes shut, almost, the fragile balls thrown into the air for her to shoot." She did the same stunts she had always done. She smashed glass balls from every angle, even lying on her back over a chair. She laid her gun on the ground, then picked it up and fired after the targets had been thrown. She shot backwards using a mirror to sight. The hardest feat of all, she said, was smashing five balls thrown at once before any hit the ground.[11]

Annie had a new feat, probably learned from Will Rogers or Fred Stone, in which she twirled a lariat with her left hand and shot a gun with her right. Annie posed for a picture, lariat slung over her shoulder. Unlike the old serious-looking photographs with Buffalo Bill, in this one Annie had a big smile on her face—and a curly brown wig on her head. The papers were calling her "America's shooting star" and "the absolute queen in her sphere," and were comparing her to Joan of Arc and Abraham Lincoln, since her early home life "had been no less humble."

When the Young Buffalo Wild West played Greenville, Ohio, on May 5, 1913, *The Courier* lavished Annie with praise. "She has made a proud record," the paper said, "by her wits, her activity, her genius, her naturalness, her brightness of mind, her courteous nature and her bravery." [12] The paper implored "every patriotic citizen of Darke County" to attend the show and cheer for Annie to demonstrate "love for 'Our Own.'" Though Annie had not lived in Greenville for years and it was doubtful that many people there really knew her, the town embraced her, and she returned its affection.

Annie hadn't forgotten her roots, and the older she became the more apparent it was that they still were very much a part of her. In a gesture, perhaps, of growing sentimentality, she gave away free Young Buffalo show tickets that May to residents at the Darke County Children's Home and then served free ice cream and other refreshments to the children. She repeated the gesture later that year when Young Buffalo played Cambridge, Maryland, on September 3. In a letter, Frank invited the managers of any orphan's home in Cambridge to bring the children to the Young Buffalo show as Annie's guests. Free refreshments were promised. [13]

According to legend, Annie Oakley had been giving away free tickets and buying ice cream for children all during her years with Buffalo Bill's Wild West. But this simply does not appear to be true. Buffalo Bill's Wild West did hold an "Orphan's Day," most notably at the Chicago World's Fair in 1893. However, Annie's name was not connected with it. No account exists until 1913 of Annie giving anything away to poor children.

It wasn't that she didn't like children. In fact, she and Frank befriended Johnny Baker's two girls, Gladys and Della. Frank was Gladys's godfather, and Annie, in a photograph she had made into a brooch, was pictured holding the girls lovingly. And judging from the way Annie treated her nieces, it seems obvious that she cared about children and perhaps would have liked to have had some of her own. The subject, though, certainly never came up in interviews, and even Annie's niece Irene Patterson did not recall hearing the Butlers talk about it. Al-

Annie Oakley as she appeared with the Young Buffalo Wild West, 1911. (Courtesy of the Circus World Museum, Baraboo, Wis.)

though there is no way to know, it is possible that Annie and Frank never had children out of pure practicality. Annie Oakley, after all, was a working woman preoccupied with making a living. She was dedicated to her career, and to the money it brought. Annie began her stage career when she was about twenty-two years old, joined Buffalo Bill's Wild West when she was going on twenty-five, and stayed until she was forty-one. Where was there time to stop and have a baby? What would the lapse have done to her career—and her pocketbook?

But it can be surmised that Annie Oakley felt deeply about children and her own early struggles in the world. Why else had she singled out those at the Darke County Children's Home for free tickets and ice cream? And perhaps most telling, though never well documented, were contributions Annie made over a number of years to the education of at least nineteen young women. Who the women were or where they went to school is not known, though they reportedly lived in various parts of the United States. Annie, who seldom talked about her charitable acts, apparently had met the women during her travels. One of the few documented accounts of the women is found in the Worcester, Massachusetts, *Evening Gazette* of June 17, 1912, which reported that Annie then was educating her eighteenth child, Elizabeth, "a beautiful girl 18 or 19 years of age."

"You smile when you think of Annie Oakley and 18 children," the *Gazette* wrote, "but all of the 18 have been adopted children. They have all been given high school and business educations, and then started on the road to success." According to Annie, she had not legally adopted the young women but simply helped them out with money as it was needed. The contributions said much about an Annie Oakley who once told the Newark *Sunday News* that she had acquired her education "among the birds and the wild flowers." She wasn't ashamed of it, but she certainly seemed to have regrets. Maybe Annie Moses never had a formal education, but Annie Oakley, in whatever healing way it afforded, could make sure that some other young woman did.[14]

Life on the road had not left much time for Annie Oakley to return to school, and here she was in 1913, still on the road with the Young Buffalo show. It had taken her to 139 towns in seventeen states. Americans, just as they had been doing for years when the circus or the Wild West came to town, lined the sidewalks to watch the street parade. They listened to William Atterbury's Cowboy Band as it lumbered by in a big wagon drawn by eight horses. They saw a band of dark-skinned Dahomians, a half-dozen spirited Cossacks, twenty cowgirls, twenty cowboys, and a mule-drawn stagecoach, which harbored two squaws and two papooses. The "original 20-ox team" pulled a prairie schooner. Clowns rode burros, and a wagon rolled by "crowded with buxom and comely harem inmates, realistic enuf [sic] to lure every male in Peoria to the performance." Oriental music drifted through the air, tom-toms thumped, a calliope played, and a thousand Americans cheered.[15]

Annie Oakley of the Wild West, whose enduring fame arose from a spectacle such as that, rode in at least one street parade that year in a civilized, 1911 model Packard. "She Rides in an Automobile Now," the headline read. Still more surprising, she was dressed "like a Washington debutante." Whatever had happened to the original wild and woolly western performers? Why, the newspaper said, it seemed as if they had "become infected with regular downeast airs."[16] Anyone who knew the real Annie Oakley knew that that had been true for a very long time.

As the Young Buffalo season closed, fifty-three-year-old Annie Oakley rode in her last street parade and gave her last performance as a Wild West star. It came in Marion, Illinois, on October 4, 1913. And then, Annie Oakley retired, built herself a new home in Maryland, and settled down to live happily ever after.

21.

A House on Hambrooks Bay

Annie Oakley and Frank Butler retired to a two-story cottage on Hambrooks Bay, along the eastern shore of Maryland. It was a pleasant house with a wide front porch overlooking a mile of blue water. One day in 1914 Frank sat on the porch and counted forty-two oyster boats coming in from the Choptank River. The oysters were taken into the canning houses in Cambridge, shucked, packed in boxes, and sent all over the country. Frank, who always seemed so interested in life, had been into town to watch the work and explore Cambridge, which he described as a town with "four banks, several fine churches, but no saloons." He talked of canvasback ducks, wild geese, quail, herring, perch, crabs, and, of course, oysters, and encouraged his busy New York friends to come down for a weekend in this "sportsman's paradise" only "two hundred miles from Broadway."[1]

An old friend from Cambridge, Dr. Samuel Fort, went out to Hambrooks Bay one day to visit the Butlers. He found the genial Frank, now sixty-four, in good health and with "his stock of good stories and caustic wit" still on tap. "It is doubtful if there is a citizen in all Cambridge who does not know him," Fort wrote, "and to be his friend is an open card introduction wherever you go." Dr. Fort found Annie "still the same patient, cheerful, kindly little woman" he'd always known.[2] She'd placed her trophies here and there around the house and piled her scrapbooks on a table.

Fort also met the Butlers' new dog, Dave, a black, white, and tan purebred English setter, whom they'd named after Fred Stone's partner, Dave Montgomery. Annie had been wanting a bird dog for some

197

time, and one fall day Frank drove to East New Market, Maryland, and bought her one. He found Dave penned up in a dirty kennel without much food. Frank looked the dog over, patted him on the head, and decided that he would do. Dave jumped up in the wagon beside Frank and snuggled close. Frank covered him with a blanket and took him home, where Dave soon became a member of the family. The Butlers loved their dog as they would have loved a child.[3]

Annie set about training Dave, took him hunting every other day, and soon bragged that he could stand, back, and retrieve, "all of which I have taught him without using a whip." She loved Dave so much that she pampered him, even ironing his ears. "Dave loved it," said Annie's nephew by marriage Rush Blakeley, who was present a number of times when Annie was ironing clothes. Annie would look over at the dog, lying nearby, and say, "You want your ears ironed, Dave?" And the dog would come over and rest his head between her knees. "She'd spread his big floppy ears on her legs," Blakeley said, "and then she'd iron them gently—with a cool iron of course."[4]

"Dave is a member of the family," Dr. Fort wrote. "And if you can find a warmer welcome than meets you at the door, from this family I don't know where to find it." Annie and Frank showed the doctor around their place. Out in the cove was a private oyster bed, and a little farther out, a ducking blind. A clay pigeon trap, for a little practice now and then, sat on a knoll.[5]

That summer, Annie's niece Fern came to visit. "We did enjoy the boating and fishing, and later in the fall, the hunting," she wrote. "The house was only a few hundred feet from the beautiful bay, and it was heavenly to sit on the porch and look over the bay and dream." Fern remembered especially how the traveling man Frank Butler had always wanted a strawberry bed. So he hired a nurseryman to come out and set one. But Frank didn't have the patience to be a gardener. "He thought that the plants should blossom right away," Fern said, "and because they did not he thought the plants had not been set right, so every few days he would change some of them. He kept moving the young plants until he killed most of them."[6]

Annie loved the hunting and fishing around Cambridge as much as Frank did. Before the hunting season ended, she had killed quail, rabbits, and squirrels, and still was hunting ducks. "While there has been a great deal of game bagged here, I am pleased to say there is plenty left over," she wrote to the *American Field*. "When I say there was more than 1,700 game licenses taken out in this county (Dorchester), the reader can imagine the amount of hunting that was done." [7]

When they weren't in the field, the Butlers liked to have a go at the birds at the Du Pont shooting grounds in Cambridge and commented on its "fine colonial buildings and ground," donated by Mr. Du Pont. They were impressed, too, with Cambridge's new hospital, the gift of Mrs. Du Pont. Not surprisingly, it was during Annie's first year in Cambridge that she wrote the booklet, *Powders I Have Used*. It was published by the Du Pont Company.

That summer Annie gave an exhibition at the Dorchester County Fair and made plans to go to Florida for the winter. Annie and Frank had been attracted to the South ever since Frank's days with the Union Metallic Cartridge Company. They had traveled for a time with the company's southern squad and spent parts of 1908 and 1909 in Louisiana, Alabama, Georgia, North and South Carolina, and Florida, where they had visited the lake country around Leesburg. Ever since, they had dreamed of spending a winter there.

Their first chance came after the close of the Young Buffalo season of 1911. They took a room at the Lakeview Hotel, a comfortable, two-story building with big windows and a wide porch, railed and pillared. They would be back many times and in all would spend four seasons there. "Flowers are in bloom and peach trees in blossom," Frank wrote from the Lakeview one winter. "All this while in front of me lies a paper with the staring head lines, 'Many People Frozen to Death up North.'" [8]

The lakes were teeming with fish, and the quail hunting was superb. "No need to go more than a few miles to get the limit, which is fifteen birds to each gun," Frank wrote. He called Leesburg a "sportsman's paradise," and the Lakeview, a hotel "whose landlord knows how and does cater to sportsmen." [9] The quail hunting was so good that Annie said she and Frank seldom returned to the hotel without their limit. It became their habit to distribute their kill to the hotel guests who, Annie said, "appreciated them greatly." Sometimes they went after wild turkeys, deer, 'possum, or doves. "The other day we returned with a magnificent specimen of wild turkey, which was killed by Mr. Butler," Annie wrote to old friends in Nutley. "It weighed eighteen pounds and was in fine condition, and made an unusually good dinner." [10]

Another day, Annie brought home a trophy of a different kind—a seven-foot, four-inch rattlesnake, which she had almost stepped on while hunting. "I happened to look at the ground less than a pace distant and saw the rattler," Annie said. "It was coiled and ready to strike. Another step forward and I would have received the strike. I never did such quick thinking in my life as was crowded into that second. I sprang backward and at the same instant raised my gun and fired quickly." The shot went true, and the rattler was killed where it lay, its head blown off. "I took it back to the hotel with me and had it skinned, and the skin tacked to a board," Annie said.[11]

Someone took a picture of Annie and her rattlesnake, and Annie enclosed it in a letter to friends up North. Beware of rattlers and water moccasins, she wrote, then took the opportunity to tell of another Florida hazard—the land sharks. "They print alluring advertisements in pamphlet form, and they catch the gullible by the thousands," she wrote. "We have met hundreds of people here who were making their way back to their homes in the North after having been induced to come down here by the false statements made to them. In many cases their trip South meant the investment and spending of every dollar they had in the world." To the frugal Annie Oakley, land sharks were no better than a dangerous rattlesnake.

During Annie Oakley's years in the South, she gave exhibitions now and then to raise money for this cause or that. On January 19, 1911, she gave an exhibition at the Leesburg baseball grounds to raise money for the Leesburg Band. In connection with Annie's exhibition, the Florida Hunter and Fisherman's Club held a target shoot, charged admission, and raised $150 for the band. That evening, the band said thanks by giving a concert at the Lakeview.[12]

There had been an exhibition at the Polo Grounds in New York to aid the Actors' Fund and one in Maryland to help the Dorchester County Fair. The mature Annie Oakley, financially set for life herself, became more charitable as the years progressed. One day when she was performing in Winston-Salem, North Carolina, she read in the local newspaper about a pregnant woman left penniless when her husband was killed in a mining accident. Perhaps thinking of her own mother's predicament when Jacob Moses died, Annie sent a letter, along with a check for four dollars, to the widow, care of the newspaper.

"I enclose check for ten per cent of the salary I received yesterday for shooting in Winston-Salem," Annie wrote to the editor. "I hope the citizens of your prosperous 'Twin-Town' will do likewise, and thereby place the grief-stricken little widow, as well as the little life soon to begin, beyond want for awhile." A four-dollar gift may not have seemed like a lot of money from a woman as well off as Annie Oakley, but it was a tithe of her pay, and it must have seemed a proper and practical sum. "Our duty is that which lieth nearest," Annie would say, "and how many futile attempts to place square pegs in round holes would be spared if this were remembered." [13]

Despite the Butlers' idyllic winters and the vows to settle down in Maryland, all was not perfect: Annie seemed restless. "[Frank] and I were always wondering," Fern Campbell Swartwout wrote, "how long she would be satisfied to stay in the cozy place we had there, among such good friends." Annie, who once said, "You can't cage a gypsy," admitted her dissatisfaction. "We had our own boat, dogs and oyster bed, and settled down to 'live happy ever after.' But I couldn't do it," she said. "I went all to pieces under the care of a home. As Mr. Butler puts it, I am a complete failure as a housekeeper." [14]

That was exactly how Frank put it. "Her shooting record is much better than her housekeeping mark," he said. "Riding, shooting and dancing came natural to her but she's a rotten housekeeper. Her record in this department is seven cooks in five days." Though Frank didn't say so, the string of cooks undoubtedly was another example of just how particular Annie could be. She had been just as picky about the Cambridge house itself and, according to writer Peter Carney, had drawn up plans to have it built "her way." Men, she told Carney, didn't know how to build a house to suit a woman. Annie wanted square rooms, no projecting closets, and a sink "at a heighth over which a woman did not have to break her back" and "a hundred and one little things." [15]

The particular Annie Oakley also had a restless side. Nothing proved it more than a trip she, Frank, and Fern took in the summer of 1915, only one year after they had "settled down." They rented an automobile and took off on a pleasure trip, intending to travel from Cambridge to San Francisco. They drove to Baltimore, then into western Maryland and through West Virginia, Ohio, and Indiana. As if they never had traveled before, the Butlers took an interest in everything they saw. Frank noted that automobile factories and machine shops were running at full force in Detroit, but heavy rains had left thousands of acres of corn and wheat under water and washed out many bridges. He took special note of the traveling shows they saw along the way. He counted six stranded companies, one of which stood six feet under water.

"The show business is in very bad straits," Frank told a Dayton reporter, who then inquired whether Annie Oakley had given up show business for good. In a surprising answer for one who already had stated her intentions to retire, Annie responded: "No, I haven't given it up for good, but only until they are willing to pay the salary I ask. Instead of spending all my salary I saved a large part of it and now I can afford to be independent." [16]

The story was different with Buffalo Bill. The showman who had been talking of retiring for almost twenty years was still performing— and still in debt. He had lost money in a mining venture and made the mistake of accepting a loan from Denver newspaperman Harry H. Tammen. In 1913, while Annie was finishing her tour with the Young Buffalo show, Tammen attached the Two Bills Show and auctioned off its paraphernalia. A prairie schooner sold for twenty dollars, Cody's silver-mounted saddle for twenty-five, and Indian pads and bridles for twenty-five cents apiece. It was a sad day, and Cody once referred to Tammen as "the man who had my show sold at sheriff's sale, which broke my heart." The Colonel went into the movie business after that, then traveled with Tammen's Sells-Floto Circus and Buffalo Bill's Wild West. [17]

It was during those dark days that Annie and Frank met up with Cody during their cross-country tour. Frank was surprised at how old Cody looked. "He is quite feeble and seems to be living his last days," Frank said. Perhaps he sensed that he and Annie never would see Buffalo Bill again. [18]

22.

At the Carolina

The Carolina was the finest hotel in Pinehurst. It stood four stories tall, had elevators, steam heat, electric lights, and telephones in every room. Some suites had private baths and sleeping porches open to the clear North Carolina air. The Carolina was a model of elegance. It drew wealthy northerners who came down from Boston and New York every season to vacation in the pleasant sandhill country just forty miles west of Fayetteville. They arrived in the fall when the gum trees showed their first tints of crimson and the goldenrod and the Joe-Pye weed turned the fields yellow and white. They drove down in their automobiles or rode in Pullmans over the Seaboard Air Line Railroad. Some came in their private rail cars, which they parked along the siding at the Pinehurst depot.

Pinehurst was a charming village of winding paths and driveways, all planted in flowers and shrubs. It had a dozen stores, three schools, a chapel, a library, a post office, and its own newspaper, the Pinehurst *Outlook*, published every Saturday. In its pages, one read of Pinehurst's most ubiquitous visitors, the golfers. They teed off every day by the hundreds on one of the village's three eighteen-hole courses. After their rounds, they went back to the Carolina, took off their hobnailed boots, sat around tea tables, and talked about the day's "foozles and miracles on the links."[1]

Pinehurst was ideal for golf. The sandy soil absorbed moisture well, and the climate was temperate. By 1915, the village had become a mecca not only for golfers, but all kinds of outdoorsmen. They canoed in the Lumbee River, went on long horseback rides into the pine forests or took a motor car down to historic Cheraw, South Carolina. They bowled, or played tennis, croquet, billiards, polo, or baseball. Pinehurst had an excellent dog kennel, a stable full of horses—and a trapshooting range.

Annie Oakley had competed in a tournament there as early as January 23, 1909.[2] She fell in love with Pinehurst, and in December 1915, she and Frank decided to spend the season there. They took up residence at the Carolina Hotel in what would be the first of many seasons. To be sure, the Carolina was a long way from the cheap boardinghouses that Annie and Frank had known as a young couple. With their reputations long established and their finances set, they turned in their later years to a pleasant sportsman's life among the well-to-do in places like the Lakeview in Leesburg, and now the Carolina in Pinehurst. But no matter how well off they appeared to be, Annie and Frank were as frugal as ever. They earned their keep at the Carolina by teaching at the Pinehurst gun club. Frank worked at the skeets, Annie at the trap and rifle range.

As they had done for years, Frank Butler threw the targets up and Annie Oakley shot them down; demonstration at the gun club in Pinehurst, N.C., about 1920. (Courtesy of the Tufts Archives, Pinehurst, N.C.)

Their lives settled into a pleasant routine. Annie enjoyed getting up at four in the morning and heading down to the stables for a fox hunt. She wore a tweed jacket, high boots, and a black, broad-brimmed hat. She saddled her horse and took off down the Carthage Road, through the woods, over the brush, and to McKenzie's pond in pursuit of "old reynard." The weekly hunts, Annie said, kept her "vital." She raced at the Pinehurst jockey club, entered a setter named Roy in a dog show (and took first place in the pointer class), and, of course, went after the quail.[3]

One of her fondest memories was the day she introduced three women to the hunt. It didn't matter that their bag was light. At noon, Annie built a hot fire, took a bird she had shot, and impaled it on a stick. When she placed a piece of bacon inside the bird to flavor it, her companions were delighted. "My, how they did enjoy that meal!" Annie said.[4] Though she had been adored by women for a lifetime, it wasn't often that she got to enjoy their company in the field.

Frank was happy in Pinehurst, too. One day, he took a seventy-mile canoe trip down the Lumbee River. Always full of details, he wrote to friends in Cambridge: "This river has a current of about six miles an hour, and more crooks and bends than any river I have ever seen."[5] Another day he took a group of Boy Scouts on an outing in the woods, where they studied path finding, signs, scents, and sounds.

Life was easy at the Carolina. The orchestra played every Sunday night, and the ladies gathered every Monday morning in the Three Oaks Tea Room for their weekly bridge game. On Saturday nights, Frank and Annie sometimes went to the dances in the Carolina ballroom. At one costume dance, on Valentine's Eve, 1919, Annie Oakley wrapped a string of beads around her neck and stuck a wealth of pheasant feathers in her hair. Appropriately, the western girl went to the dance as an Indian squaw. She danced with a white Indian chief named Manning and carried off first prize as the most popular and perfectly costumed person at the ball.[6]

On Christmas, Santa Claus took his station between the foyer and the dining room, greeted guests with jovial holiday wishes and ushered them in to eat. Annie and Frank always took their meals in the Carolina dining room, where Frank admired the waitresses. There were a good hundred of them, dressed in such pretty uniforms, Frank said, that it was "enough to make a sick man want mince pie for breakfast."[7] The Carolina cuisine and table service were unsurpassed in the South, and only white help was employed, a fact that Frank noted in a letter he wrote home to Cambridge. He said white help was the rule at nearly all first-class hotels in the South.

That Frank mentioned it at all raises the question of racism. The question was pertinent for Annie, as well. On at least one occasion, she used the word *darkey* to describe a black soldier. It happened during a shooting exhibition she gave for a black regiment during World War I. Annie apparently had her reservations about the black men's ability to fight—but her feelings soon changed. "After seeing these men and talking with some of them, I have a different opinion of them," she said. "They are going to be real fighters. . . . I was very much amused," she continued, "at one enthusiastic darkey whom I overheard talking about me to one of his mates. 'If we only had 'dis Joan of Arc to lead us, we'd get to Berlin so fas' dat Kaiser's heart would stop beatin'.'"[8] Annie's amusement and choice of words make it easy to point a finger at her today. But right or wrong, she was a product of her times. Never a crusader, she was conservative in her views, as undoubtedly also were most of the well-to-do guests who frequented the Carolina.

The hotel's list of distinguished personages was long. It included John Philip Sousa, Alexander Graham Bell, Will Rogers, Theodore Roosevelt, and Warren G. Harding, whom Annie was proud to meet. Harding, then a U.S. senator from Ohio, seemed just as pleased to meet her. "I feel highly honored at meeting Ohio's most distinguished daughter," Harding said to Annie. "I am equally pleased to meet our next President," she replied. At that, Harding blushed: "I'm not so sure." "I am," was all Annie had to say.[9]

Frank and Annie made better friends with Pinehurst owner Leonard Tufts, whose father, James, had founded the village as a haven for tuberculosis sufferers. When doctors advised Tufts that tuberculosis might be contagious, he abandoned his plan and turned his eight-thousand-acre estate into a resort. Pinehurst advertising, like that of many other hotels and resorts, now stipulated "No consumptives allowed." Over the years, Annie and Frank became so identified with Tuft's village that the *Outlook* called them "permanent fixtures." They returned year after year, arriving in November when the Carolina opened and staying until April when it closed. In the summer, they headed to New Hampshire, where Annie gave shooting lessons at another fashionable hotel, the Wentworth in Portsmouth, also managed by H. W. Priest.

During Annie Oakley's years at Pinehurst, she took a great interest in teaching women how to use a gun. Her lessons came about quite by accident one day when she overheard the wife of a wealthy New Yorker talking to some other women in the Carolina ballroom. "My, how I wish I were a man so that I could shoot," the woman was saying. Amused, Annie walked up and introduced herself. "Your sex does not prevent you from learning to shoot," Annie said, and then she invited the woman to the target range for a lesson. Annie handed her a .22-caliber rifle and admonished her not to point it at anyone unless she meant to kill. She taught her to grasp the gun and how to stand just so, leaning a little forward. Annie was a good teacher. When the woman quit the range that day she carried a card with a perfect bull's-eye.

"That was the beginning," Annie said. After that her classes increased in number so quickly that she devoted two hours to them every morning. She charged no fee. She would be repaid, she said, if women became "shooting enthusiasts." Within months, she registered her seven-hundredth pupil and was telling their success stories around the Carolina. One woman from the Back Bay of Boston, Annie said, came to her "as frightened at the sight of a rifle as a rabbit is of a ferret." The woman progressed rapidly, and her husband bought her a fine pistol. It came in handy back in Boston one day when she found a man in her room "with the silverware packed and ready to depart." "She didn't become flustered," Annie said, "but got her revolver out, covered the man and 'phoned the police." Then she gave all the credit to Annie Oakley and the lessons she had had at Pinehurst.[10]

As she always did, Annie occasionally gave shooting exhibitions at Pinehurst. At one, during the week of February 11, 1917, seven hundred people came to watch, including a reporter from the *Outlook*. "Without practice or preparation," he wrote, Annie Oakley "commenced a bit of close rifle work in the neighborhood of Frank Butler and her setter Dave that spoke a world of confidence." She started on coins flipped into the air, broke marbles on the fly, shot a cigarette out of Frank's hand, and put a hole through an apple on Dave's head. "Dave plays his part of the game," the reporter said. "He threw what was left of the apple into the air, caught it in his mouth and danced about in an ecstasy to exhibit the puncture."[11] Annie had been doing such stunts for more than thirty years—so long that she didn't practice much or even think about them anymore. When the man from the *Outlook* asked for a program, she laughed. "Why, I never bother with a program any more," she said. ". . . We no longer plan anything. When we get to the field we pull off an impromptu shoot, and run the stunts along as long as the crowd wants them, and suit the show to the audience."[12]

Annie Oakley gives a shooting lesson in Pinehurst, N.C., c. 1920. (Courtesy of the Tufts Archives, Pinehurst, N.C.)

Annie Oakley shoots an apple off Dave's head, c. 1917. (Courtesy of the Garst Museum, Greenville, Ohio)

Her exhibitions at Pinehurst were like so many she had given over the years for the Union Metallic Cartridge Company. She "scrambled eggs" in midair, cracked nuts, and rolled a tin can over the ground. She shot a pistol, the *Outlook* said, "after the fashion of a society belle"—by scrutiny in a little mirror. But the general consensus was that Annie Oakley probably didn't need the mirror. She could have shot without seeing the target at all, if it would only make a little noise. Though she was fifty-seven years old, Annie was doing the same tricks, with the same speed and accuracy, that she had done as a young woman in the Wild West arena. Annie Oakley never would lose her touch on the trigger.[13]

It was during Annie Oakley's happy years at Pinehurst that William F. Cody died. The Colonel had spent his last year writing a series of autobiographical articles for *Hearst's* magazine, touring the East with his own moving pictures, "The Indian Wars," and lecturing on preparedness for the war now raging in Europe. He joined the Miller & Arlington Wild West Show for the season of 1916, earning one hundred dollars a day and one third of the profits. But still, he was so far in debt that he often had to draw his salary in advance to keep ahead of his creditors. And Cody was getting so old and weak that he sometimes had to be helped onto his horse behind the scenes. Johnny Baker and John Burke were with him in his last season, one so alternately cold and rainy, then hot and sticky, that it took its toll on Cody's health. That winter, on January 10, 1917, he died while visiting his sister May in Denver.[14]

Telegrams, phone calls, and letters poured in from everywhere at the news that Buffalo Bill was dying. Hourly bulletins on his condition went out, and Boy Scouts kept vigil on May's porch at 2932 Lafayette Street. Stories of his last hours told how Cody, knowing he was near death, said: "Let's forget about it and play high five." Annie Oakley heard the card stories in Pinehurst, and didn't believe a word of them. "He practically never played cards," she said in an interview with the Pinehurst *Outlook*. "The popular pastime of clothing him with the attributes of the daredevil and the casual cowboy are pure fiction. . . . Like all really great and gentle men he was not even a fighter by preference. His relations with everyone he came in contact with were the most cordial and trusting of any man I ever saw."[15]

Annie Oakley did not go to Denver that winter to see the Colonel's body lying in a state under the Colorado capitol rotunda. Though she was reported to be in a "sombre mood" and had paid high tribute to Cody in the *Outlook* as "the kindest-hearted, broadest minded, simplest, most loyal man" she ever knew, she did not go to Denver, either, for Cody's funeral, which had been delayed until June when a burial site had been carved out of the granite atop Lookout Mountain. Annie Oakley was never one to live in the past. She was busy at the Carolina that June, teaching the ladies at the rifle range and struggling to get more revolvers for her burgeoning classes. So many revolvers were required for the troops in Europe that Smith & Wesson had been unable to fill an order she had put in for her ladies.[16]

How different Annie's fate seemed from Cody's. She had saved her money, moved on, and left show business behind. When she eulogized the Colonel that year, it isn't surprising that she talked in terms of finances. Always so frugal and so reasonable herself, Annie shook her head sympathetically at Cody's troubles. "It may seem strange that after the wonderful success attained that he should have died a poor man," she said. "But it isn't a matter of any wonder to those that knew and worked with him. The same qualities that insured success also insured his ultimate poverty." His generosity and kindhearted attitude helped him make friends and handle people, but by the same token, Annie said, "he was totally unable to resist any claim for assistance that came to him, or refuse any mortal in distress."

"The pity of it," she said, "was that not only could anyone that wanted a loan or a gift get it for the asking, but that he never seemed to lose his trust in the nature of all men, and until his dying day was the easiest mark above ground for every kind of sneak and gold brick vendor that was mean enough to take advantage of him." [17] Annie told the story of a snowy day in New York when she, Frank, and Cody were leaving Madison Square Garden by the stage door on their way to get some supper. As they opened the door, they saw a group of vagrants huddled around. Rather than hurrying on, Cody dug in his pocket for some money, and when he found none, he turned to Frank. "Butler, how much have you got with you?" he asked. Between them, Annie, said, she and Frank scraped up twenty-five dollars. "Lend it to me," Cody said. "With that," Annie recalled, "he turned and said in the most cheerful and wholehearted manner: 'Here boys, here's a dollar apiece. Go get a square meal and a bunk. It's too rough for a fellow to cruise around out here in the blizzard this night.'

"There were twenty-three of them," Annie said, "which left us just enough for a frugal fare. Of course, he paid it all back in the morning— the usual end of his receipts." [18]

Though Annie never was so free with money herself, she respected Cody. "Good bye old friend," she wrote that January. "The sun setting over the mountain will pay its tribute to the resting place of the last of the great builders of the West, all of which you loved, and part of which you were." [19]

As Cody was being buried on Lookout Mountain, the United States was preparing to enter World War I, which had been raging in Europe for three years. On June 5, 1917, only two days after Cody's funeral, more than 9 million men went to their local polling places to sign up for the country's first Selective Service draft. The United States, swayed by Allied propaganda and infuriated by submarine warfare, had declared war on Germany on April 6. Americans got behind the "war to end war." They bought Liberty Loan Bonds; donated money, books, and sweaters to the Red Cross; and converted their backyards into vegetable gardens. They'd taken the president's words to heart: To win this war, Americans would have to cut their "wastefulness and extravagance."

Guests at the Carolina Hotel read about a new food-rationing plan ordered by Herbert Hoover of the U.S. Food Administration. A two-ounce bread ration had been ordered for patrons of hotels, restaurants, and dining cars, and life at the Carolina wouldn't be quite the same. Every Monday and Wednesday were to be wheatless days, and Tuesday was to be a meatless day. No one at the Carolina seemed to mind, though. Patriotism was in favor.[20] On March 23, 1918, Mrs. Charles R. Marsh, wife of a captain in the U.S. Navy, stood on a platform in the Carolina ballroom and made an impassioned appeal for the French hospitals in Avignon. In weeks, the Germans would be on the Marne River, only thirty-seven miles from Paris. As Mrs. Marsh talked, three women "armed themselves with a bushel basket each" and went among the guests at the Carolina seeking donations. They filled the baskets "well nigh full of greenbacks," the *Outlook* said, "totaling something over $400."

Frank Butler and Annie Oakley burned with patriotism like everyone else. Frank pasted the "American Creed" in Annie's scrapbooks and wrote a poem called "Come Across:"

> There are folks who say we're fighting
> For a world's democracy
> That we're sending men and millions
> Just to set the Boches free,
> But we're out to kick the kaiser,
> And we're in the fight to stay.
> For the honor of Old Glory,
> And to save the U.S.A.[21]

Annie and Frank had been right about the kaiser with the crippled arm, whom they'd met so long ago in Berlin. He was being blamed now for starting the great war. "I expected it," Frank said. "We gave an exhibition before the kaiser a number of years ago, and we were not with him five minutes before we both agreed that he gave us a warlike feeling. His atmosphere reeked with love of conflict."[22] Suddenly, Annie Oakley's cigarette stunt before Prince Wilhelm so many years ago took on new significance. Why, with an errant shot, she could have prevented the great war. "An American Woman Who Could Have Shot Kaiser, She Leveled Her Rifle Directly at His Head but Hit Only His Cigarette," said a headline in the Philadelphia *Public Ledger*. Annie Oakley reflected, "If I shot the kaiser, I might have saved the lives of several millions of soldiers. I didn't know then that he would swing the iron fist and shake the universe." She continued, "Perhaps it was well for both of us that humans lack foresight." Frank told how he sat down and wrote a letter to the kaiser, saying that Annie Oakley would like to repeat the shot. Wilhelm never answered.[23]

Annie was so patriotic that she offered to raise a women's regiment for "home defense," a remarkable idea considering it came so far ahead of its time and from someone as conservative as Annie Oakley. No feminist in the traditional sense, Annie would have nothing to do with the growing women's movement. She would march in no parades, carry no banners—and never considered wearing unladylike bloomers, though they would have come in handy over the years.

"There is nothing so detestable as a bloomer costume," Annie once said. Though she wanted women to learn how to shoot, she stipulated, "Do not think that I like women to go in for sport so that they neglect their homes. I don't like bloomers or bloomer women."[24] When the *Outlook* ran a notice on April 22, 1916, that a party of suffragettes had arrived in Pinehurst to outline a campaign for women's rights in the South, Annie certainly did not knock on their door. In fact, she wasn't even sure women should get the vote, a position that was more conservative even than Buffalo Bill Cody's. "Why not," Cody once said of women voting. "Times have changed, and, whereas, a woman would have been hooted a few years back if she had dared to work in an office along with men, now we recognize that so long as she does her work well and is womanly, she is far better there than wasting her time at home playing with the cat."[25]

Annie Oakley was never so all-embracing. "If only the good women voted," she would say. She said she believed in the equality of the sexes "in the wage-earning field," but wasn't so certain about suffrage. "About this she does not have much to say," one reporter wrote. "But you get the impression that she never has been strong for equal rights as this generation understands the term." The reporter had it exactly right. Annie Oakley was part of a different generation, conservative, and rather old-fashioned. She shook her head at modern ideas like husbands and wives living apart and separate vacations for married couples.[26]

But when it came to guns and to women protecting themselves there was no one more modern and more liberal than Annie Oakley. She was completely serious about her women's regiment. She wired a telegram to Secretary of War Newton D. Baker: "I can guarantee a regiment of women for home protection every one of whom can and will shoot if necessary," it said.[27] Annie had discussed the idea with former president Theodore Roosevelt, who had been talking for months about raising a volunteer division, leading it to Europe, and storming the Germans out of the trenches. But a women's regiment was a different matter, and Annie found Roosevelt not only opposed to her idea, but with "strong and forcible opinions" against it. Secretary of War Baker apparently was opposed, also, because nothing more was said of Annie's telegram.

Interestingly, years before when Annie still was with Buffalo Bill's Wild West she had volunteered her services during the Spanish-American War. The country had been feverish with war as the Wild West opened its season that year of 1898. William F. Cody talked of raising a company of sharpshooters and had volunteered himself to go to the Cuban front. John Burke told the Brooklyn *Eagle* on April 25, 1898, that so many Wild West hands were talking of going to war that he was worried the show would be crippled. Though Burke said nothing of Annie Oakley, she quietly had written a letter to an old Ohio acquaintance, William McKinley, who had become president of the United States. On April 5, 1898, she received a courteous but noncommittal reply from John Porter, secretary to the president, and nothing more ever was said about Annie's offer.[28]

Despite opposition, old and new, Annie would not budge from her position on a woman carrying a gun. "Surely, the great war has revealed many instances when a woman with a pistol and no fear of using it might have been spared torture, shame and death," she said. "I have often and persistently maintained that women should be prepared: not necessarily for war, although it would not be undesirable to have them ready for extreme emergencies in war time, but to defend themselves."[29]

For a woman who was not much of a feminist in the traditional sense, Annie Oakley certainly sounded like one of those "bloomer women" on this issue. "I have always maintained that outside of heavy, manual labor, anything a man can do a woman can do practically as well," she would say. "Certainly this is true in the use and manipulation of firearms."[30] If anyone cared to argue, Annie pointed to her pupils at Pinehurst. "As I have taught nearly 15,000 women how to shoot, I modestly feel that I have some right to speak with assurance on this subject. Individual for individual, women shoot as well as men."[31]

There was no other issue on which Annie ever spoke so forcefully and with such conviction. It stemmed, undoubtedly, from her deep pride and independence. She had made her own way in the world, from the time she was ten years old. The Victorian image of the helpless woman did not fit her. Annie was a contradiction on this issue and this issue alone. So concerned with her reputation and her image as a lady, bloomers and all that was associated with them were out of the question for her. On the other hand, her mastery of a gun was the ultimate in the unfeminine. It gave her a strength that she was not about to deny. And though she never would have called herself a feminist, she was one despite herself, in her own way, in the only way she knew—at the target range. It was there that she passed her strength along to other women.

"I want to see women rise superior to that old-fashioned terror of firearms," she said. "I would like to see every woman know how to handle them as naturally as they know how to handle babies." It was a point that Annie Oakley would stress over and over again. She thought women should learn to protect themselves, and a gun was the best way to do it. "I have had an ideal for my sex," she said. "I have wanted them to be able to protect their homes." [32] She encouraged women to keep a revolver in a drawer by their bed and to carry a pistol when they were out alone, just as she did. Annie hid it in the folds of an umbrella, which she carried when she was out at night anywhere she feared the slightest danger. It was a remarkable thing for a woman to do at the turn of the century. Annie meant business, and even demonstrated her umbrella technique in a series of pictures in the Cincinnati *Times-Star*.

"If I were accosted, I could easily fire," Annie said. "A woman cannot always rely on getting help just by calling for it." She told of an Ohio woman who had been "attacked by a brute as she was walking home from work." The woman ran screaming to a streetcar, and leaped for the rail, crying "Save me! This man will murder me!" Annie said, "The man followed, explained that she was his wife, she was drunk and he was taking her home. . . . And the conductor rang the bell and went off and left her to be brutally killed. . . . You see, if she had had a gun—!" [33]

Annie Oakley, an abused child grown into a prideful woman, seemed determined that no one would take advantage of her again. "It is a common remark that woman's only weapon is her tongue," Annie said, "but though this might have been true half a century ago it is not as true now." She was adamant. She berated the New York legislature for forbidding people to have firearms in their homes and went so far as to suggest that every school should have a rifle range and a competent shooting instructor for both boys and girls. [34]

Though a women's regiment never was raised, Annie still was determined to do her part for the war effort. Through the National War Work Council of the Young Men's Christian Association and War Camp Community Service, she volunteered to visit several army cantonments, which had been built hurriedly that spring to train American soldiers. At her own expense, Annie set out to visit the camps one by one, planning to give two exhibitions a day to thousands of soldiers.

On May 22, 1918, she was at Camp Crane in Allentown, Pennsylvania, for the camp's first spring holiday. She stood by her gun table, down in the oval before the grandstands. She looked a small, white-haired woman, though the Camp Crane *News* found her "young in spirit." Her name probably was known to every soldier present, though many hadn't yet been born back in the days when Annie Oakley's name was whispered with that of Sitting Bull. Annie Oakley belonged to the horse-and-buggy days, and how strange she must have seemed amid the airplanes and tanks of World War I.

The Allentown *Democrat* recognized the poignancy of the moment. The young soldiers, it said, were privy that day to "an exhibition of shooting such as the old fairgrounds never saw before and is hardly likely to witness again."[35] Annie Oakley, showing "remarkable vitality and vivaciousness," picked up a pistol from her gun table and "split the ace of hearts, placed on a board." Frank Butler turned the card sideways then, and Annie split it in two edgewise. She shot over her shoulder, using a mirror to sight, and shot an apple from Dave's head. Aiming from the hip, "she made a tin can look like a sieve" and shot "to bits" pieces of coal and coins tossed in the air. She wrecked a tin can sitting on a wooden box with one blow from a dum-dum bullet, used by the German armies, then demolished the box with a second shot. She "drew cheer after cheer from the soldier boys as she performed one feat after another" with rifle, shotgun, and revolver. When she finished, hundreds of soldiers gathered around to offer their congratulations. Someone remarked that if Uncle Sam had one regiment of crack shots like Annie Oakley, they would clean up the German army.[36]

The more camps Annie visited, the more caught up in the war she became. "Oh! What wouldn't I give to get a good old 'high-power' to my shoulder, station myself where the Huns were trying to advance and knock those square-heads down as fast as they came in view—and believe me, I could do it," she said. "You can't visit the camps and escape being inoculated with the 'On to Berlin' spirit which is rampant in our army. Why, you know, there's no question about it in my mind—those boys of ours are going to be in Berlin and have the despised Kaiser on his knees before you realize it."[37]

Annie and Frank became so enthusiastic about the army that "they can talk about nothing else," one newspaper said. "Honestly, words fail me when I attempt to describe my reception at the camps where I gave exhibitions." Annie said. "I'm the happiest woman in the world because I had the opportunity to 'do my bit' in a way which was best suited to me." [38]

Her days at the army camps, she would say, were greater even than her glory days with the Wild West. She pasted numerous letters of thanks from camp commanders in her scrapbooks and had this to say about her experience: "It has been my good fortune when with Col. W. F. Cody to shoot before thousands of enthusiastic people . . . and there have been some proud and happy moments in my life when I rode into the big tent and heard the cheers of the thousands. But those days can't compare with the experiences I so recently have had when I was entertaining the boys who will fight for us 'over there.'" [39]

Even Dave had become a patriot. He spent his spring and summer raising money for the Red Cross. Dave sat on a stool with a sign attached to his stand. "I am doing my bit are you?" it read. "Let Me Find

A family portrait: Annie Oakley, Dave, and Frank Butler, c. 1920. (Courtesy of the Garst Museum, Greenville, Ohio)

Your Money for the Red Cross." Spectators liked the game. They tucked a quarter or a dollar or maybe a larger sum in a handkerchief and brought it up to Dave, "The Red Cross Dog." After Dave smelled the handkerchief, they hid it within one hundred yards of his stand. With that, Dave hopped down and went hunting. If he found the handkerchief, the money inside went to the Red Cross. If he didn't find it, well, "what's the use of guessing," the papers said. "Dave never fails, for he is a genuine win the war patriot—'doing' and not 'talking,' so to speak." One day in Portsmouth, New Hampshire, Dave found $1,625.

Dave traveled everywhere with the Butlers. He was so well-behaved that he was a welcome guest even at hotels that did not allow dogs. He always slept on a mat in the bathroom of Annie and Frank's room. "Dave frisks into the corridors and lobbies like the great traveler that he is," one newspaper said. "He is never surly and seems to say a how-d'-ye-do to people he passes." [40]

Only one thing prevented Annie, Frank, and Dave from touring every army cantonment in the country—money. "I'm only sorry that I can't afford to continue the exhibitions," Annie said. "You see, Mr. Butler and I paid our own expenses in visiting the camps and giving the exhibitions and we just can't afford to continue it indefinitely." Though they were as conscious of money as ever, the Butlers were not greedy. Reports that summer said they had turned down an offer of eighty-five dollars a day to give a series of exhibitions under contract. The war effort mattered more to them. [41]

Their tours of the army cantonments done, Annie and Frank rested for a time at the house in Cambridge, then returned to Pinehurst for the winter. In August the Allies took Soissons, and by October the Americans were fighting in the Meuse Valley and the wooded hills of Argonne. The Austro-Hungarian army crumbled in late October, and on November 9, 1918, the kaiser abdicated. The war ended two days later. Americans crowded Times Square and hurled confetti from office windows. In Pinehurst, the patriots held a parade and a day of track athletics. Annie Oakley was there "armed to the teeth with about ten rifles." She celebrated the end of the war by giving an exhibition.

23.

Trouble on the Dixie Highway

On a spring afternoon in May 1919, Annie Oakley visited the Ringling Brothers and Barnum & Bailey Circus in Philadelphia. She came down out of the stands that day to pay a visit to circus man Cy Compton, an old friend from the Wild West. She made her way over the muddy paths between the dressing tents and shook hands all around backstage.

"I'm only one of the good old has-beens," she said to a reporter who happened to be among the crowd.[1] Annie Oakley never was one to delude herself. Though her choice of words was harsh, the truth was that Annie Oakley *was* "a good old has-been" when it came to show business. World War I had brought an end to the golden era of the Wild West show, which had made a legend of Annie Oakley. Even the big street parades were dead, a casualty of city traffic. Americans were flocking now to a new kind of entertainment—the motion picture. By the middle of the 1920s the industry had become the fourth largest in the nation, and by 1927 there were 20,500 motion-picture theaters in the country.[2] Americans cheered Mary Pickford, Charlie Chaplin, and Douglas Fairbanks now. Annie Oakley belonged to a past era.

If Annie Oakley longed for the good old days of the show business, she certainly did not say so. At nearly sixty years old, Annie seemed to have had her fill of royalty and public attention. At least it seemed so to a reporter in Detroit who interviewed her on July 2, 1921, while she was in town visiting Fern Campbell Swartwout, who was living at 4137 Commonwealth Avenue. The reporter sat in Fern's living room that day and talked to Annie, who had spread out her scrapbooks for him. She opened them more and more now, using them as a conversation piece. Frank sat beside her and Dave nosed at her knee as she thumbed a book for the reporter's benefit. He watched her closely, noticed "no suspicious glistening in her eyes" and concluded that "peace has settled on a clamorous life." Yes, Annie answered his question, she had knocked a cigarette out of Kaiser Wilhelm's mouth. But that was long ago. The conversation, as usual with Annie Oakley, turned to the present. She was in Detroit, she said, to see a specialist about some throat trouble. "I'm going to ask him really to build a new body on my old feet," she said, "and when he gets that done I'll tell him to put on new feet, also." Though she joked about being old, the reporter found her youthful. "Annie Oakley—The Annie Oakley," he wrote, "has found what Ponce de Leon sought in vain. She has come upon the spring of everlasting youth." Annie's hair was white, but her eyes twinkled. For the reporter's benefit, she got up out of her chair in Fern's parlor that July, placed the palms of her hands on the floor without bending her knees, and walked on all fours about the room. "Let me see any of your girls of today do that," Annie said.[3]

A proud woman always, Annie bristled when she read a column by a correspondent from the New York *Tribune*, who had seen her one day at the Carolina Hotel and written that she no longer was "a short-skirted, dashing girl of the plains, but a nice little old lady with spectacles and knitting." The report, which appeared in the famous "Conning Tower" column, touched a nerve with Annie Oakley, and she sat down and fired off a letter to the *Tribune*, dated February 8, 1917.

"My Dear Mr. Conning Tower Man," she wrote. "What did I hear you say? 'She is a little white haired lady who wears spectacles and knits?' I am guilty as to the first two charges owing to two trains trying to pass on the same track, but did not succeed. . . . Not guilty as to knitting. I graduated from the knitting school at the age of eight years. . . . So your correspondent, Mr. White, could not see at close range when he mistook the embroidering for knitting. Why did I give up the Arena? Because I made hay in the hay day of my youth, and felt that I had earned a change."[4] White hair and spectacles hadn't destroyed Annie Oakley's spunk.

She was back at the Carolina in the fall of 1919, and wrote of fox hunts, of her bronc Fred, her dog Dave, and long hunts in the pine forests in quest of quail. "A twelve or fifteen mile trip makes me sleep and

Annie Oakley and Frank Butler return from the hunt, Pinehurst, N.C., c. 1920. (Courtesy of the Tufts Archives, Pinehurst, N.C.)

dream again of the days when I ran bare-footed over hill and dale chasing the wild bees and butterflies," she said.[5]

The older she got, the more sentimental—and charitable—she became. In addition to the young women she was putting through school, she took an interest in tuberculosis, a disease that had claimed two of her sisters (Elizabeth and Lydia) and put thousands of soldiers in Veterans Bureau hospitals after the war. She looked in on patients in the sanatoriums near Pinehurst and occasionally gave exhibitions to raise money for them. At one exhibition in Pinehurst, on March 19, 1920, she marked pennies with a bullet, and sold her autographs and a little pamphlet called *Annie Oakley, Her Career and Experiences.* On the front was a sketch of her birthplace in Woodland, on the back a picture of Dave. Inside was a poem by Frank, called "What Did You Do?"

> Did you give him a lift? He's a brother of Man
> And bearing about all the burden he can.
> Did you give him a smile? He was downcast and blue
> And the smile would have helped him battle it through.
> Did you give him your hand? He was slipping down hill
> And the World, so I fancied, was using him ill.
> Did you give him a word? Did you show him the road
> Or did you just let him go on with his load?[6]

Annie and Frank raised a hundred dollars that day and gave the money to the Farm Life School in Eureka, North Carolina. A few weeks later they were in Montrose, North Carolina, where they gave another exhibition on behalf of tuberculosis patients in a nearby sanatorium. Annie occasionally looked in on the patients and was said to have treated them as her "special charges." She was in the habit of taking them a "candy treat."

Annie's way of paying for the candy spoke volumes about her. According to the Philadelphia *Public Ledger,* she "rose early in the mornings during violet-blooming time and picked the shy flowers all day." She made them into bunches, then sold them to guests at the Carolina for less than the going price at the local florist shop. What the florist thought of Annie's business, the paper did not say, but she was quite pleased with the arrangement herself. She felt there must be some sacrifice in her giving, and "not merely the charity of unthinking others."[7]

It probably was during the spring of 1920 that Annie made another sacrifice to fight tuberculosis. Exactly when she did it, and why, she never said. But at some time she broke up her valuable gold medals, had them melted down, and contributed the money to a sanatorium. The act showed just how far behind her she had put the glory days and just how much zeal she could hold for a cause in which she believed. In one of the few contemporary accounts of the incident, Annie told the Charlotte *Observer* that during her life she had won a total of twenty-seven medals for shooting. "These medals she no longer has," the *Observer* wrote, "as some four years ago she broke them up and sold them for the benefit of a Tuberculosis Sanitarium near Pinehurst."[8]

A few years after melting down her medals, Annie Oakley said goodbye to Pinehurst, as well. She had decided to take a rest, she said, and

would retire to the house on Hambrooks Bay.[9] Before leaving, she went
down to the gun club that Leonard Tufts had built and smashed one
hundred clay targets in a row, shooting from the sixteen-yard line. The
feat, accomplished on April 16, 1922, was said to be a new world's
record among women shooters.[10]

As always, the writers gathered round. They wanted to hear of the old
glory days and liked to tell of a lithe, brown-haired girl who could "out-
shoot William Tell in her sleep." They wrote of Sitting Bull and the bad
horse Dynamite, and tried to guess how old Annie Oakley was. No one
seemed to know, and even now, at almost sixty-two, Annie wouldn't tell.[11]

While Annie was saying goodbye to friends at Pinehurst, Fred Stone was
up on Long Island planning the biggest charity event of the summer—
a Motor Hippodrome and Wild West show to benefit the Occupational
Therapy Society, which maintained workrooms for disabled soldiers.
The show was to be held on July 1, 1922, at the Mineola fairgrounds.
Stone assembled a group of Broadway stars, lined up a few society belles
to sell peanuts and ice cream, and invited an old-timer he knew would
be a crowd-pleaser: Annie Oakley.

She arrived in Amityville on the daily express from New York City on
June 22. Fred Stone was too busy to greet her at the train depot, but he
sent an entourage from his show. They came dressed in western outfits
and riding in an old stagecoach drawn by four mules. Stone, who was in
the movie business now, had picked the coach up from a movie lot in
California. It must have seemed the proper welcome for Annie Oakley.

She got off the train that day, hopped up in the shotgun seat on the
stagecoach, and rode out the Long Island Turnpike to Stone's place.
There was her picture, big as life, in the New York *World*. Annie Oakley
"holds up Fred Stone's stage coach in the wilds of Long Island," the
caption read. It was only the beginning of a week of publicity for a star
the newspapers hadn't seen in years.[12]

"Annie Oakley has come back," wrote a reporter from the New York
Tribune, who apparently was too young to know that Annie Oakley had
been a brunette, not a blonde. "Out of the memories of hot summer
afternoons under a canvas tent, out of dreams in which cowboys and
Indians enternally clatter around a smiling young woman with long
yellow braids and an unerring rifle, she came yesterday to take part in
Fred Stone's benefit circus. . . .

"She carried over her shoulder the gun which Buffalo Bill himself
gave her many years ago, and at her side tramped her husband, at whom

Portrait of Annie Oakley, c. 1920. (Courtesy of the Buffalo Bill Historical Center, Cody, Wyo.)

she has been shooting for forty years, but never hurt. The gun and the husband remain unchanged, but the Annie Oakley of childish impressions has gone. In her place," the young reporter wrote, "stands a white-haired, sweet-voiced little woman in a black dress with an old-fashioned lace choker." [23]

Old-fashioned though she may have looked, Annie said she was in perfect condition and had come to Long Island to help out the "poor injured soldiers." She never shot nowadays except at charities, she said, "but a day or two of practice will show you that Annie Oakley can come back."

Determined and proud as ever, she did indeed prove it. That July first, she skipped into the arena as of old, wearing a knee-length skirt and a khaki-colored silk blouse, open at the throat, and set off with a bright red tie. On her head, as always, she wore a hat with a high crown and a broad brim. It only partially covered her white hair, though, and hesitatingly, almost apologetically, she put on a pair of spectacles. But the rest was the Annie Oakley of old. There was that quick little hop, skip, and jump, and a bow so familiar that Anne Whitney Hay of the *Morning Journal* described it as "Annie Oakleyish."

"She makes a sudden little run forward," Hay wrote, "stands on one toe with her other leg flung out horizontally, ducks her body in a bow and then scampers a few feet displaying a neat pair of gaiters above well shaped calves." She seemed coy as she "cavorted around the ring, skipping and blowing kisses." Though she was almost sixty-two years old, her eyes and her muscles were as true as ever. "The balls looped up against the sky and fell in showers of black pieces," the *Tribune* wrote. "The venerable Miss Oakley lay on her back over a chair and shot them, or she shot them between hops and skips. It made no difference."

And only a few feet from Annie "boldly stood" Frank Butler, a bit stoop-shouldered and white-haired himself now. He threw plates and tossed balls for Annie to puncture, then swung a white ball on a cord around his head while his "crackshot Quaker wife" nipped it "just as clean as a whistle."

"After that," said the New York *Herald*, "she skipped and curtsied in recognition of the storm of applause." Then the young reporters of 1922 flocked to Annie Oakley just as their counterparts had done in another century. They took her picture and pulled her aside for interviews. Anne Whitney Hay gazed into a face with a well-shaped mouth and a generous smile. Hay asked Annie whether it was true that a free baseball pass was named after her.

"She nods 'yes,'" Hay wrote, "then asks you if her hat is on straight." When Hay wanted to know the secret of handling a gun, Annie told her it was "like pianny-playing in one way. You have to keep your fingers supple and in practice or you miss now and then." For Hay's benefit, Annie stretched her slender hands and wriggled her fingers to show how pliable and responsive they were.

A rare film clip, which turned up in recent years at the Buffalo Bill Historical Center in Cody, Wyoming, shows Annie performing at the Mineola fairgrounds that Saturday. Interestingly, the clip also shows Annie coming in and out of a door and making a number of facial expressions for a movie camera. The clip lends credence to a report in the New York *Herald* of June 28, 1922, that Annie Oakley was thinking of making a comeback. "She is considering an offer to go into the movies," the *Herald* wrote. "If the taste of publicity she gets next Saturday (at the Hippodrome) proves agreeable she may say yes and move to Hollywood."

The prospect of a sixty-two-year-old Annie Oakley going into the movies was not absurd, especially considering Annie's friendship with Fred Stone, who had been making films since 1918 when he did circus stunts in *Under the Big Top*. Stone had appeared in the cowboy pictures, *Johnny, Get Your Gun, The Duke of Chimney Butte,* and *Billy Jim*. Will Rogers was making motion pictures, also, six of them in 1920 alone. Whatever Annie's plans were, Stone and Rogers may well have had a hand in them.[13] Annie had come out of retirement before and probably wasn't above doing it again if the arrangements—and the price—were right. "Oh, yes," she had told a reporter in 1915. "I have been offered several positions with the movies, but so far I have turned them down. They don't want to pay enough and until they do I will not be seen in the movies."[14]

As late as July 1921, a report had surfaced that Annie was planning to pick up her career again. Though nothing ever came of it, it was rumored that she was to star the next season in a new Wild West show conceived by George C. Moyer, general agent of the John Robinson Circus.[15]

Further proof that Annie Oakley was thinking about coming out of retirement came in October 1922, when she appeared at the forty-ninth Brockton fair in Massachusetts. The fair had opened on the hottest October 5 anyone could remember in Brockton, but one hundred thousand people had gone to the fairgrounds anyway. Among them was reporter Miles E. Connolly, whose sole purpose that day was to obtain an interview with Annie Oakley. He arrived at the fairgrounds late, though, and missed her performance. Distraught, he took off frantically in search of her. He wound his way though the crowds, past hawkers, acrobats, and high divers. He hurried past booths that smelled of frankfurters and popcorn and excused himself when he bumped into a child licking an ice cream cone. He passed old couples and young, balloons and bands, cattle shows and horse races. The scene, Connolly wrote, was "delirium, racket, shrieks, laughter, dust, smoke, automobiles, and what not." At last, his shirt damp with perspiration, he found the dressing room, and the woman he sought.

"I assure you she was worth finding," he wrote that hot October day. She stood at the door, a petite woman with a pleasant face, though years in the sun had crossed it with lines, which stood out when she smiled. As she invited Connolly inside, he commented on the madness without. Annie Oakley looked out the door and nodded. "All this," she said, and with a sweep of her hand she enveloped the passing crowd. "All this has its glamour. All this has its lure, especially after 38 years of it, but still, home is best." Before Annie even shut the door, Connolly was smitten. She picked up a newspaper, spread it out on her trunk, and invited him to sit down. He found her a "sensitive little woman with the air of one who has looked out on a wood-and-meadow world all her life through a parlor window." She seemed too gentle for the crack of a rifle.[16]

A less romantic Annie Oakley talked in more practical terms. The Brockton fair had been her first paid performance in years, she said— and some of the best money she had ever made. For five exhibitions of five minutes each, she had received seven hundred dollars. Perhaps thinking back to the days when she had to scrimp to buy hair ribbons, she and Frank sat down that October and calculated: seven hundred dollars for twenty-five minutes' work. That meant Annie Oakley could make $5 million a year if she wanted to put in ten hours a day, six days a week. "You think that some money for twenty-five minutes performance, but I have done much better than that," Annie said.[17]

But, tragically, any plans Annie Oakley may have had for a career comeback or a stint in the movies ended shortly after she pulled in that fee at the Brockton fair. The episode that would bring an end to the healthy and happy days of Annie Oakley's life began on November 2, 1922, when she, Frank, and Dave boarded a boat for Florida, where they planned to spend another season among friends at the Lakeview Hotel.[18] They docked in Jacksonville a few days later, put Dave on a train for Leesburg, and proceeded onward themselves by automobile.

Annie Oakley with seven-year-old Eddie Huff, who had qualified as an expert marksman by hitting an apple at 150 feet. This photograph appeared in the *New York Times*, September 17, 1922. (Courtesy New York Times Pictures)

They rode with some friends, Mr. and Mrs. J. J. Stoer, who had a chauffeur-driven Cadillac.

On Thursday, November 9, they were driving along the Dixie Highway about forty-six miles north of Daytona when tragedy struck. According to the Daytona *News* of November 10, 1922, the Stoer's chauffeur, a Mr. Young, lost control of the car after he passed another vehicle and was trying to turn back onto the brick road. The Cadillac "jumped over an embankment and turned turtle. Annie was pinned under the car, her hip and right ankle fractured. A. Mr. B. Benson of Fort Pierce, who the *News* said was following in a car behind the Cadillac, stopped, helped extricate Annie, lifted her into his car and drove her to Daytona, where she was admitted to Bohannon Hospital.[19]

Frank, who was not injured, went on to Leesburg, where he picked up Dave and brought him to Daytona to be near Annie. Frank and Dave took a room across from the hospital and spent the next six weeks there, crossing the street every day to visit Annie. In a touching story Frank later wrote called *The Life of Dave, As Told by Himself*, he described from Dave's point of view that troubled November when Annie lay in a bed at Bohannon Hospital.

"She looked very feeble and could only put out one hand to stroke my head," Dave wrote. "By putting my feet on a chair I managed to get close enough to lick her ear. . . . I didn't like the nurses there, as they seemed rough and hurt my mistress when they moved her." In time, Annie improved and spent hours in her hospital room brushing and combing Dave. "She was always so gentle and careful in combing and brushing me that I enjoyed having it done," Dave said. "I often wondered if any other dog had a mistress as good and gentle as mine."[20]

Finally, with a brace on her leg and walking with crutches, Annie moved to the Lakeview Hotel in Leesburg sometime around the first of the new year. Her half-sister, Emily Brumbaugh Patterson, came down from Ohio to look after her because Annie would spend several more weeks in bed.[21] She missed her walks and her exercise, she said, but her days were cheered by the thoughtfulness of friends, whom she thanked, as in the old days, in an open letter to the *American Field*.

"Since my accident, I have received nearly 2,000 letters and telegrams, also loads of flowers from many kind and thoughtful friends," she wrote. "Only someone like myself, who has suffered and laid for weeks in a hospital, knows what such messages of sympathy mean and I certainly do appreciate all that my friends have done for me." She was still using crutches, she said, and getting along as well as could be expected. She was cheered because her doctors had promised that, in time, she would fully recover.[22] But the truth was that Annie Oakley never would walk again without a brace on her leg.

Annie's life took another tragic turn that February at the Lakeview. Dave had left her side temporarily to go for a walk with Frank. As they walked, probably not far from the hotel, Dave spotted a squirrel and took off after it. He darted into the street just as an automobile came around a corner. The car hit Dave, killing him instantly. Annie and Frank were heartbroken. They buried Dave under a tree in Leesburg, then marked his grave with a simple stone bearing his name. Letters of sympathy came from friends who knew how much Dave had meant to the Butlers.[23]

A grieving Frank sat down and wrote his story, *The Life of Dave*, which was printed in the Newark *Sunday Call* of June 24, 1923, under an editor's note that said: "This is a plain story of a dog bearing the plain name Dave, but not a plain dog himself. He was a beautiful setter, owned by Frank E. Butler and his wife, Annie Oakley Butler, and for ten years he was their faithful companion. Wherever they lived, and ofttimes they put up at the finest hotels in the land, Dave was ever a third guest. Everywhere that Annie went the dog was sure to go."

Dave's death, coupled with the accident on the Dixie Highway, marked a sad turning point in Annie Oakley's life. Though Annie would be up and around again, and would even shoot again, her life never would be the same.

24.

Home to Darke County

Spring brought the Philadelphia Phillies baseball team to Leesburg, where they took spring training on the big diamond out at Cooke Field. Pitcher Jimmy Ring, who would chalk up 112 strikeouts in 1923, and slugger Cy Williams led the roster that year. They were out with the rest of the team, batting and fielding balls one Tuesday afternoon when an automobile pulled up under the big stone archway at Cooke Field.

A stalwart man who looked to be in his late sixties stepped out of the car, walked around to the other side and opened the door for a woman who looked from the diamond to be a little old lady. Her hair was white and her right leg, below the knee, was in a brace. Everyone in Leesburg knew Annie Oakley, and the sight of her stopped baseball practice that day. She carried crutches, but she seemed undaunted as she took Frank Butler's hand and slid out of the car.[1] Annie Oakley was up and around again and she'd come out to the open spaces of Cooke Field to try her hand once again at the traps.

"I haven't shot since October 8," she said. "Still I think my eye is good and maybe I'll be able to shoot fairly straight." With that, she hobbled toward the baseball diamond, where Frank Butler, just as he had done for so many years, was busy setting up a table and spreading it with her shotguns and rifles. The baseball players, accompanied by a number of curious little boys, sat down in the bleachers to watch.

Abandoning her crutches, Annie leaned totally on her left leg and began an exhibition described as "little short of miraculous." She winged pennies tossed in the air at twenty feet and sent them spinning across the diamond, "where a riot ensued" among the little boys, who made a mad scramble for them. And then she threw five eggs in the air with her left hand and broke them all before they hit the ground, a stunt "she performed several times" while the Phillies applauded.

When Annie had finished, the players gathered around and told her about some women sharpshooters they knew back in Philadelphia. The women, who shot for the Drexel Institute team, had never lost a match. Annie said she had heard of the team and had seen photographs of the members. "I only wish I had the opportunity to give them a little instruction," she added. "I can tell by the photographs . . . that they do not hold their rifles quite right. I could rectify that easily and make them better than they are, even if they never have been beaten." [2]

Crippled though she was, Annie was in good spirits. That October, she and Frank attended the John Robinson Circus in High Point, North Carolina, and in early November they stopped by the Pinehurst fair, where Frank told the *American Field* that Annie "fast was recovering from her injuries." Though she still was wearing a brace, Annie sounded optimistic about her health, as well. "Why, I have been told three different times by various doctors that I would never get on a horse again! But I always did!" she told the Philadelphia *Public Ledger* that fall. There was a shade of triumph in her voice. "Maybe I will again, even with this," she said, touching the brace on her leg. "In spite of this!" [3]

She was cheerful and uncomplaining, though her troubles had made her more philosophical. She took up a motto, and had it copyrighted by the Elliott Service Company of New York and printed on a card. "Aim at a high mark," it said, "and you'll hit it. No, not the first time, nor the second time and maybe not the third. But keep on aiming and keep on shooting for only practice will make you perfect. Finally, you'll hit the bull's eye of success." [4]

It was a simple motto, written by a down-to-earth woman who was full of common sense. For all her fame, she had lived life in a simple way, finding her pleasures in the fields, the flowers, and the hunt. And the older she grew, the more sentimental and nostalgic she became. She talked more and more of the idyllic days of her childhood, referring to Ohio, as she always had, in words of endearment. Not surprisingly, after Annie recovered from the car wreck on the Dixie Highway, she decided to go home again.

Her niece Bonnie Ann and Bonnie Ann's husband, Rush Blakeley, were living in the Ohio countryside, just a few miles from the North Star crossroads. They were eager for their famous relatives to visit, and one winter, Rush harnessed a one-horse dray and took it into Greenville to meet Annie and Frank at the train station on Front Street. Annie alighted from the train, her leg still in a brace and her trunks in tow. She took a carriage seat up front by Blakeley, while Frank sat on a trunk in the back. They rode up the old Celina Road, past Pikesville, Beamsville, and Dawn, and turned into a large farmhouse not far from Ansonia.[5]

There, Annie and Frank settled into a corner bedroom and would remain for the next few months. In one of the few intimate glimpses we have of the Butlers, Rush Blakeley recalled those days. He noticed that Frank Butler "was what you might call a loafer when it came to chores," but that, for Annie, Frank split wood for a little stove inside their bedroom. "Annie loved a wood stove," Blakeley said, especially the hot fire she made by burning the tops of hardwood trees that had been lumbered off the Blakeley place. "She said it brought back childhood memories."

Rush noticed that Annie kept her clothes "as neat as a pin," and that Frank was a stickler for neatness, too. He was "always very trim and neat and his shoes were always shined." Annie, who wore glasses now, kept busy washing clothes, ironing, or sitting around the kitchen table mending and talking to her niece Bonnie. "I remember thinking once, 'imagine the world's greatest sharpshooter wearing glasses,'" Blakeley recalled. "Seems like she was always doing something. She liked to cook and helped my wife prepare a lot of meals, especially when we had steaks. Frank and Annie were partial to T-bones."

Frank took long walks in the fields, but Annie stayed behind. Walking was hard for her. "They didn't socialize," Blakeley said, "but you might say Frank was a pretty regular down at the Christian Church services in Dawn, even if he was an Irish Catholic." Annie never went to church with Frank, Blakeley said, but they both liked to accompany him when he and Bonnie went in to Ansonia where they shopped. In Ansonia, Annie frequented the National Bank, where she said she had five thousand dollars deposited. The Butlers, ever conscious of finances, paid Blakeley thirty dollars a week for room and board.

That summer, Annie and Frank returned to North Carolina, where they took up residence at the Mayview Manor in Blowing Rock, a resort along the lines of Pinehurst. Guests played tennis or golf, went trout fishing or horseback riding and shot traps at the new gun club, which the Butlers had come to help establish. They spent the season in a leisurely way, promenading about the hotel veranda or sitting in a cozy corner of the lobby, where reporter Henry E. Dougherty of the Charlotte *Observer* interviewed them one day. He found Annie to be "a frail little woman with a bright, infectious smile," and Frank, a man "hale and hearty." Dougherty marveled most that the Butlers were "perhaps the only theatrical couple in the world—or in all history—that has been married 42 years."[6]

Comfortable as they were, and despite a rumor that they were thinking of buying a house in nearby Greensboro, the Butlers left North Carolina late that fall, never to return. They caught a train and headed back to Ohio for good, arriving in Dayton on a cold December day in 1924. Annie wore a round wool hat, which covered her forehead almost to the eyes. Her hair had grown long again, and it flowed white down her back. Despite her age, a reporter from the Dayton *Sunday Journal* found her still "an undying tribute to outdoor life." She impressed him as a "woman of unusual force of character, unassuming manners and rare modesty." She told him that she was planning to settle in Dayton, where her sister Emily lived at 2334 Salem Avenue.[7]

Annie and Frank took "a cozy apartment," probably in the North Dayton View section and within months moved to a two-story white house at 706 Lexington Avenue. It was a large house with a front porch supported by three stone pillars. Here, Annie and Frank would spend the last healthy days of their lives.

They took an interest in the Amateur Trapshooting Association, which had just built a clubhouse and trapshooting grounds in the city of Vandalia, just a few miles north of Dayton. The recently purchased grounds would serve as the permanent home of the ATA and the site of the annual Grand American Handicap. One Tuesday in August 1925, Annie and Frank went to Vandalia to watch the yearly championships. Annie took a seat on the veranda of the big new ATA building and watched the trapshooters move from score to score. Anyone who didn't know her, said the Dayton *Daily News*, would never have recognized Annie Oakley in the "unassuming old lady, who occupied an inconspicuous seat on the veranda."[8]

But Annie Oakley was so well known among trapshooters that scarcely had she arrived on the grounds before she was surrounded by an admiring group of men and women. When a photographer approached her, Annie stood up and swung a gun to her cheek to please him. She hadn't felt its old, familiar caress for some time, but no one would have guessed it. "The old snap was there," the *News* wrote. Her eyes gazed proudly along the barrel and the heavy gun did not waver in the least. "For remarkable vigor, robustness and reliability," the *News* decided that Annie Oakley had no equal.

But the truth was that Annie Oakley was not in the best of health. She was developing anemia, which would make her tired and pale. Still, she seemed full of "pep and ginger" that summer and fall of 1925. For those who doubted it, she danced a jig, leg brace and all. The Newark *Star Eagle* captured a photograph and ran it in its pages of October 6, 1925. "For me," Annie said, "sitting still is harder than any kind of work." [9]

That winter in Dayton, Annie tried to write her autobiography, but she seemed unable to finish it. Apparently looking for help in preparing the memoirs, Frank contacted a writer in New York City, a Mr. Shaw, who expressed interest in the project in a letter to the Butlers dated March 3, 1926. "I was particularly interested when I learned that it was your wish to write of your historical associations in a manner worthy of their value and not to have them presented in the light, sensational style of a good many writers of today," Shaw wrote. [10] No deal with Shaw was ever made, however, and Annie Oakley would not live to see her manuscript published.

The *Billboard*, looking backward that spring as well, ran an old photograph, taken in 1883, of the shooting team of Butler and Oakley. It showed a mustachioed man with black hair who stood straight and tall beside a handsome young woman with flowing dark hair. In her hand she held a long rifle, and at her feet lay a white poodle, whose name, of course, was George. "This One Really Is 'Back Yonder,'" the caption read. The old photograph touched a sentimental note with the sensitive Frank Butler. He clipped it out of the *Billboard*, pasted it on a page in Annie's scrapbooks, picked up a pen, and wrote just below the picture: "Happy days long gone." His words must have been directed to Annie because he signed them, "Jimmie." [11]

Elsewhere, thoughts were turning to the future. A farsighted R. J. Middaugh, third vice president of the Amateur Trapshooting Association, proposed that the association buy the old house at North Star where Annie had grown up. He wanted to move the house to the ATA grounds and furnish it with mementos of Annie's life. [12] This never came about, however, and the house later was sold at auction and eventually demolished.

That Annie's thoughts had turned toward the decline of life was apparent by October 1925, when she and Frank took a room at the Robert Treat Hotel in Newark, New Jersey, where they told a reporter from the *Star Eagle* they had come "on business" for a week. Though they didn't reveal the nature of their business, undoubtedly it was conducted at the Essex County Surrogate Court. There, on October 7, 1925, "Annie Oakley Butler" signed her last will and testament, Docket No. 2826-C.

"I give and bequeath to my half-sister, Mrs. Emily Patterson, now residing at Ansonia, Ohio, the sum of One Thousand Dollars," Annie dictated. "I give and bequeath to my sister, Mrs. Huldie Haines, now residing at Royal Oak, Michigan, the sum of One Thousand Dollars. I give and bequeath unto my brother, John Mozee, now residing at McCurtain, Oklahoma, the sum of One Thousand Dollars."

So it was that Annie Oakley, as adamant about the name Mozee as ever, doled out her life's savings. She gave three thousand, in trust, to her sister Ellen Grabfelder, then residing in Ansonia, and paid special attention to three nieces: Huldie's daughter, Fern Campbell Swartwout; and Emily's daughters, Bonnie Blakeley and Irene Patterson. If Frank died before she did, Annie directed that each niece was to receive six thousand dollars. Another five thousand was to go to John's daughter, Elsie G. Lindsey of McCurtain, Oklahoma, and one thousand each to six nephews: Bernard, Chelcy, and Lee Mozee of McCurtain, and Orville Patterson and Lee and Harold Campbell of Detroit. In all, her will disposed of thirty-five thousand dollars.

Annie bequeathed her clothes, jewelry, and other personal effects to be divided equally among her three sisters, Ellen, Emily, and Huldie, and her four nieces, Fern, Bonnie, Irene, and Elsie. Of all her valuables, Annie mentioned only one by name, the three drawings of herself on horseback, made so long ago by the Hardy sisters during the magical year in London. She wanted Frank to have the drawings; only he could know how really happy were those "happy days long gone."

Frank's will, signed that same Wednesday in October, gave one of the few clues to his former life in the days before he met Annie Moses. In his will, Docket No. 2825-C, Frank remembered his former wife, Elizabeth, and his daughter, Kattie. In forty years' worth of newspaper stories, their names never had been mentioned. Frank must have kept track of them, though. Elizabeth was Mrs. Howard Hall now, and she lived at 21 North Twenty-Sixth Street in Camden, New Jersey. Kattie was Mrs. Kattie Wagner of 1327 Wanamaker Street, Philadelphia. Frank bequeathed one thousand dollars to each. He also remembered his godchild, Mrs. Leslie White of Golden, Colorado, who was the former Gladys Baker, the daughter of Wild West shooter Johnny Baker. He gave her also one thousand dollars. He bequeathed all his jewelry and guns to his brother, William J. Butler of Joliet, Illinois.

Old New Jersey friends, William Longfellow of Nutley and Spencer S. Marsh of Newark, were appointed executors of the wills, and W. L. Morgan of Newark and Carl A. Feick of Short Hills witnessed the signing. Obviously touched by the process, Annie had this to say when she talked to the man from the *Star Eagle* back at the hotel: "After traveling through fourteen foreign countries and appearing before all the royalty and nobility I have only one wish today. That is that when my eyes are closed in death that they will bury me back in that quiet little farm land where I was born." [13]

Back home in Darke County, Annie and her niece Bonnie had gone for a ride through the old country haunts one day in 1925. Annie rode back to Woodland, now called Willowdell, and was delighted to find that the houses and general store still stood where they had when she was a girl. Perhaps it was that day that she and Bonnie stopped by the Brock Cemetery, where her nephews were buried. The cemetery was just up the road from Ansonia, where Bonnie and Rush were living. Soon after, Annie bought a plot there, announcing that that was where she wished to be buried. [14]

Though she still was getting around, Annie was in declining health. As early as January 1925, the *Billboard* reported that Annie had turned down "a flattering offer" to appear with the Miller Brothers 101 Ranch Wild West Show in the coming spring. "Ill health," the *Billboard* said, "caused Miss Oakley to abandon thoughts of further trouping." That winter, according to the Dayton *Daily News*, Annie had failed to finish her autobiography "due to ill health." She had been seeing a doctor, who had "ordered her to remain absolutely quiet," and "not to engage in anything strenuous." [15]

By February 1926 Annie's health was bad enough that it worried Fred Stone's wife, Allene, who corresponded with Annie for a short period that winter. Allene, Fred, and their daughter Dorothy were on the road appearing in their current show, the *Stepping Stones*. Allene wrote her letters to Annie on stationery from various hotels. In one letter, from the Book-Cadillac Hotel in Detroit, Allene told Annie that Huldie and Fern had come to the theater to see the show. They must have told Allene that Annie wasn't feeling well. "We are all so sorry you have not been well," Allene wrote. "I know the 'stuff' you are made of 'Missie.' You will be well and strong again because you are just a little lady made of steel wires."

When *Stepping Stones* played Columbus the next week, Annie made the trip down from Dayton to see her old friends. She took a copy of her unfinished autobiography along and left it with the Stones to read. They hadn't yet started it, though, by the time they took her to the train station for the trip back to Dayton. Allene, apparently feeling badly about that, wrote a letter to Annie that Saturday, this time on stationery from the Neil House in Columbus, promising to begin reading the manuscript early in the week. Allene had fond memories of Annie's visit.

"I never want a better picture of you than your *flying* over the platform after your train giving that 'red cap' all he could do to keep up with you," she wrote. "First I was alarmed and then I realized there was [no] reason to be: You are guided and *up-held* always. The Bible says Annie dear, 'Underneath are the Everlasting Arms,' and that is what upholds you always." [16] What was Allene alarmed about? That Annie, flying over the platform in her leg brace, might fall? Or did her concern go deeper?

That May, just three months after her visit with the Stones, Annie wrote to Leonard Tufts at Pinehurst that she was so sick she was only able to be up about half the time. Frank was not well, either. "His throat gives him considerable trouble," Annie wrote. [17]

Annie was in bed at the house on Lexington Avenue that spring when she had a surprise visitor, Will Rogers. He had been lecturing around the country and writing a weekly Sunday column, which appeared in about two hundred newspapers and was estimated to reach 35 million readers. For a time he also wrote a daily column called "Worst Story I Have Heard Today." It was under that heading that Rogers sat down and wrote a column about Annie Oakley after visiting her in Dayton. In it, he celebrated Annie Oakley at the height of her fame.

"This is not the worst story," he wrote on April 30, 1926.

It is a good story about a little woman that all the older generation remember. She was the reigning sensation of America and Europe during all the heyday of Buffalo Bill's Wild West show. She was their star. Her picture was on more billboards than a modern Gloria Swanson. It was Annie Oakley, the greatest woman rifle shot the world has ever produced. Nobody took her place. There was only one. I went out to see her the other day as I was playing in Dayton, Ohio. She lives there with her husband, Frank Butler, and her sister. Her hair is snow white. She is bedridden from an auto accident a few years ago. What a wonderful christian character she is. I have talked with Buffalo Bill cowboys who were with the show for years and they worshipped her. She for years taught the fashionable people at Pinehurst, N.C., to shoot. America is worshipping at the feet of Raquel Miller, the Spanish lady. Europe talked the same of Annie Oakley in her day, and she reigned for many a year. I want you to write her all you who remember her and those that can go see her. Her address is 706 Lexington Avenue, Dayton, Ohio. She will be a lesson to you. She is a greater character than she was a rifle shot. Circuses have produced

Profile of Annie Oakley at the height of her career. This photograph appeared in *Army and Navy Magazine*, July 29, 1893. (From Cooper, *Annie Oakley: Woman at Arms*)

the cleanest living class of people in America today, and Annie Oakley's name, her lovable traits, her thoughtful consideration of others will live as a mark for any woman to shoot at.

Americans read Will Rogers's column, and they did write. On May 15, Frank told Leonard Tufts that Annie had received one thousand letters in the few days since the column appeared. "I had nothing to do with the article," Frank wrote to Tufts. "In fact, didn't know anything about it until letters started coming in."[18] The letters that came that May were full of nostalgia and good wishes. An admirer in San Francisco wrote:

> Dear Miss Oakley,
> I read Will Rogers story the other day. So glad to learn you are still here, for you gave me endless pleasure when I was a boy. . . . May God's blessings be upon you always, Miss Oakley.
> > Sincerely,
> > One whom you pleased years ago.

The urbane and popular Charles Dillingham, who staged musicals on Broadway, wrote from the Globe Theatre in New York:

> Dear Annie,
> I was so sorry to learn that you had been so badly hurt in an automobile accident. I read Will Rogers' beautiful tribute to you, which also gave me your address. The last time I saw you I was taking a French artist down to Fred Stone's and you gave us a wonderful exhibition of shooting, and yesterday Fred got in from the road and he, Mrs. Stone, Dorothy and I were talking of you, so I thought I would send you a little line to let you know that so many people love you and think of you and are praying for your recovery.

One of many strangers, William H. Trantham, wrote from Washington, D.C.:

> Dear Miss,
> I am sure that a great many people, besides myself, feel grateful towards Will Rogers for telling us about you, altho all I know of you—is what I could learn by attending the wild west show, yet I believe you are as good as our friend Mr. Rogers says you are.

H. R. ("Hy") Everding remembered distinctly that he had seen Annie's "marvelous shooting act" at the Chicago World's Fair in September 1893, and Francis S. Wells wrote from Boston that he had played for a short time with the Buffalo Bill band and remembered meeting Annie. "I certainly hope that the future will bring you much of the joy and sunshine that you deserve," he wrote on May 5, 1926. Odell L. Whipple asked his secretary at the C. F. Droop & Sons Music Co. in Washington, D.C., to type a letter for him. "You can be sure that millions remember you and the thrill you gave them and are praying for your restoration to health," he dictated on May 1. Businessman George Van Wagner typed a letter on stationery from the Torrington Typewriter Exchange at 60 Main Street, Torrington, Connecticut.

> Dear Mrs. Butler,
> As my memory goes back it seems as if it must have been all of thirty years ago when I first saw you with Buffalo Bill's show and you were teamed with Johnny Baker in shooting glass balls thrown in the air. I know now I must have looked funny with my eyes bulging and my mouth open as you would brake one after the other and it seemed impossible for you to miss. . . . One of my greatest wishes are that you will recover your health speedily and be able to again enjoy the great out door's where you once shone in your art as no other woman ever did or ever will I believe.[19]

Even a thousand wishes, however, were not enough to make Annie Oakley well. That summer, she moved home to Darke County, again staying near Ansonia with Bonnie and Rush Blakeley. "Annie's health wasn't too good. She got tired awful easy. Said it was anemia," Rush Blakeley said later. "Frank wasn't too good either." Frank wanted to go south for the winter, but Annie didn't. When she told him to go without her, he left Ansonia alone. According to Fern Campbell Swartwout, "he left her with a heavy heart and only went because he thought he was pleasing her."[20] Frank, thinking he would go to Pinehurst with Fern, wired her in Detroit where she was living. She wasn't able to go at the moment, however, and she had Frank come to Detroit until arrangements could be made.

Before traveling to Michigan, Frank stopped in New Jersey, where he attended a shooting match in Morristown in late August. From there, he wrote to Leonard Tufts: "Annie is out in Ohio with her niece on a farm. She is in very bad health. Doctors don't give me *much* hope. Don't know yet if we will get to Pinehurst or not this year. Haven't seen any place we *like better*. But doubt if we can afford it. *Three years* doctor bills put a lump in our bank account."[21]

Frank wasn't well, either, and when he reached Fern's home, she fixed up a room for him and wrote about how grateful he was. "Many times he had said he knew he could depend upon me, for if ever Missie died before he did he knew he would be helpless."[22]

While Frank lay ill in Michigan, Annie was getting worse in Ohio. "She seemed to be failing fast," Rush Blakeley said. "It wasn't long before Annie asked to be taken to a home in Greenville where she could be near Dr. Husted, her friend and physician." On a fall day the Blakeleys drove her into town, and Annie took a room in the Zemer and Broderick boardinghouse at 227 East Third Street.[23]

There, on October 11, 1926, Dr. W. H. Matchett, not a Dr. Husted, paid his first visit to an ailing Annie Oakley. He walked down a quiet street, lined with trees, and turned in at a two-story house. He walked up the wooden steps, then climbed a stairway just inside the door. In a room at the top of the stairs lay a pale, white-haired woman whom Matchett would be back to visit regularly for the next three weeks.

Other visitors came. On Saturday, October 23, Harriett Zemer, Lorietta Bollinger, and George A. Katzenberger—the son of the old storekeeper—gathered around as witnesses as Annie made a codicil to her will. She had decided to give her sixty-six shares of Du Pont stock, in trust, to her sister Ellen, who still was living in Ansonia. Other changes, dealing with money for her nieces, hinged on whether Frank died before she did. She must have known he was near death, too.

Another visitor came that October. Her name was Louise Stocker, an undertaker who worked at her father's funeral home at Walnut and Fourth Street in Greenville. Louise Stocker's visit proved just how modest Annie Oakley was. "She wanted a woman to handle her body and I was the only female licensed embalmer and funeral director in those parts, maybe in the whole state," Stocker said. She found Annie pale and very weak. "She said she had no strength left and was ready to die," Stocker said. "Then she said softly and simply that she wanted me to embalm her." Annie also said she wanted to be cremated. She pointed to a trunk sitting against the wall and asked Stocker to open it. "It was full of personal things," Stocker said, "pictures, souvenirs, mementos of her travels, items of clothing, all personal and all labeled with the names of those to receive them, relatives and friends." Among the items, neatly placed between sheets of tissue paper, was an apricot-colored dress of fine georgette silk. That dress, Annie told Stocker, was the one she wanted to wear during her funeral service. The dress was only half-hemmed, so Stocker took it and completed the job.[24]

And so it was, as October slipped into November, that Annie Oakley died. She died late in the evening, at eleven o'clock on Wednesday, November 3, 1926. Dr. Matchett, who had visited her just the day before, hurriedly filled in her death certificate. Her name: Annie Oakley Butler. Occupation: Expert marksman. Cause of death: Pernicious anemia.

The story went out over the Associated Press wire on November 4: "In the hills of Darke county, Ohio, where the girl, Annie Oakley, learned to handle a rifle will rest the ashes of the noted marksman, who was perhaps the greatest shooter of all time. . . . She was the friend of monarchs and the confidante of Sitting Bull."

The word reached Fern Campbell Swartwout in Michigan, and she broke the news to Frank. "He never ate a bite after she went. He said he could not swallow," Fern wrote.[25] While Frank lay dying, Louise Stocker embalmed Annie's body and dressed it in the apricot dress, as she had wished. Annie's face was so pale that Stocker colored it with cosmetics.

On Friday morning, November 5, unknown to the press that had loved Annie Oakley as much as anyone, her body was taken to a brick house at Tecumseh and East Main Street and laid on a bed. There, in the home of Fred and Hazel Grote of Greenville, Reverend Christian C. Wessell led a private funeral service. Annie's friends were so intent on keeping the services private that they lied to reporters, telling them the service was to be the following morning. "Annie Oakley Funeral Is Held Hurriedly," said a headline in the *New York Times* of November 6. The story told how "friends admitted they had announced the funeral for Saturday, that it might be held without the presence of the curious."

By Friday afternoon, the funeral was over. Annie's body was placed in a coffin and put in a hearse for the eighty-mile ride to Cincinnati, where it was cremated. "We brought her ashes home in an urn," Louise Stocker said. Fred Grote made a strong oak box for the urn, encased it in cement, and put it in a vault at Stocker's Funeral Parlor for safekeeping against thieves.[26] And there the urn was to stay, awaiting the death of Frank Butler.

The wait was not long. On November 21, 1926, just eighteen days after Annie died, Frank died at Fern Campbell Swartwout's home in Michigan. There was difficulty in filling out his death certificate. No one knew the date of his birth, so they guessed that he was "about 76 years old." No one knew, either, the place of his birth, except that it was somewhere in Ireland. His occupation was easier: Showman. Cause of death: Senility.[27]

Frank's body, which according to his wishes was not cremated, was brought back to Darke County. Another service was held at the brick house at Tecumseh and East Main, and again, Reverend Wessell officiated.

And then, on Thanksgiving Day, November 25, 1926, Annie Oakley made her last trip past the old Public Square where she had sold her quail and rabbits to G. Anthony and Charles Katzenberger so long ago. The old home folks carried her remains up north, past Ansonia and Versailles and the fields and forests that were so familiar to Annie Oakley. Just south of the village of Brock, they turned off Highway 127 into a little cemetery hemmed on all sides by fields and trees.

Up North Star way, just five miles distant, the rabbits scampered over the fields and the quail darted from their covey, just as they had done years ago when the girl Annie Moses sat on a moss-covered log with Jacob Moses's old Kentucky muzzle-loader resting across her knee. The forests weren't so thick anymore, but still this quiet farmland was home to Annie Oakley. They buried her under a plain headstone that bore a simple inscription: [28]

Annie Oakley
At Rest
1926

Right beside her, under an identical headstone that bore the name Frank Butler, they buried the man who had discovered and loved Annie Oakley. The woman who had become one of the best-loved Americans of all time was gone, but her legend would not die.

Epilogue

Annie Oakley's gravestone still can be found in the old Brock Cemetery. Every July, during ¡"Annie Oakley Days," the old home folks make the pilgrimage up Highway 127 to honor their most famous daughter. A few miles away and just below the North Star crossroads, a stone marks the site of Susan Shaw's old house, torn down long ago. To the east is Woodland, now called Willowdell. A marker along Spencer Road in Patterson Township says Annie Oakley was born "not far from here." Today, the fields are planted in soybeans and corn. Down in Greenville, some of Annie's guns are on exhibit at the Garst Museum, and the house where she died, at 227 East Third Street, still stands on a tree-shaded street. For those who care to look, the reminders of Annie Oakley's life are still to be found, though it is in the American imagination that she truly lives on.

Her name is as familiar today as it was in the old days of Buffalo Bill's Wild West, though Americans now seem to know of her life in only a vague way. It is the name that lives still, synonymous with the Old West, and that despite a surprising lack of commercialization.

There have been a few comic books, a few motion pictures, and the ABC television show, "Annie Oakley," in which a blond, pig-tailed Gail Davis played Annie from 1954 to 1957. In 1954, the program was second on the list of top children's shows, and in 1959 and 1960 reruns aired on Saturdays and Sundays. But probably the single biggest contributor to Annie's modern-day fame was the 1946 Broadway musical *Annie Get Your Gun*, in which Ethel Merman immortalized Annie

Oakley with those popular Irving Berlin tunes, "You Can't Get a Man with a Gun" and "There's No Business like Show Business."

But we shouldn't confuse Annie Oakley with the brash Ethel Merman. As Fred Stone said, people always seemed surprised upon meeting Annie Oakley. They expected to find a big, blustery sort of person, and the petite woman with the quiet voice took them by surprise. But we shouldn't let that fool us, either. Annie Oakley was competitive and resolute, a woman who made it in a man's world when that was an unusual thing to do. Though she never cared for feminism in a political sense, she became and has remained a symbol of the liberated woman.

Notes

Chapter 1: A Darke County Girl

1. See *The History of Darke County, Ohio* (Chicago: W. H. Beers, 1880); Frazer E. Wilson, *History of Darke County Ohio from Its Earliest Settlement to the Present Time*, 2 vols. (Milford, Ohio: Hobart Publishing, 1914), 1:351.

2. Annie Fern Swartwout, *Missie* (Blanchester, Ohio: Brown Publishing, 1947), 3. There is no record of Annie Oakley's birth. The Darke County Courthouse lost its records before 1867 in a fire. The date of birth, however, is recorded on her death certificate as August 13, 1860. Family records also put the date as 1860. The birthdate sometimes is disputed because Annie lied about her age and insisted throughout much of her life that she was born on August 13, 1866.

Susan Moses also had given birth to another daughter, Sarah Ellen, in 1857, giving Annie four sisters: Mary Jane (born April 22, 1851), Lydia (born August 6, 1852), Elizabeth (born April 5, 1855), and Sarah Ellen (born April 4, 1857). A fifth child, Catherine (born March 17, 1859), died in infancy, on November 8, 1859.

For the Moses family, see U.S. Department of Commerce, Bureau of the Census, *Eighth Census of the United States, 1860: Population*, 1:681; genealogy provided by Toni Seiler, director, Garst Museum, Greenville, Ohio.

3. See Annie Oakley, *The Story of My Life* (n.p.: NEA Service, 1926); and *Annie Oakley: Her Career and Experiences* (Pinehurst, N.C., March 19, 1920).

4. Oakley, *The Story of My Life*.

5. Philadelphia *Public Ledger*, May 18, 1919.

6. Wilson, *History of Darke County*, 1:349. The story that Annie's brother taught her to shoot was well entrenched by the time of her death, although it was an unlikely story considering he was only six years old at the time. In her obituary in the *New York Times*, November 6, 1926, C. G. and Lee Moses, sons of John, told "how 'Aunt Ann,' when a small girl, would secretly follow her brother on hunting expeditions until they were so far from home he would not send her back. Then she would beg to shoot his heavy shotgun. After many such excursions he agreed she could shoot at a bird. First, however, he loaded the gun with two extra drams of powder, in the hope it would 'cure' her of the desire to shoot. The 'kick' fractured her nose, but she killed the bird." Interestingly, in a newspaper interview shortly before his death, John Moses denied that he had taught Annie to shoot. According to the untitled clipping at the Garst Museum, dated

March 21, 1949, John "said people got the idea he taught Annie to shoot. He added that this was very false. He said he never liked guns and hardly ever hit where he aimed."

7. Knoxville (Tenn.) *Sentinel*, May 1, 1899.

8. Oakley, *The Story of My Life*, chap. 1.

9. Swartwout, *Missie*, 13.

10. U.S. Department of Commerce, Bureau of the Census, *Ninth Census of the United States, 1870: Population*, 1:412A. The 1870 census does not list Annie as a member of the Susan and Daniel Brumbaugh family. (Susan Moses married Brumbaugh on August 12, 1867.) Annie's absence probably means she had moved away from home before the census was taken in that part of Darke County on July 27, 1870, but she was not listed, either, on census records taken in the south of the county or at the Darke County Infirmary earlier that year. Perhaps she was in the process of moving, or "The Wolves" (see below) did not report her.

11. See Wilson, *History of Darke County*, 513–16; and Robert E. Perry, *Treaty City: A Story of Old Fort GreenVille* (Bradford, Ohio, 1945), 44. For Allen LaMott, see George W. Calderwood, "The Darke County Boy," quoted in Wilson, *History of Darke County*, 1:267, 272.

12. Oakley, *The Story of My Life*, chap. 2.

13. Nancy Ann Edington obituary, August 20, 1903, Annie Oakley Scrapbooks, hereafter cited as AOSB.

14. See Oakley, *The Story of My Life;* and Isabelle S. Sayers, *Annie Oakley and Buffalo Bill's Wild West* (New York: Dover, 1981), 4, quoting Frank Edington.

15. See *A Biographical History of Darke County Ohio, Compendium of National Biography* (Chicago: Lewis Publishing, 1900), 457, 527; and *Atlas of Darke County, Ohio, 1875–1888*, no publisher listed.

16. London *Dramatic Review*, June 10, 1887.

17. Nashville (Tenn.) *Banner*, March 28, 1908. She expressed the same sentiment in the London *Evening Express*, September 28, 1891: "I don't know how I acquired the skill, but I suppose I was born with it."

18. Brighton (England) *Guardian*, October 14, 1891.

19. Annie Oakley, *Powders I Have Used* (Wilmington: DuPont Powder Company, 1914).

20. Ibid.

21. *The Story of American Hunting and Firearms, from Outdoor Life* (New York: E. P. Dutton, 1976), 139–45.

22. Oakley, *Powders I Have Used*.

23. See Anne Whitney Hay, "Annie Oakley Still Pulls a Wicked Trigger," New York *Morning Telegraph*, July 16, 1922; and unidentified clipping, AOSB 1912–on. Records at the Garst Museum show that a $200 note on the house was paid off on March 9, 1876.

24. See Brighton (England) *Guardian*, October 14, 1891; and New York *Journal*, July 29, 1894.

Chapter 2: The Fancy Shooters

1. Captain Adam Bogardus, *Field, Cover and Trap Shooting*, ed. Colonel Prentiss Ingraham (New York: Orange Judd, 1884). On passenger pigeons, *Collier's Encyclopedia*, 1984 ed. The American ornithologist, John J. Audubon, told of watching one flock of pigeons that took three hours to pass. He estimated that the formation was a mile wide and contained more than one billion birds.

2. New York *Sun*, July 5, 1878. Glass ball targets were relatively new in the United States. In use in England since about 1830, they did not come to America until 1866. The balls were of various colors and were formed of blown glass. They were packed in sawdust

or wood shavings, about 300 in a barrel, and were used as an alternative to killing pigeons. Ralph Lindsay, "The Evolution of the Clay Pigeon," *American Shotgunner* (August 1982): 14–18.

3. New York *Times*, July 6, 14, 1878.

4. New York *Times*, August 22, 1880. Deerfoot Park had been renamed Brooklyn Driving Park.

5. Jaroslav Lugs, *A History of Shooting* (Feltham, Middlesex, England: Spring Books, 1968).

6. Ibid., 179.

7. Ibid., 182.

8. *New York Times*, August 21, 1884.

9. See *New York Times*, April 15, September 27, October 5, November 13, 1874.

10. For family history see Swartwout, *Missie*, 61–63; and U.S. Department of Commerce, Bureau of the Census, *Tenth Census of the United States, 1880: Population*, Will County, Illinois.

11. Swartwout, *Missie*, 62–63.

12. According to the Cincinnati *Commercial*, January 2, 1891, Frank Butler "years ago figured as one of the Austin Brothers."

13. Jack Burton, *In Memoriam—Oldtime Show Biz* (New York: Vantage Press, 1965); Joseph and June Bundy Csida, *American Entertainment: A Unique History of Popular Show Business* (New York: Watson-Guptill, 1978); Harlowe R. Hoyt, *Town Hall Tonight: Intimate Memoirs of the Grassroots Days of the American Theatre* (Englewood Cliffs, N.J.: Prentice-Hall, 1955); Glenn Hughes, *A History of the American Theatre 1700–1950* (New York: Samuel French, 1951); Douglas Gilbert, *American Vaudeville: Its Life and Times* (New York: Dover, 1940); Bernard Sobel, *A Pictorial History of Vaudeville* (New York: Citadel Press, 1961); and Parker Zellers, *Tony Pastor: Dean of the Vaudeville Stage* (Ypsilanti: Eastern Michigan University Press, 1971). For the number of shows, see *New York Times*, September 1, 1875.

14. Cincinnati *Enquirer*, April 3, 1881.

15. See Sells Brothers Circus Route Book, 1881; Greenville, Ohio, *Democrat*, September 21, 1881; and Robert L. Parkinson of Circus World Museum, Baraboo, Wisconsin, personal communication, August 30, 1983.

16. See Sells Brothers Circus Courier, 1881, in Sayers, *Annie Oakley and Buffalo Bill's Wild West*, 6; and Greenville (Ohio) *Democrat*, September 21, 1881.

17. Pittsburgh (Pa.) *Dispatch*, February 4, 1903. According to the Cincinnati *Enquirer*, March 27, 1881, one F. C. Butler of Newark was registered at the Burnet House.

Chapter 3: Butler and Oakley

1. Cincinnati *Enquirer*, April 9, 1881. No contemporary account of the match ever has been found. John Steinle, manuscript curator at the Cincinnati Historical Society, personal communication, November 25, 1981. On Frank's shooting career, see *Forest and Stream*, January 29, 1910.

2. See Pittsburgh (Pa.) *Dispatch*, February 4, 1903; Charlotte (N.C.) *Observer*, July 6, 1924; and Dayton (Ohio) *Sunday Journal*, December 14, 1924. In the *Observer*, correspondent Henry E. Dougherty interviewed Annie and Frank at a North Carolina gun club in 1924. He wrote: "They related the occasion when Frank Butler, then the crack shot of the nation, was invited to participate in a shooting match in an Ohio town near Cincinnati. That was 43 years ago [1881]. . . . He went out to the little town. He was given an ovation, such as any here might receive, but all about him the people were whispering. After a time a 16-year-old [*sic*] girl came upon the scene.

"I noticed that she was receiving extraordinary attention, said Butler in continuing the story. . . . She licked me fairly and squarely. I was amazed—and fascinated. Well, I fell in love with her—and a year later we were married."

In the Dayton *Sunday Journal*, Frank told how Baughman and Butler were "headliners" at a Cincinnati theater but were "unable to book steady work." To "keep them going," Frank had been entering local matches for side bets. Thus, the match with Annie came about. "On the day of the match Butler was very much surprised to find that his opponent was a young girl of 15 [*sic*] years," the *Sunday Journal* wrote. "She won the match by one bird."

"'Right then and there I decided if I could get that girl I would do it,' Butler told the writer. He soon afterwards signed a contract with a circus but corresponded with the girl, Annie Oakley, and within a few months they were married."

3. The Sells Brothers Circus played Greenville, Ohio, on September 24, 1881. Perhaps this is when Annie saw Frank perform.

4. Courtney Ryley Cooper, *Annie Oakley, Woman at Arms* (New York: Duffield, 1927), 65–67. Cooper said he found the poem among Annie's memorabilia and that it was dated in Quincy, Illinois, on May 9, 1881. At the bottom, he said, was the "almost boyish notation": "Written and composed for my little girl by her loving husband. Frank E. Butler." The notation is confusing because it would seem to nullify any theory that Annie and Frank had met only that spring. A possible explanation is that Frank added the notation sentimentally in a later year. Perhaps May 9, 1881, was the day they met or the day they first corresponded. At least one time in the Annie Oakley scrapbooks, Frank added exactly such a sentimental notation years after the clipping was pasted in the scrapbooks.

5. Swartwout, *Missie*, 59.

6. Ibid., 64.

7. Rush Blakeley interview at 321 Chippewa Street, Greenville, Ohio, May 13, 1981.

8. Ibid. In her autobiography, Annie Oakley stated that she and Frank Butler were married on August 23, 1876. By adding on the six years that Annie usually subtracted from her age, the marriage date becomes, more realistically, the summer of 1882.

9. See Newark (N.J.) *Sunday Call*, October 1, 1916; Detroit *Free Press*, July 5, 1921; Philadelphia *Public Ledger*, May 18, 1919; Erie (Pa.) *Daily Times*, n.d., AOSB 1912-on; and John R. Claridge, executive director of the Erie County Historical Society, personal communication, November 9, 1983.

10. George C. D. Odell, *Annals of the New York Stage*, 15 vols. (New York: Columbia University Press, 1939), 11:544; and Sayers, *Annie Oakley and Buffalo Bill's Wild West*, 7.

11. Greensboro (N.C.) *Daily News*, December 30, 1923; *Billboard*, May 9, 1925, 75. That Annie Oakley went on the stage in 1882 is proved in a number of newspaper accounts, including the London *Evening News and Telephone*, June 10, 1887. "How long have you been shooting in public?" a reporter asked her. "Since 1882," she said. In *Shooting and Fishing*, n.d., AOSB 1902-8, Frank Butler told the story of a woman shooter who accidentally had killed her partner on stage. Frank said the incident occurred "along about 1879 or 1880, before Annie Oakley commenced shooting." In 1905, when Annie was under oath and testifying during a trial, she was quoted in the Wilmington (Del.) *Every Evening*, October 31, 1905, as saying "she was a professional wing and rifle shot since June, 1882."

12. Untitled clipping, n.p., April 7, 1904, AOSB 1903-5. Annie made this statement while under oath during a series of libel trials.

13. See Swartwout, *Missie*, 41–42, 268–69; Toni Seiler, personal communication, March 26, 1982; and Marcy Heidish, *The Secret Annie Oakley, A Novel* (New York: NAL, 1983), 123.

14. Newark (N.J.) *Sunday News*, May 11, 1902.

15. Oakley, *Story of My Life*, chap. 5.

16. Untitled clipping, n.p., August 13, 1923, AOSB 1921-25. On artificial lights, see Gilbert, *American Vaudeville*, 17; and *New York Times*, October 24, 1881.

17. Newark (N.J.) *Sunday News*, May 11, 1902.

Chapter 4: Little Sure Shot

1. Walter Havighurst, *Annie Oakley of the Wild West* (New York: MacMillan, 1954), 52.

2. See Stanley Vestal, *Sitting Bull, Champion of the Sioux* (Norman: University of Oklahoma Press, 1932), 232-50; and Point St. Charles, Ontario, Canada, *Times*, August 10, 1885. This description of Sitting Bull was taken from an account written seventeen months after Sitting Bull was in St. Paul.

3. This visit was before the tour of fifteen cities of the United States, which began in St. Paul, Minnesota, on September 15, 1884.

4. St. Paul *Dispatch*, March 17-22, 1884.

5. Ibid., March 18-19, 1884.

6. Untitled clipping, n.p., August 13, 1887, AOSB 1887-91.

7. Ibid. Annie's flippant remarks seem uncharacteristic of her. It is possible the interviewer put his own slant on what she had to say. Annie also discussed her adoption by Sitting Bull in the Pinehurst (N.C.) *Outlook*, January 6, 1917.

Chapter 5: A Whole World of Wonders

1. Ottawa (Kans.) *Daily Republican*, August 21, 1884. The Sells Brothers Circus was the third largest outfit on the road in 1884, behind only Barnum and Bailey and Adam Forepaugh. See John and Alice Durant, *Pictorial History of the American Circus* (New York: A. S. Barnes, 1957), 63-67; and Robert L. Parkinson, personal communication, August 30, 1983.

2. See Paola, Kans., *Times*, August 14, 1884; and (Emporia) *Kansas Daily Republican*, September 3, 1884.

3. Sells Brothers Circus Route Book, 1884.

4. New Orleans *Daily Picayune*, November 1884-April 1885.

5. Oakley, *The Story of My Life*, chap. 6.

6. New York *Clipper*, November 29, 1884.

7. New Orleans *Daily Picayune*, December 8, 12, 1884.

8. "Camp sketches," n.p., August 13, 1887, AOSB 1887-91.

9. Ibid.

10. New Orleans *Daily Picayune*, December 15, 1884.

11. Richard Walsh, with Milton S. Salsbury, *The Making of Buffalo Bill* (Indianapolis: Bobbs-Merrill, 1928), 242-43.

12. New Orleans *Daily Picayune*, March 9, 16, 1885.

13. Untitled clipping, n.p., August 13, 1887, AOSB 1887-91.

14. Ibid.

15. Oakley, *The Story of My Life*, chap. 6. According to the Cincinnati *Commercial* of January 2, 1891, Annie Oakley was an honorary member of the Independent Gun Club. It may have been there that she went to practice before trying out for Buffalo Bill's Wild West. For her nine-hour feat, see Philadelphia *Item*, December 30, 1888; London *Evening News and Telephone*, June 10, 1887; and Buffalo Bill Wild West programs. For her earlier rifle feat, see London *Evening News and Telephone*, June 10, 1887.

16. Untitled clipping, n.p., August 13, 1887, AOSB 1887-91.

17. Frank Butler to *Shooting Times* (London), October 14, 1887. Here are Frank's words: "As regards Miss Oakley shooting a shotgun, nearly every shooter east of the

Rocky Mountains knows that for the first three years before the public Miss Oakley did nothing but rifle and pistol shooting, and gave it up because she could not get a living salary for doing it."

18. See the *Referee* (London), n.d., AOSB 1887–91; Lugs, *A History of Shooting*, 169–73; and unidentified clipping, AOSB 1921–25.

19. See Lindsay, "The Evolution of the Clay Pigeon," 18; and Fred Missildine, with Nick Karas, *Score Better at Trap and Skeet* (New York: Winchester Press, 1971), 17–34. Clay targets were invented by Cincinnatian George Ligowsky, who promoted the new targets in a much publicized national tour by Carver and Bogardus in the early 1880s. Over several months the two competed in twenty-five clay bird matches at various gun clubs around the nation.

Chapter 6: Buffalo Bill and His Wild West

1. Chicago *Tribune*, December 19, 1872; New York *Herald*, April 1, 1873; New York *Tribune*, April 1, 1873.

2. Sarah J. Blackstone, *Buckskins, Bullets, and Business: A History of Buffalo Bill's Wild West* (Greenwood Press, Westport, Conn., 1986), 128; Chicago *Daily News*, May 5, 1893 (quotation).

3. See Don Russell, *The Lives and Legends of Buffalo Bill* (Norman: University of Oklahoma Press, 1960); Allen Johnson and Dumas Malone, eds., *Dictionary of American Biography* (New York: Charles Scribner's Sons, 1930), 260–61; *The New Encyclopaedia Britannica*, 15th ed., s.v. "William F. Cody"; and *The National Cyclopedia of American Biography* (New York: James T. White, 1907), 483.

4. Blackstone, *Buckskins, Bullets, and Business*, 133–34.

5. New York *Herald*, June 26, 1886. For other good descriptions of the Wild West show in action see "The Summer Show," Boston, n.p., June 13, [1899?]; and Boston, n.p., June 17, 1900, Nate Salsbury Scrapbooks, hereafter cited as NSSB.

6. Oakley, *The Story of My Life*, chap. 6. For their arrival in Louisville, see Louisville *Commercial*, April 25, 1885; New York *Clipper*, April 18, 1885, 71; and untitled clipping, n.p., August 13, 1887, AOSB 1887–91.

7. Untitled clipping, n.p., August 13, 1887, AOSB 1887–91; and Oakley, *The Story of My Life*, chap. 6.

8. There is not much information on where the nickname Missie originated. In her autobiography, Annie Oakley wrote that Cody called her Missie. However, in *Missie*, 174–75, Fern Campbell Swartwout said that Annie acquired the name in France, when a "little French maid of whom she was very fond" began calling her Missie.

9. Pinehurst (N.C.) *Outlook*, January 20, 1917.

10. See Buffalo Bill's Wild West program, 1896, 22; and Russell, *The Lives and Legends of Buffalo Bill*, 297.

11. Oakley, *The Story of My Life*, chap. 6.

Chapter 7: In the Arena

1. *New York Times*, April 7, 1901.

2. Dexter Fellows and Andrew Freeman, *This Way to the Big Show* (New York: Viking Press, 1936), 73.

3. Toledo (Ohio) *Blade*, July 27, 1896. For her outfit, see Toledo (Ohio) *Blade*, July 27, 1896; Joliet (Ill.) *Daily News*, August 27, 1903; Chicago *Daily News*, July 26, 1898; New York *Sun*, May 20, 1894; Syracuse (N.Y.) *Post*, August 6, 1895; and photographs.

4. Swartwout, *Missie*, 248; Irene Patterson Black, personal communication, Octo-

ber 2, 1990. According to Swartwout, *Missie*, 203, Annie had thirty-five different costumes, all very much of the same style.

5. New Orleans *Daily Picayune*, October 27, 1900; Portsmouth (Mass.) *Times*, June 8, 1900; Dallas *Morning News*, October 12, 1900.

6. New York *Evening News*, June 3, 1897.

7. Dallas *Morning News*, October 12, 1900; *Sporting Life*, n.d., AOSB 1896–1901.

8. New York *Tribune*, July 22, 1894; Providence (R.I.) *Journal*, June 1, 1897; Fall River (Mass.) *Evening News*, June 3, 1897; Springfield (Mass.) *Republican*, May 22, 1897; Nottingham (England) *Daily Express*, August 25, 1891.

9. See Boston *Daily Advertiser*, May 25, 1897; and *Sporting Life*, n.d. [1895?].

10. "Notes from England," n.p., n.d., AOSB 1893–95.

11. Toronto *Mail and Express*, July 6, 1897; Newport (Mass.) *Herald*, June 22, 1899; and Washington, D.C., *Times*, April 25, 1901.

12. In the New York *Recorder*, October 6, 1894, Annie was quoted as saying she could run the hundred-yard dash in thirteen seconds.

13. See London *Figaro*, May 11, 1892; and unidentified clipping, AOSB 1887–91.

14. New York *Sun*, May 20, 1894; Kansas City *Star*, n.d., AOSB 1896–1901.

15. New York *Sun*, May 20, 1894; New York *Commercial*, August 4, 1894.

16. Minneapolis *Times*, n.d., AOSB 1896–1901.

17. Chicago *Daily News*, July 16, 1901; Chicago *Daily News*, n.d., AOSB 1893–95; and Akron (Ohio) *Press*, n.d., AOSB 1912–on.

18. Chicago *Daily News*, May 5, 1893.

19. Fellows and Freeman, *This Way to the Big Show*, 73.

20. See Brighton (England) *Guardian*, October 14, 1891; and Nottingham (England) *Daily Express*, August 25, 1891.

21. Basil Tozer in *Rod and Gun* (London), n.d. [1891?], AOSB 1887–91.

22. Brighton (England) *Guardian*, October 14, 1891.

23. Walsh, *The Making of Buffalo Bill*, 252; Fellows and Freeman, *This Way to the Big Show*, 74.

24. Ralph Greenwood of *Shooting and Fishing*, in *New York Times*, September 13, 1894.

25. Swartwout, *Missie*, 106.

26. *Shooting and Fishing*, n.d., AOSB 1893–95.

27. Unidentified clipping, AOSB 1887–91.

28. See Frank Butler to *Shooting Times*, n.d., AOSB 1887–91; Frank Butler to *American Field*, January [1890?], AOSB 1887–91; and untitled clipping, n.p., May 26, [1888?], AOSB 1887–91.

29. See Knoxville (Tenn.) *Sentinel*, May 1, 1899; and Evansville (Ind.) *Journal News*, June 19, 1908.

30. Fellows and Freeman, *This Way to the Big Show*, 73.

Chapter 8: A Season with Sitting Bull

1. See Walsh, *The Making of Buffalo Bill*, 182–84; *The Journalist*, August 14, 1886; David A. Curtis, quoted in Cincinnati *Commercial Tribune*, May 7, 1897; and Fellows and Freeman, *This Way to the Big Show*, 83.

2. Buffalo (N.Y.) *Courier*, June 13, 1885.

3. Cooper, *Annie Oakley, Woman at Arms*, 121–24.

4. Buffalo (N.Y.) *Courier*, June 13, 1885; Russell, *The Lives and Legends of Buffalo Bill*, 316.

5. Buffalo (N.Y.) *Courier*, June 13, 1885.

6. *Dramatic Review* (London), June 10, 1887.

7. See Boston *Post*, July 28, 1885. According to Vestal, *Sitting Bull, Champion of the Sioux*, 35–36, 112, 183, Sitting Bull adopted a number of people during his lifetime, including an Assiniboin Indian boy, a mail carrier named Frank Grouard whom he captured on the trail between Fort Hall and Fort Peck, and a man of mixed ancestry named Johnny Brughiere who was fleeing a murder charge. In later years, Annie's adoption by Sitting Bull was mentioned in the Wild West program.

8. St. Louis *Republican*, October [4?], 1885; St. Louis *Sunday Sayings*, October 4, 1885 (quotation).

9. Boston *Globe* and Boston *Evening Traveller*, July 31, 1885.

10. See Buffalo (N.Y.) *Courier*, June 13, 1885.

11. Pinehurst (N.C.) *Outlook*, January 6, 1917. The Custer battle was always a very touchy subject with Indians. According to Standing Rock agent James McLaughlin, it was not easy to get them to tell what happened at the battle because they feared they were being examined for the purpose of singling out men for punishment.

12. Detroit *Evening Journal*, September 5, 1885; St. Louis *Republican*, October [4?], 1885; Grand Rapids (Mich.) *Evening Leader*, September 12, 1885.

13. See Montreal *Herald*, August 14, 1885; and Montreal *Daily Star*, August 12, 1885.

14. Toronto *Globe*, August 24, 1885.

15. St. Louis *Sunday Sayings*, October 4, 1885.

16. See Vestal, *Sitting Bull, Champion of the Sioux*, 250; Harry Blackman Sell and Victor Weybright, *Buffalo Bill and the Wild West* (New York: Oxford University Press, 1955), 145.

17. Hamilton (Ontario, Canada) *Daily Spectator and Tribune*, August 27, 1885.

18. See New York *Clipper*, June 20, 1885; Oakley, *The Story of My Life*, chap. 6; and Swartwout, *Missie*, 97–98.

Chapter 9: Summer in New York

1. Charles Lockwood, *Manhattan Moves Uptown* (Boston: Houghton Mifflin, 1976). For Erastina, see New York *Star*, June 26, 1886; New York *Sun*, June 26, 1886; *New York Times*, June 26, 1886; *Brick Pomeroy's Democrat*, July 10, 1886; and New York *Mail and Express*, July 23, 1886.

2. New York *Herald*, June 26, 1886; New York *Morning Journal*, June 26, 1886; New York *Sun*, June 26, 1886; New York *World*, July 5, 1886.

3. See Chicago *Daily News*, May 5, 1893, and n.d., AOSB 1893–95; *Rod and Gun*, n.d. [1887?], AOSB 1887–91; and New York *World*, July 31, 1886.

4. New York *World*, July 5, 1886.

5. See untitled clipping, n.p., 1886, NSSB; New York *Morning Journal*, July 5, 1886; New York *Morning Journal*, August 1, 1886; and New York *Star*, August 1, 1886.

6. See New York *World*, July 25, 1886; and New York *Mail and Express*, July 27, 1886.

7. Oakley, *The Story of My Life*, chap. 7.

8. See St. Louis *Republican*, May 13, 1886; and St. Louis *Post Dispatch*, May 11, 1886.

9. Ibid.

10. To mark Annie's birthday that summer at Erastina, the *National Police Gazette* ran a story about her on August 14, 1886, one day after Annie's twenty-sixth birthday. Interestingly, the date given for her birth is 1866, proving that she had begun lying about her age by that summer.

11. Oakley, *The Story of My Life*, chap. 7.

12. New York *Herald*, June 27, 1886.

13. Oakley, *The Story of My Life*, chap. 7; New York *Clipper*, July 10, 1886; and n.p., July 1886, NSSB.

14. Oakley, *The Story of My Life*, chap. 8; Kansas City *Star*, April 3, 1902.
15. New York *World*, July 31, 1886.
16. See Joseph Durso, *Madison Square Garden, 100 Years of History* (New York: Simon and Schuster, 1979), 34; Lockwood, *Manhattan Moves Uptown*, 296–97; and Sell and Weybright, *Buffalo Bill and the Wild West*, 152–55.
17. New York *Herald*, November 25, 1886.
18. New York *Clipper*, March 4, 1887. The only person who wasn't impressed with Annie's new stunt was a female rider named Emma Lake, who wrote to the *Clipper* to say that she had been doing that same feat every day for the past six weeks at the West-end Training Academy in Jersey City. Emma's letter brought results. Within days, Cody and Salsbury hired her as a lady rider for the Wild West.
19. New York *Clipper*, December 11, 1886, March 12, 1887.
20. That Annie could perform horseback stunts from various positions was confirmed by the Newark (N.J.) *Sunday Call*, November 6, 1892. "It seemingly [makes] no difference to her whether she sits upright on the horse, lies extended, or faces forward or backward," the paper said. "Her shots from under a horse's neck made with the animal on a run would cause a Comanche to turn green with envy." The Hardy sisters often drew for London's *Sporting and Dramatic News*.
21. Newark (N.J.) *Sunday Call*, n.d., AOSB 1893–95. The incident on the elevator occurred in the winter of 1894–95 while Annie was in England starring in the play, *Miss Rora*.
22. London *Evening News*, June 10, 1887.
23. Oakley, *The Story of My Life*, chap. 8.
24. Ibid.
25. See ibid.; and New York *Clipper*, October 16, 1886. In her autobiography, Annie Oakley confused the date of the Newton fair with an appearance she made a week later at Oak Point, New York, on October 16, 1886. She was unable to shoot at Oak Point because of the stitches in her hand.
26. Dayton (Ohio) *Daily News*, May 30, 1926; Annie Oakley to the New York *Tribune*, February 8, 1917, AOSB 1912–on.
27. See Philadelphia *Item*, December 30, 1888; and "Camp Sketches," n.p., August 13, 1887, AOSB 1887–91. This match took place in Danville, Illinois, on March 10, 1884.
28. Oakley, *The Story of My Life*, chap. 8.
29. See *Shooting and Fishing*, March 18, 1893; and unidentified clipping, AOSB 1887–91.
30. Oakley, *The Story of My Life*, chap. 8. Joseph Shaw was Susan Moses's third husband. Her second husband, Daniel Brumbaugh, died on November 4, 1870. Susan married Shaw on November 25, 1874. Joseph Shaw died on April 25, 1887, less than a month after Annie left for England.

Chapter 10: The Magical Year in London

1. See *New York Times*, April 1, 1887; "Bon Voyage," n.p., April [1?], 1887, Johnny Baker scrapbooks, hereafter referred to as JBSB; Walsh, *The Making of Buffalo Bill*, 263–65.
2. New York *Tribune*, April 30, 1887; London *Times*, April 15, 1887; and London *Daily News*, April 16, 1887.
3. See the *Illustrated London News*, April 16, 1887; London *Morning Post*, April 12, May 5, 1887; London *Daily News*, April 15, 18, 1887; and London *Times*, May 10, 1887.
4. London *Evening News and Telephone*, May 10, 1887; and London *Daily Telegraph*, May 10, 1887.

5. Walsh, *The Making of Buffalo Bill*, 266. Everyone seemed pleased with the Wild West except the Earl's Court neighbors, who complained about the traffic and said that their houses were peppered with shot and fragments of glass balls from the Wild West's fancy shooters. *Bat* (London), October 4, 1887.

6. See London *Daily Telegraph*, April 29, 1887; London *Times*, April 29, 1887; London *Morning Post*, May 5, 1887; and *Encyclopaedia Britannica*, 1974 ed., s.v. "Alexandra."

7. See "A Few Glimpses Behind the Scenes," Knoxville (Tenn.) *Sentinel*, May 1, 1899; Oakley, *The Story of My Life*, chap. 9; London *Daily Chronicle*, May 6, 1887; "Camp Sketches," n.p., August 13, 1887, AOSB 1887–91; and unidentified clipping, AOSB 1921–25.

8. See London *Daily Chronicle*, May 6, 1887; London *Daily Telegraph*, May 6, 1887; London *Times*, May 6, 1887; and Oakley, *The Story of My Life*, chap. 9.

9. See Manchester newspaper (name unknown), April 28, 1887, Johnny Baker scrapbook; *Pall Mall Gazette*, April 26, 1887; *Echo*, April 27, 1887; London *Daily Telegraph*, April 22, 1887; and London *Sunday Times*, May 8, 1887.

10. *Court and Society Review*, April 27, 1887; New Castle (England) *Chronicle*, April 30, 1887; *Eastern Daily Press*, April 25, 1887; *Dramatic Review*, n.d., AOSB 1887–91; and unidentified clipping, JBSB 1887. The St. Stephens *Review* of May 6, 1887, said that Cody's mail was averaging more than a thousand letters a day, so many that he didn't bother to open them all.

11. Springfield (Mass.) *Union*, October 26, 1887.

12. See *Referee* (London), n.d., AOSB 1887–91; *Rifle*, n.d. AOSB 1887–91; London *Evening News*, April 19, June 10, 1887; *Sportsman*, May 4, 1887; *Bat*, September 27, 1887; *Rod and Gun*, n.d., AOSB 1887–91. Over the years, reporters would speak of her as almost childlike in her winning ways, and many commented on her girlish voice and personal magnetism.

13. *Topical Times*, May 14, 1887.

14. See New York *World*, January 8, 1888; and Oakley, *The Story of My Life*, chap. 10. Over the years she would receive thousands of letters from admirers (and a few cranks), and many proposals of marriage, mostly from men she didn't even know. "When I first went with the Wild West I used to get five or six proposals of marriage a week, but now I don't get so many," she told the Knoxville (Tenn.) *Sentinel* on May 1, 1899. "I suppose people have found out that it did them no good." For Frank's duties with the Wild West show, see the Toledo (Ohio) *Blade*, August 15, [1899?], AOSB 1896–1901.

15. Toledo (Ohio) *Blade*, August 15, [1899?], AOSB 1896–1901.

16. See Greensboro (N.C.) *Daily News*, December 30, 1923; and *American Field*, n.d., AOSB 1893–95; Swartwout, *Missie*, 141.

17. *Rifle*, n.d., AOSB 1887–91; Springfield (Ohio) *Daily Union*, October 29, 1887; and *American Field*, November 19, 1887 (quotation).

18. "Camp sketches," n.p., August 13, 1887, AOSB 1887–91.

19. *Society Times and Tribune* (London), July 16, 1887; *Rod and Gun*, n.d., AOSB 1887–91, and Oakley, *The Story of My Life*, chap. 10.

20. Oakley, *The Story of My Life*, chap. 10.

21. See the *Truth* (London), May 23, 1889; and Swartwout, *Missie*, 133.

22. "Camp sketches," n.p., August 13, 1887, AOSB 1887–91.

23. *Encyclopedia Americana*, 1982 ed., s.v. "Victoria."

24. See London *Times*, May 11, 12, 1887; *London Illustrated News*, May 21, 1887; London *Daily Telegraph*, May 12, 1887; Pinehurst (N.C.) *Outlook*, February 3, 1917; Chicago *Inter Ocean*, June 7, 1896; *ERA* (London), May 16, 1887; and Philadelphia *Item*, April 6, 1888.

25. Russell, *The Lives and Legends of Buffalo Bill*, 331.

26. Philadelphia *Public Ledger*, May 18, 1919.

27. See *St. Stephens Review* (England), May 6, 1887; *Referee* (London), n.d., AOSB 1887-91; London *Evening News*, May 10, 1887; *American Field*, n.d., AOSB 1887-91; and Oakley, "Powders I Have Known."
28. Frank Butler to *American Field*, n.d., AOSB 1887-91.
29. Charles Lancaster, *Illustrated Treatise on the Art of Shooting*, 4th ed. (London: McCorquodale, 1892).
30. See Frank Butler, letter to editor, n.p., n.d., AOSB 1887-91; and *American Field*, n.d., AOSB 1887-91.
31. Oakley, *The Story of My Life*, chap. 9.
32. See Lancaster, *Illustrated Treatise on the Art of Shooting;* T. T. Cartwright to *American Field*, n.d., AOSB 1887-91; Milton J. Shapiro, *A Beginner's Book of Sporting Guns and Hunting* (New York: Messner, 1961), 40-41; and Annie Oakley to Charles Lancaster, December 8, 1888, quoted in Lancaster, *Illustrated Treatise on the Art of Shooting*, 224. Too much "drop" meant that the stock of Annie's gun was bent at too great an angle to suit her body. When she pressed her cheek to the stock, her eye did not align perfectly down the barrel and, consequently, her aim was off.
33. *Rod and Gun*, November 22, 1890.
34. See Frank Butler to *American Field*, 1887, AOSB 1887-91; *Field* (London), June 18, 1887; *Item*, 1887, AOSB 1887-91; London *Evening News*, June 13, 1887; *Sporting Life* (London), June 13, 1887; *Shooting Times*, n.d., AOSB 1887-91.
35. "Miss Oakley's Pigeon Shooting," n.p., n.d., AOSB 1887-91.
36. See Pinehurst (N.C.) *Outlook*, February 3, 1917; London *Evening News*, June 17, 1887; Oakley, *The Story of My Life*, chap. 9; and Walsh, *The Making of Buffalo Bill*, 272.
37. Frank Butler to *American Field*, n.d., AOSB 1887-91.
38. See London *Evening News*, July 19, 1887; *Bat* (London), July 26, 1887; and *Weekly Dispatch*, July 24, 1887.
39. See London *Evening News*, July 21, 1887; *The Society Times* (London), July 30, 1887; and London *Sunday Chronicle*, July 24, 1887.
40. Glasgow *Evening News*, December 1, 1891.
41. See *American Field*, [1887?], AOSB 1887-91; and London *Evening News*, May 10, 1887.
42. Dayton (Ohio) *Sunday Journal*, December 14, 1924.
43. Oakley, *The Story of My Life*, chap. 9.
44. See "The Wild West Rampant" and "Miss Annie Oakley," *Breeder and Sportsman*, August [1887?], AOSB 1887-91; and *Shooting Times*, October 14, 1887. Annie's grudge against Lillian Smith lasted at least until February 1889 when, through the pages of the *American Field*, she refused to accept a shooting challenge from Lillian, who apparently was calling herself the champion. "I will say that for many reasons which it is not necessary to mention here, it is impossible for me to enter in any competition with Miss Smith," Annie wrote. "The word 'champion' I have never used myself. . . . If the title benefits her any . . . I hope she will make better use of it than she did when she visited Wimbledon" (unidentified clipping, AOSB 1887-91).
45. Sacramento (Calif.) *Record Union*, quoted in "Miss Annie Oakley," *Breeder and Sportsman*, August [1887?], AOSB 1887-91.
46. Carter also said Lillian lied about breaking twenty balls on a swinging target inside of thirty seconds. He kept track over a number of days. "The lowest time Miss Smith made on any day I was present was 35 seconds," he wrote. One day it took her forty seconds, and then she hit only eighteen balls. Almost every day, Carter wrote, two or three balls dropped off the target at one shot, an occurrence that apparently was noticed by other spectators in the arena because "there was some hissing."
47. Oakley, *The Story of My Life*, chap. 10.
48. London *Evening News*, October 31, 1887.

49. Unidentified clipping, AOSB 1887–91.
50. *Topical Times* (London), October 22, 1887.

Chapter 11: Riding with Pawnee Bill

1. See unidentified clipping, AOSB 1887–91; Philadelphia *Item*, July 8, 1888; New York *Clipper*, May 5, June 9, 1888.
2. See Pinehurst (N.C.) *Outlook*, March 9, 1918; *American Field*, n.d., AOSB 1887–91; Rochester (N.Y.) *Post-Express*, September 5, 1888; Easton (Pa.) *Express*, January 31, 1888.
3. Pinehurst (N.C.) *Outlook*, March 9, 1918.
4. See New York *Herald*, January 30, 1888; Rochester (N.Y.) *Post-Express*, September 5, 1888; New York *Star*, February 23, 1888; New York *Clipper*, March 3, 1888; Philadelphia *Item*, n.d., AOSB 1887–91; *American Field*, n.d., AOSB 1887–91; Pinehurst (N.C.) *Outlook*, March 9, 1918; and Oakley, *The Story of My Life*, chap. 11.
5. See Boston *Daily Globe*, April 20, 1888; Toronto *Empire*, n.d., AOSB 1887–91; Newark (N.J.) *Sunday Call*, April 21, 1889; Reading (Pa.) *Eagle*, April 14, 1889; *American Field*, April 13, 1889; New York *Herald*, n.d., AOSB 1887–91; *Times and Dispatch* (no city listed), April 13, 1889, AOSB 1887–91; and unidentified clipping, AOSB 1887–91.
6. "Miss Oakley Breaks a Record," Philadelphia *Item*, December 19, 1888; Toronto *Forest and Farm*, October 20, 1888 (quotation).
7. Baltimore *American*, October 31, 1888.
8. See Philadelphia *Commercial Gazette*, June 17, 1888; New York *Tribune*, November 30, 1888; and "Trap and Trigger," n.p., n.d., AOSB 1887–91.
9. *Dictionary of American Biography*, s.v. "Tony Pastor."
10. See "Tony Pastor and His Great Co." scrapbooks, fall season 1887, and various accounts in AOSB 1887–91.
11. *New York Times*, May 21, 22, 1888.
12. Oakley, *The Story of My Life*, chap. 11. For Lillie's canceled Belgian tour, see Don Russell, *The Wild West: A History of the Wild West Shows* (Fort Worth: Amon Carter Museum, 1970), 32–33.
13. See Glenn Shirley, *Pawnee Bill: A Biography of Major Gordon W. Lillie* (Lincoln: University of Nebraska Press, 1958); and Russell, *The Lives and Legends of Buffalo Bill*, 296–97.
14. Unidentified clipping, AOSB 1887–91.
15. See Shirley, *Pawnee Bill*, 115–19; and Philadelphia *Daily News*, July 4, 1888.
16. See Philadelphia *Times*, July 31, 1888; Philadelphia *Public Ledger and Daily Transcript*, July 31, 1888; Philadelphia *Inquirer*, July 31, 1888; and Camden (N.J.) *Courier*, July 31, 1888.
17. Oakley, *The Story of My Life*, chap. 12.
18. Ibid.
19. Pawnee Bill advertisement, AOSB 1887–91; Shirley, *Pawnee Bill*, 124.
20. Frank Butler, letter to the editor, n.p., n.d., AOSB 1887–91.
21. For descriptions of Annie Oakley in *Deadwood Dick*, see New York *Clipper*, December 8, 1888, February 2, 1889; Bridgeton (N.J.) *Morning Star*, December 22, 1888; Philadelphia *Press*, December 25, 1888; Philadelphia *Inquirer*, December 25, 1888; *North American*, December 25, 1888; Paterson (N.J.) *Morning Call*, January 8, 1889; Paterson (N.J.) *Daily Press*, January 8, 1889; West Chester (Pa.) *Local News*, January 5, 1889; Baltimore *Sun*, January 15, 1889; Baltimore *American*, January 15, 1889; Oakley, *The Story of My Life*, chap. 12; unidentified clipping, AOSB 1887–91.
22. Baltimore *Sun*, February 26, 1889.

23. Swartwout, *Missie*, 163.
24. For the Newark rifle club, see Newark (N.J.) *Journal*, February 20, 1889; Newark (N.J.) *Evening News*, February 20, 1889; and Philadelphia *Item*, n.d., AOSB 1887–91. For the Butte rifle club, see letter to editor, *American Field*, n.d., AOSB 1887–91; and for the sermon, unidentified clipping, AOSB 1887–91.

Chapter 12: A Postcard from Paris

1. Joseph Harriss, *The Tallest Tower: Eiffel and the Belle Epoque* (Boston: Houghton Mifflin, 1975).
2. Unidentified clipping, AOSB 1887–91.
3. See New York *Herald-Paris*, May 12, 1889; and *New York Times*, April 28, 1889.
4. See Oakley, *The Story of My Life*, chap. 12; and Pinehurst (N.C.) *Outlook*, Early Season Number, 1917.
5. Oakley, *Powders I Have Used*, 5.
6. New York *Herald-Paris*, July 28, 1889.
7. See *New York Times*, August 28, 1889; untitled clipping, Bangor, Maine, n.p., July 1906, AOSB 1905–8; and report from "The wanderer," n.p., August 29, 1889, AOSB 1887–91.
8. See New York *World*, January 8, 1888; untitled clipping, Bangor, Maine, n.p., July 1906, AOSB 1905–8; *American Field*, n.d., AOSB 1887–91; Oakley, *The Story of My Life*, chap. 15; and Brighton (England) *Guardian*, October 14, 1891.
9. Oakley, *The Story of My Life*, chap. 13. For the king of Senegal, see "Notes from Paris," n.p., July 19, 1889, AOSB 1887–91; and Brighton (England) *Guardian*, October 14, 1891.
10. "Shooting Notes from Paris," Frank Butler to *Shooting and Fishing*, November 6, 1889; Oakley, *Powders I Have Used*, 5.
11. W. W. Greener, *The Gun, and Its Development* (New York: Bonanza Books, 1881; rpt., 1910), 537. Ira Paine died in Paris on September 10, 1889, of inflammation of the bowels. "Poor Ira," Frank wrote home. "He left a reputation that no one in his line will ever eclipse." Frank said Paine had visited him and Annie only two days before he died.
12. "Notes from Paris," n.p., July 19, 1889, AOSB 1887–91.
13. See unidentified clipping, AOSB 1893–95; *Kentish* (England) *Express and Ashford News*, December 20, 1890; *Shooting Times*, December 27, 1890; and London *Field*, December 27, 1890. According to newspaper accounts, the targets varied from a playing card to a calling card to a photograph. An ace of hearts target, pasted in Annie's scrapbooks, measured three and a half by two and three eighths inches and sported a little picture of Annie in the left corner. The heart itself, in the middle of the card, was about three quarters of an inch square. She perforated this particular target in New York on March 10, 1893. According to printing on the card, she hit the heart with twenty-five shots in twenty-seven seconds at a distance of twelve yards. The card showed that none of Annie's bullets had missed the heart by more than one quarter of an inch.
14. Annie Oakley to *American Field*, n.d., AOSB 1887–91.
15. See Oakley, *The Story of My Life*, chap. 14; and Frank Butler, "Three Months with Italian Sportsmen" *Shooting and Fishing*, n.d., AOSB 1887–91.
16. See Pinehurst (N.C.) *Outlook*, Winter Golf Number, 1917; and n.p., April 23, 1890, AOSB 1887–91.
17. Oakley, *Powders I Have Used*, 6.
18. Oakley, *The Story of My Life*, chap. 15.
19. Ibid., chap. 13.
20. See Swartwout, *Missie*, 177; and Oakley, *The Story of My Life*, chap. 13.
21. Pinehurst (N.C.) *Outlook*, December 23, 1916.

22. For Naples, see Butler, "Three Months with Italian Sportsmen"; for Annie's ten-dollar gift, Cardiff (Wales) *Evening Express*, October 2, 1891.
23. William F. Cody to Annie Oakley and Frank Butler, January 27, 1891, on file at Brigham Young University Library, Provo, Utah.
24. Annie Oakley, letter to *Shooting and Fishing*, January 25, 1891. For reports of her death, see *Shooting and Fishing*, December 31, 1890; Cincinnati *Enquirer*, December 31, 1890; Cincinnati *Commercial*, January 2, 1891; Baltimore *American*, January 11, 1891; New York *Clipper*, January 17, 1891; New York *Daily Graphic*, n.d., AOSB 1887–91; "Death of Annie Oakley," *Weekly Breeder and Sportsman*, n.d., AOSB 1887–91; and unidentified clipping, AOSB 1887–91.
25. Frank Butler letter to Al Bandle, "She is Not Dead," n.p., n.d., AOSB 1887–91; and *American Field*, n.d., AOSB 1887–91. The first paper to report Annie's death apparently confused her name with that of Alice Oatley, an American singer who had died.
26. Pinehurst (N.C.) *Outlook*, February 17, 1917.
27. Ibid.; Philadelphia *Public Ledger*, May 18, 1919.
28. *Shooting Times*, n.d., AOSB 1887–91.
29. See Edinburgh *Evening Dispatch*, November 11, 1891; Manchester (England) *Courier*, July 21, 1891; *Eastern Bells*, December 1891; and "'Little Sure Shot' the Winner," n.p., n.d., AOSB 1887–91.
30. See *Belgian News*, May 29, 1891; London *Weekly Dispatch*, May 8, 1892; London *Weekly Times and Echo*, May 8, 1892; *Mistress and Maid*, May 11, 1892; London *Daily Chronicle*, June 7, 1892; *The People*, n.d., AOSB 1887–91; and unidentified clipping, AOSB 1887–91.
31. *Kensington Society*, July 14, 1892.
32. *Cycle Record*, September 3, 1892; London *Figaro*, May 11, 1892.
33. See Streatham *News*, June 11, 1892; *Mistress and Maid*, May 11, 1892; *Daily Chronicle*, June 7, 1892; *Daily Graphic and Penny Illustrated News*, n.d., AOSB 1887–91; and unidentified clipping, AOSB 1887–91.
34. *Moonshine*, October 1, 1892; and "Ally Sloper's Half-Holiday," n.p., n.d., AOSB 1887–91.
35. Cardiff (Wales) *Evening Express*, September 28, 1891; Brighton (England) *Guardian*, October 14, 1891.
36. New York *World*, January 8, 1888.

Chapter 13: A Press Sweetheart

1. New York *Press*, August 11, 1894.
2. *Forest and Stream*, n.d., AOSB 1887–91; Cincinnati *Post*, December 26, 1899.
3. *World* (no city listed), June 29, 1893. The cowboys were listed as receiving four pounds, or $20. For the $150 a week figure, see Knoxville (Tenn.) *Sentinel*, May 1, 1899; and Scranton (Pa.) *Truth*, March 16, 1904. For the average worker's pay, see *Historical Statistics of the United States, Colonial Times to 1970, Part I* (Washington, D.C.: U.S. Department of Commerce, Bureau of the Census, 1975), 165. Accounts differ on how much Annie Oakley made. The *London Tid-Bits*, May 28, 1892, said she made $375 a week; and the Greenville *Daily Tribune*, March 19, 1895, AOSB 1896–1901, said she made "about $500 a week." However, the $150 figure seems more reliable. In the Scranton *Truth*, she was testifying under oath, and in the Knoxville *Sentinel* she is quoted directly.
4. Fellows and Freeman, *This Way to the Big Show*, 72. For the *Clipper* story, New York *Clipper*, October 16, 1886, February 11, 1888. The *Clipper* was hard to come by in Europe, and Annie had been delighted to see a man reading it in a train car in Germany. When she let him know that she wanted to look at it, "he promptly and curtly let me know that I would have to pay four marks (about 96 cents) for it," Annie said. "No sooner said

than done. That amount I did pay, and quickly, too. I was determined to have it, and that at almost any price."

5. See London *Evening News*, April 19, 1887; Newark (N.J.) *Sunday News*, May 11, 1902; *Sydenham, Forest Hill, and Crystal Palace Times*, May 28, 1887.

6. Swartwout, *Missie*, 84–85.

7. New York *Tribune*, June 28, 1922.

8. New York *World*, October 29, 1892; Sussex (N.J.) *Register*, June 25, 1893; unidentified clipping, AOSB 1893–95, quoting Kansas City *Journal*, January 12, 1893.

9. See "Amy Leslie at the Fair," Chicago *Daily News*, May 2, 1893; and Chicago *Inter Ocean*, April 27, May 2, 1893.

10. See Emmett Dedmon, *Fabulous Chicago: A Great City's History and People* (New York: Atheneum, 1953; enlarged ed., 1981), 220–37; Edo McCullough, *World's Fair Midways* (New York: Exposition Press, 1966), 41–49; Chicago *Record*, May 22, 1893; Chicago *Herald*, October 22, 1893; and Chicago *Times*, October 27, 1893.

11. See Chicago *Herald*, April 27, 1893; and Chicago *Inter Ocean* April 27, 1893.

12. Chicago *Telegram*, August 20, 1893; Walsh, *The Making of Buffalo Bill*, 303–4; Chicago *Globe*, October 10, 1893; and Chicago *Times*, September 13, 1893.

13. Amy Leslie, Chicago *Daily News*, n.d., AOSB 1893–95.

14. Edward T. James, ed., *Notable American Women 1607–1950: A Biographical Dictionary* (Cambridge, Mass.: The Belknap Press of Harvard University Press, 1971), vol. 2, s.v. "Amy Leslie."

15. Joliet (Ill.) *Daily News*, August 27, 1903, quoting Chicago *Daily News*.

16. Amy Leslie, *Some Players* (Chicago: Herbert S. Stone, 1899), 149–66, 396–415, 549–62.

17. See "Conning Tower" column, New York *Tribune*, January 11, 1917, and Annie Oakley's response, February 8, 1917, AOSB 1912–on.

18. "Notes of the Rod and Gun," *Gameland*, March 1893; London *Evening News*, June 10, 1887.

19. Joliet (Ill.) *Daily News*, August 27, 1903, quoting Chicago *Daily News*.

20. Unidentified clipping, AOSB 1893–95; *Forest and Stream*, July 15, 1893.

21. Greenville (Ohio) *Courier*, November 4, 1893; *American Field*, n.d., AOSB 1893–95; Chicago *Inter Ocean*, September 10, 1893; New York *Commercial Advertiser*, June 9, 1894.

Chapter 14: At Home in Nutley

1. See Ann A. Troy, ed., *Nutley, Yesterday, Today* (Nutley, N.J.: The Nutley Historical Society, 1961), esp. 84–90, 122–26; Sheryl Weinstein, "When Nutley Was Bloomsbury," *New Jersey Monthly* (December 1980): 139–40; New York *Herald*, March 11, 1894; and Harry Emerson Wildes, *Twin Rivers: The Raritan and the Passaic* (New York: Farrar & Rinehart, 1943).

2. Newark *Sunday Call*, November 6, 1892; n.p., November 26, 1892, AOSB 1887–91; Nutley (N.J.) *Sun*, March 13, 1936.

3. See New York *News*, April 16, 1894; "Electricity at the Wild West," *Electrical World*, September 15, 1894.

4. New York *Morning Journal*, June 16, 1894; Troy, ed., *Nutley, Yesterday, Today*, 198–99. The no-closet legend also may have stemmed from another house Annie had built much later, which had no *projecting* closets.

5. Havighurst, *Annie Oakley of the Wild West*, 161.

6. Unidentified clipping, AOSB 1893–95; Passaic (N.J.) *Daily News*, n.d., AOSB 1893–95.

7. Nutley (N.J.) *Review*, n.d., AOSB 1893–95.

8. *Forest and Stream*, n.d., AOSB 1893-95, and July 15, 1893.
9. Gloan to *American Field*, n.d., AOSB 1893-95; Joliet (Ill.) *Daily News*, August 27, 1903, quoting Chicago *Daily News*.
10. See Newark (N.J.) *Sunday Call*, n.d., AOSB 1893-95; and *Sporting Goods Gazette*, n.d., AOSB 1893-95.
11. New York *Herald*, March 11, 1894.
12. New York *Sun*, March 25, 28, 1894.
13. For accounts of the circus, see Newark (N.J.) *Evening News*, February 2, 1894; New York *Herald*, March 11, 1894; Belleville (N.J.), n.p., March 31, 1894; Newark (N.J.) *Daily Advertiser*, March 23, 1894; New York *Tribune*, March 28, 1894; New York *World*, March 28, 1894; New York *Press*, March 28, 1894; New York *Sun*, March 25, 28, 1894; and *Harper's Weekly*, n.d., AOSB 1893-95.
14. See New York *Tribune*, May 10, 1894; Brooklyn *Eagle*, May 10, 1894; New York *Sun*, May 13, 1894; Kings County (N.Y.) *Journal*, May 12, 1894; New York *Sunday Recorder*, May 13, 1894; Brooklyn, n.p., April 15, 1894, NSSB.
15. The truth was that the three weren't living in their tents at all. Cody had taken a flat over the Eighth Ward Bank on Thirty-ninth Street, and Salsbury had rented a house on the corner of Benson Avenue and Bay Twenty-sixth Street. No one gave Annie's address, though she told the New York *Sun* that her most comfortable hours were those spent in her carpeted tent on the Wild West lot.
16. New York *World*, May 13, 1894.
17. Ibid.; New York *American and Mercury*, July 31, 1894.
18. See "Electricity and the Wild West," *Electrical World*, September 15, 1894; and Brooklyn *Standard*, July 7, 1894.
19. Ibid.
20. New York *Recorder*, n.d. [1894?], AOSB 1893-95; *Shooting and Fishing*, n.d., AOSB 1896-1901; unidentified clipping, AOSB 1896-1901; Kings County (N.Y.) *Journal*, July 18, 1894.
21. New York *Recorder*, n.d. [1894?], AOSB 1893-95.
22. New York *Commercial*, June 16, 1894.
23. See New York *Recorder*, September 25, 1894, and n.d., AOSB 1893-95; New York *Herald*, September 24, 25, 1894; Ronald W. Clark, *Edison: The Man Who Made the Future* (New York: G. P. Putnam's Sons, 1977), 176; and Matthew Josephson, *Edison* (New York: McGraw-Hill, 1959), 392-94. Annie Oakley appeared at Edison's Black Maria probably in May or November 1894. According to the New York *Recorder*, she appeared on the same day as "a bevy of Gaiety Girls" from England and El Capitaine, "the beautiful trapezist."
24. See Brooklyn *Weekly*, August 18, 1894; New York *Journal*, April 16, June 8, 1894; and New York *Tribune*, October 6, 1894.
25. Swartwout, *Missie*, 208; Russell, *The Lives and Legends of Buffalo Bill*, 378.
26. *New York Times*, October [7?], 1894; New York *Tribune*, October 7, 1894.

Chapter 15: Village on Wheels

1. Russell, *The Lives and Legends of Buffalo Bill*, 378; "Official Route of Buffalo Bill's Wild West," 1895, 1896.
2. Detroit (Mich.) n.p., n.d., NSSB.
3. Swartwout, *Missie*, 89. Cody's compartment was comfortable too. "His car is palatial," one reporter wrote. "In every nook and corner" were photos of Indian warriors and generals, and "rifles, paintings and bric-a-brac." In one conspicuous spot sat a photograph of General Nelson A. Miles, surrounded by American flags. That Cody was "a stickler for comfort" was apparent by an electric fan that whirred and a pitcher of lemonade that he kept in his tent at the showgrounds. See London (Ontario, Canada)

Press, July 10, 1887; Nashville (Tenn.) *American*, May 1, 1899; and Scranton (Pa.), n.p., May 22, 1899, NSSB.

4. Fellows and Freeman, *This Way to the Big Show*, 72.

5. See St. Louis *Globe-Democrat*, May 18, 1896; North Platte (Neb.) *Daily Telegraph*, September 3, 1898; and Milwaukee *Sentinel*, August 25, 1896.

6. Boston, n.p., June 15, 1899. NSSB.

7. See Atchison (Kans.) *Globe*, September 20, 1898; and Emporia (Kans.) *Gazette*, September 17, 1898.

8. See Philadelphia *Times*, April 25, 1895; and Waterbury (Conn.) *Democrat*, May 28, 1895.

9. Swartwout, *Missie*, 255.

10. Oakley, *Powders I Have Used*, 11.

11. *Rod and Gun*, n.d., AOSB 1887–91.

12. See Wheeling (W.Va.) *Intelligencer*, May 28, 1901; Hartford (Conn.) *Times*, May 27, 1898; and Hartford (Conn.) *Post*, May 27, 1898.

13. For the road experiences related here, see Stamford (Conn.) *Telegram*, May 24, 1898; Lawrence (Kans.) *Daily Journal*, October 2, 1900; Trinidad (Colo.) *Chronicle News*, September 10, 1898; Topeka (Kans.) n.p., September 19, 1898, NSSB; Beloit (Wis.) *Daily Free Press*, August 23, 1900; Quincy (Ill.) *Journal*, June 20, 1896; and Muskegon (Mich.) *Daily Chronicle*, August 12, 1896.

14. See Wausau (Wis.) *Weekly Record*, September 10, 1896; Detroit *Free Press*, July 30, 1900; and unidentified clipping, NSSB.

15. Manchester (N.H.) *Mirror and American*, June 4, 1897; Worcester (Mass.) *Telegram*, June 12, 1897.

16. Newark (N.J.) *Sunday News*, May 11, 1902.

17. M. B. Bailey, ed., *Buffalo Bill's Wild West Route Book* (Buffalo, N.Y.: Courier, 1896).

18. See Sioux Falls (S.D.) *Argus-Leader*, September 17, 1896; and Bailey, *Buffalo Bill's Wild West Route Book*.

19. Kansas City *Star*, October 19, 1896.

20. See unidentified clipping, AOSB 1896–1901; and Bailey, *Buffalo Bill's Wild West Route Book*.

21. Bluffton (Ind.), n.p., July 8, 1896, AOSB 1896–1901.

22. See Oakley, *The Story of My Life*, chap. 6; Swartwout, *Missie*, 207; and Bailey, *Buffalo Bill's Wild West Route Book*.

23. AOSB 1912–on.

24. Amy Leslie, Chicago *Daily News*, July 26, 1898, August 1899.

25. Chicago *Daily News*, August [31?], 1897.

26. Chillicothe (Ohio) *Daily News*, May 1, 1896.

27. Chicago *Daily News*, August [31?], 1897.

28. Knoxville (Tenn.) *Sentinel*, May 1, 1899.

Chapter 16: The Old Home Folks

1. See Hot Springs (Ark.) *Sentinel*, November 21, 1896; Hot Springs (Ark.) *News*, October 30, 1896; and unidentified clipping, AOSB 1896–1901.

2. *American Field*, n.d., AOSB 1896–1901.

3. "A Quail Hunt in Virginia," *American Field*, n.d., AOSB 1887–91.

4. Walter Swain to *American Field*, n.d., AOSB 1896–1901. Swain added that he had seen "many a walnut and pebble torn to atoms" by Annie's guns.

5. Oakley, *The Story of My Life*, chap. 10; unidentified clipping, AOSB 1896–1901.

6. *Gameland*, March 1893.

7. Swartwout, *Missie*, 200–201, 205–6, 224, 241–42. Annie's brother John had mar-

ried in 1884 and eventually moved his family to Oklahoma. Annie's sisters Elizabeth and Lydia had died in 1881 and 1882, both of tuberculosis, so Hulda, Sarah Ellen and Emily were her only surviving sisters.

8. Swartwout, *Missie*, 242; Rush Blakeley interview, May 13, 1981.

9. Swartwout, *Missie*, 206.

10. See Greenville (Ohio) *Daily Advocate*, November 30, 1896; n.p., February 11, 1895, AOSB 1896–1901; unidentified clipping, AOSB 1896–1901; Swartwout, *Missie*, 271.

11. Swartwout, *Missie*, 233.

12. Unidentified clipping, AOSB 1896–1901.

13. *Forest and Stream*, January 29, 1909.

14. Newark (N.J.) *Evening News*, n.d., AOSB 1902–8.

15. See *Ohio State Journal*, August 30, 1906; and Freehold (N.J.), n.p., n.d., AOSB 1902–8.

16. Greenville (Ohio) *Advocate*, July 23, 1968; Darke County (Ohio) *Early Bird Supplement*, July 20, 1981.

17. John E. Vance, "Informal Information about Our Town," n.d., Greenville (Ohio) Public Library.

18. See Greenville (Ohio) *Daily Advocate*, July 26, 1900, and n.d., AOSB 1896–1901; Greenville (Ohio) *Courier*, n.d., AOSB 1896–1901; and unidentified clipping, AOSB 1896–1901.

19. New York *World*, January 8, 1888; *Forest and Stream*, n.d., AOSB 1887–91; Charlotte (N.C.) *Observer*, July 9, 1924.

Chapter 17: End of the Road

1. See New York *Telegraph*, April 3, 1901; Freeport (Ill.) *Daily Journal*, August 24, 1900; and Scranton (Pa.), n.p., June 7, 1901, NSSB.

2. Washington, D.C., *Times*, April 25, 1901; n.p., June 1, 1901, NSSB; Chicago, n.p., July 16, 1901, NSSB.

3. Wheeling (W.Va.) *Intelligencer*, May 27, 1901.

4. N.p., June 1, 1901, NSSB.

5. The account of the train wreck is based on Charlotte (N.C.) *News*, October 28, 29, 1901; and Charlotte (N.C.) *Observer*, October 28, 29, 30, 1901.

6. All were hurt when they jumped before the collision. Williams suffered several broken ribs; Rollins had internal injuries; Cranford, a broken arm and many bruises; and Malone, a wrenched back and bruises. All except Malone were aboard the engine pulling the show train.

7. Evansville (Ind.) *Journal News*, June 18, 1908.

8. *American Field*, n.d., AOSB 1902–8.

9. Ibid.

10. See New York *Evening Sun*, January 17, 1902; and unidentified clipping, AOSB 1902–8.

11. See "Annie Oakley's Hot Bath," *Sporting Life*, quoting Amy Leslie, n.d., AOSB 1896–1901; and Amy Leslie, "Plays and Players," Chicago *Daily News*, n.d., AOSB 1902–8.

12. See New York *Evening Sun*, January 17, 1902; and unidentified clipping, AOSB 1902–8.

13. Unidentified clipping, AOSB 1902–8.

Chapter 18: The Western Girl

1. See Rochester (N.Y.) *Union and Advertiser*, January 6, 1903; Springfield (Mass.) *Republican*, December 2, 1902; Scranton (Pa.) *Tribune*, November 27, 1902; Hartford

(Conn.) *Daily Courant*, December 5, 1902; Louisville (Ky.) *Courier-Journal*, February 22, 1903; New York *Dramatic News*, October 4, 1902; Wilkes-Barre (Pa.) *Record*, n.d., AOSB 1902–8; *The Western Girl* program, AOSB 1902–8; and unidentified clipping, AOSB 1902–8.

2. See Pontypridd (England) *Chronicle*, January 12, 1895; Nottingham (England) *Evening News*, February 5, 1895; and Gloucester (England) *Chronicle*, February 2, 1895; South Wales (Great Britain) *Echo*, January 8, 1895; South Wales (Great Britain) *Argus*, January 16, 1895, and n.d., AOSB 1893–95; London *Topical Times*, n.d., AOSB 1893–95; London *Referee*, n.d., AOSB 1893–95; Newark (N.J.) *Sunday Call*, n.d., AOSB 1893–95; and unidentified clipping, AOSB 1893–95.

3. Rochester (N.Y.) *Democrat and Chronicle*, January 6, 1903.

4. See Newark (N.J.) *Evening News*, n.d., AOSB 1902–8; and Greenville (Ohio) *Daily Advocate*, April 17, 1903.

5. Wilmington (Del.) *Every Morning*, November 1, 1905.

6. See Brooklyn *Standard Union*, n.d., AOSB 1903–5; and T. C. Quinn to Mrs. Frank E. Butler, August 22, 1903, AOSB 1903–5.

7. Joliet (Ill.) *Daily News*, October 3, 1906.

8. *Forest and Stream*, April 30, 1910; Piqua (Ohio) *Leader Dispatch*, November 26, 1904.

9. See Joliet (Ill.) *Daily News*, October 3, 1906; Union City (Ind.), n.p., August 15, 1912, AOSB 1903–5; Swartwout, *Missie*, 264–65; "Make Futile Attempt to Find Some Flaw in Her Reputation," n.p., n.d., AOSB 1903–5; Greenville (Ohio), n.p., n.d., AOSB 1903–5.

10. Amy Leslie Buck to Annie Oakley, AOSB 1903–5.

11. See Newark (N.J.) *Evening News*[?], April 7, 1904, AOSB 1903–5; Rochester (N.Y.) *Post Express*, December 3, 1904; New Orleans *Item*, n.d., AOSB 1903–5; Scranton (Pa.) *Truth*, March 16, 1904; Scranton (Pa.), n.p., April 7, 1904, AOSB 1903–5; and unidentified clipping, AOSB 1903–5.

12. New Orleans *Item*, n.d., AOSB 1903–5.

13. *Forest and Stream*, January 29, 1909. During the Chicago trial, Annie had stayed in Joliet with Frank's brother, Will, who was "a prominent businessman" at A. J. Stoos & Co. on Hunter Avenue.

14. Scranton (Pa.) *Truth*, March 16, 1904.

15. Unidentified clipping, AOSB 1903–5. Because Frank Butler was a good storyteller and because no other reference to this incident appears, it is possible Frank made the story up.

16. Scranton (Pa.) *Times*, n.d., AOSB 1903–5.

17. Swartwout, *Missie*, 265.

18. Piqua (Ohio) *Leader Dispatch*, November 26, 1904.

19. Swartwout, *Missie*, 264; *Forest and Stream*, April 30, 1910.

20. *Forest and Stream*, April 30, 1910.

21. Hoboken (N.J.) *Hudson Observer* to Mrs. Frank Butler, August 26 (no year given), AOSB 1912–on.

Chapter 19: At the Traps

1. See *New York Times*, December 31, 1916, quoted in Gene Brown, ed., *New York Times Encyclopedia of Sport*, 15 vols. (New York: Arno Press, 1979), 10:38–52.

2. See Martin Rywell, *Fell's Collector's Guide to American Antique Firearms* (New York: Frederick Fell, 1963), 173–74; and *The ATA Hall of Fame and Trapshooting Museum*, Vandalia, Ohio: Amateur Trapshooting Association, n.d.

3. See *Ohio State Journal*, August 30, 1906; Freehold (N.J.), n.p., n.d., AOSB 1902–8; *Forest and Stream*, January 29, 1909.

4. Unidentified clipping, AOSB 1905–8; Annie Oakley, "Sports for Women," *Shooting and Fishing*, Christmas number, [1896?]; and "A Big Day for Trap Shooters," Paterson (N.J.), n.p., n.d., AOSB 1905–8. Frank entered and won the New Jersey State Sportsmen's Association tournament on June 7, 1905, a rainy Wednesday afternoon, at the Rahway Gun Club. Despite a steady northeast gale, Frank downed forty-eight of fifty targets to take home the state medal. See Newark (N.J.) *Evening News*, June 8, 1905; and Newark (N.J.) *Advertiser*, June 8, 1905.

5. See various clippings, AOSB 1902–8.

6. See Kansas City *Star*, March 30–April 4, 1902.

7. See *American Field*, April 13, 1889; and Philadelphia *Public Ledger*, October 28, 1923.

8. Oakley, *A Brief Sketch of Her Career and Notes on Shooting*.

9. London *Field*, July 2, 1887.

10. Buffalo (N.Y.) *Courier*, August 25, 1895.

11. "Miss Annie Oakley," *Shooting and Fishing*, November [1892?], AOSB 1893–95.

12. Oakley, *A Brief Sketch of Her Career and Notes on Shooting*.

13. The twelve-thousand-dollar purse at the Grand American Handicap was divided among sixty-three shooters, but Annie Oakley was not among them. Neither was Mrs. Johnston or Lillian Smith.

14. N.p., n.d., AOSB 1912–on; *The ATA Hall of Fame and Trapshooting Museum*.

15. See Dubois (Pa.) *Morning Journal*, April 20, 1909; and Bridgeton (N.J.) *Evening News*, July 10, [1905?], AOSB 1905–8.

16. See Rumford Falls (Maine) *Times*, August 26, 1905; Lewiston (Maine) *Saturday Journal*, August 19, 1905; Morristown (N.J.) *Daily Record*, September [?], 1907, AOSB 1905–8; and Escanaba (Mich.) n.p., n.d., AOSB 1905–8.

17. Fred Stone, *Rolling Stone* (New York: McGraw-Hill, 1945), 99–110, 131–43.

18. Ibid., 148, 149.

19. See Will Rogers, *The Autobiography of Will Rogers*, selected and ed. Donald Day (Boston: Houghton Mifflin, 1926), 184; Richard M. Ketchum, *Will Rogers, His Life and Times* (New York: American Heritage Publishing, 1973), 126, 309; and Stone, *Rolling Stone*, 170, 223.

20. Amityville (N.Y.) *Record*, n.d., AOSB 1905–8.

21. *American Field*, n.d., AOSB 1905–8.

Chapter 20: The Final Stand

1. N.p., February 11, 1895, AOSB 1896–1901.

2. See Newark (N.J.) *Advertiser*, February 16, 1908; and unidentified clipping, AOSB 1902–8.

3. New York *Press*, March 2, 1911.

4. See *Forest and Stream*, January 29, 1910; and n.p., December 25, 1909, AOSB 1905–8.

5. Don Russell, speech before the Chicago Corral of "The Westerners," January 26, 1970, quoted in "The Golden Age of Wild West Shows," *Bandwagon*, n.d.; Frank E. Butler to *Billboard*, May 10, 1919; and Newark (N.J.) *Sunday Call*, October 1, 1916.

6. Richmond (Ind.) *Palladium and Sun-Telegram*, March 21, 1911.

7. *Billboard*, n.d., AOSB 1912–on. Frank resigned from the Union Metallic Cartridge Co. in January 1910.

8. See Frank J. Pouska, "Young Buffalo Wild West Show," *The Bandwagon* (May–June 1959): 15–16; Pouska, "Young Buffalo Wild West Show Part II," *The Bandwagon* (May–June 1960): 5–6, 19–20; Russell, "The Golden Age of Wild West Shows"; and Young Buffalo Wild West program, 1911.

9. London (Ontario, Canada) *Free Press*, July 29, 1911; Nashville *Tennessean*, n.d., AOSB 1912–on; Hartford (Conn.) *Post*, June 13, 1912; *Billboard*, n.d., AOSB 1912–on.

10. Detroit *Free Press*, May 14, 1912.

11. Utica (N.Y.) *Press*, n.d.; see Akron (Ohio) *Press*, 1912; Oxford (Pa.) *News*, n.d.; Litchfield (Ill.), n.p., September 20, 1912; Union City (Ind.) *Eagle*, n.d.; Peoria (Ill.) *Star*, n.d.; Nashville *Tennessean*, n.d., all AOSB 1912–on.

12. Greenville (Ohio) *Courier*, May 3, 1913.

13. Greenville, Ohio, *Advocate*, n.d., AOSB 1912–on; Frank Butler to Robert H. Matthews, n.d., AOSB 1912–on.

14. Irene Patterson Black interview, October 1990; Newark (N.J.) *Sunday News*, May 11, 1902; New York *Tribune*, June 28, 1922. Annie had tried to attend school on occasion. After her first season with Buffalo Bill's Wild West, for example, she had spent at least part of the winter of 1886 going to school in Hagerman, Ohio. New York *Clipper*, February 27, 1886.

15. See Springfield (Mass.) *Union*, July [17?], 1912; *Billboard*, May 13, 1913.

16. Columbus (Ohio), n.p., n.d., AOSB 1912–on.

Chapter 21: A House on Hambrooks Bay

1. Frank Butler, "Two Hundred Miles From Broadway," *American Field*, n.d., AOSB 1912–on.

2. *Sports Afield*, n.d., AOSB 1912–on.

3. See "'Dave,' Annie Oakley's Wonder Dog Passes to Happy Hunting Grounds," Newark (N.J.) *Sunday Call*, June 24, 1923; and Dave's registration certificate, AOSB 1912–on.

4. Darke County (Ohio) *Supplement to the Early Bird*, July 24, 1979.

5. *Sports Afield*, n.d., AOSB 1912–on.

6. Swartwout, *Missie*, 285.

7. *American Field*, January [?] 1914, AOSB 1912–on.

8. Frank E. Butler, "Hunting and Fishing in Florida," n.p., n.d., AOSB 1912–on.

9. Ibid.

10. "Annie Oakley's Story of Winter Hunting in Florida," Newark (N.J.) *Sunday Call*, n.d., AOSB 1912–on.

11. Ibid.

12. Unidentified clipping, AOSB 1912–on.

13. Winston-Salem (N.C.) *Journal*, January 17, 1909; Dayton (Ohio) *Sunday Journal*, December 14, 1924.

14. Swartwout, *Missie*, 291; Philadelphia *Public Ledger*, May 18, 1919.

15. Greensboro (N.C.) *Daily News*, December 30, 1923; Peter Carney, "In the Shooting Field," n.p., n.d. AOSB 1921–25. Annie's Cambridge house, built without projecting closets, may explain the origin of the myth that she built her house in Nutley without any closets at all.

16. Dayton (Ohio) *Journal*, n.d., AOSB 1912–on.

17. Russell, *The Lives and Legends of Buffalo Bill*, 452–62.

18. Cambridge (Md.) *Daily Banner*, August 6, 1915.

Chapter 22: At the Carolina

1. See various issues of the Pinehurst (N.C.) *Outlook*, including January 6, December 1, 1912, December 18, 1915; John Martin Hammond, *Winter Journeys Through the South*, quoted in "Ourselves as Others See Us," Pinehurst *Outlook*, December 23, 30, 1916; Bion Butler, Raleigh (N.C.) *News and Observer*, quoted in Pinehurst *Outlook*,

April 19, 1913; and "W. A. Bristol Tells of His Visit to Pinehurst," Pinehurst *Outlook*, March 9, 1922.

2. Pinehurst (N.C.) *Outlook*, January 23, 1909, and n.d., AOSB 1902–8; and numerous clippings on Annie Oakley and Frank Butler in the South, AOSB 1912–on.

3. Pinehurst (N.C.) *Outlook*, January 6, 1917, February 2, 1918; Philadelphia *Public Ledger*, October 28, 1923.

4. Annie Oakley, "Coaching the 400," *American Shooter*, January 1, 1916.

5. Cambridge (Md.), n.p., April 2, 1916, AOSB 1912–on.

6. Pinehurst (N.C.) *Outlook*, February 22, 1919.

7. Frank Butler, letter to Cambridge, (Md.), n.p., April 22, 1916, AOSB 1912–on.

8. Ibid.; *New American Shooter*, October 1918.

9. West Chester (Pa.) *Daily Local News*, n.d., AOSB 1921–25.

10. Oakley, "Coaching the 400"; Oakley, "Woman Can Shoot," Pinehurst (N.C.) *Outlook*, January 28, 1920; Pinehurst (N.C.) *Outlook*, March 25, 1916. Among Annie's pupils was the wife of Pennsylvania governor Martin Brumbaugh, whom Annie liked to think was a distant relative because her mother's second husband was named Brumbaugh. The governor and his new bride were honeymooning in Pinehurst.

11. Pinehurst (N.C.) *Outlook*, February 24, 1917.

12. Pinehurst (N.C.) *Outlook*, March 9, 1918.

13. Pinehurst (N.C.) *Outlook*, February 12, 1916, February 24, 1917.

14. Russell, *The Lives and Legends of Buffalo Bill*, 463–72. John Burke died on April 12, 1917, just thirteen weeks after his great idol.

15. Pinehurst (N.C.) *Outlook*, January 20, 1917.

16. Ibid., March 24, 1917.

17. Ibid., January 20, 1917.

18. Ibid.

19. Ibid.

20. Ibid., February 5, 1918.

21. AOSB 1912–on.

22. Dayton (Ohio) *Journal*, July 19, 1915.

23. See Philadelphia *Public Ledger*, May 18, 1919; Cleveland (Ohio) *Plain Dealer*, May 12, 1926; unidentified clipping, AOSB 1921–25.

24. *Shooting and Fishing*, n.d., AOSB 1896–1901; "How a Woman Can Handle Firearms," n.p., n.d., AOSB 1896–1901.

25. New York *Recorder*, May 22, 1894.

26. New York *Herald*, June 28, 1922; Anne Whitney Hay, "Annie Oakley Still Pulls a Wicked Trigger," New York *Morning Telegraph*, July 16, 1922.

27. "For Home Defense," n.p., n.d., AOSB 1912–on.

28. AOSB 1896–1901.

29. Oakley, "Woman Can Shoot."

30. Dayton (Ohio) *Daily News*, May 30, 1926.

31. Oakley, "Woman Can Shoot"; Dayton (Ohio) *Daily News*, May 30, 1926.

32. Philadelphia *Public Ledger*, October 28, 1923; Dayton (Ohio) *Daily News*, May 30, 1926.

33. Philadelphia *Public Ledger*, October 28, 1923; and Cincinnati *Times-Star*, n.d., AOSB 1902–8.

34. Annie Oakley, "Why Women Should Shoot," New York *Sun*, June 3, 1894; Oakley, "Woman Can Shoot."

35. Allentown (Pa.) *Democrat*, May 23, 1918.

36. See ibid.; Camp Crane *News*, May 25, 1918.

37. *New American Shooter*, October 1918.

38. Ibid.

39. Ibid. Even Frank was impressed with Annie's shooting these days. "In her long

experience, I never saw her perform so well; her speed was s revelation to me," he said. "I think she was inspired by the fact that she was entertaining and instructing the boys who fight the Hun."

40. Various clippings, AOSB 1912–on; "Dave Dog with Almost Human Intelligence," *Record and Times Democrat* (no city listed), n.d., AOSB 1912–on. The New Madison (Ohio) *Herald*, n.d., AOSB 1912–on, quotes Frank Butler as saying that twenty-one hotels where dogs were not allowed accepted Dave as a welcome guest.

41. *New American Shooter*, October 1918; Camp Crane *News*, May 25, 1918.

Chapter 23: Trouble on the Dixie Highway

1. Philadelphia *Public Ledger*, May 18, 1919.
2. See Preston W. Slosson, *The Great Crusade and After* (New York: Macmillan, 1930), 393–94; Russell, "The Golden Age of Wild West Shows"; and *Collier's Encyclopedia*, 1984 ed., s.v. "Motion Pictures."
3. Detroit *Free Press*, July 5, 1921. Although the *Free Press* said Annie was in Detroit to see a specialist about some throat trouble, it may have been Frank who was having the trouble. He later suffered such an ailment.
4. New York *Tribune*, February 1917; and AOSB 1912–on. Note Annie's falsehood about the train wreck causing her hair to turn white. As described in chapter 17, both Annie and Frank stuck to this story consistently.
5. AOSB 1910–on.
6. Ibid.
7. See Pinehurst (N.C.) *Outlook*, March 17, April 7, 1920; and Philadelphia *Public Ledger*, October 23, 1923.
8. Charlotte (N.C.) *Observer*, July 9, 1924.
9. "All Outdoors," n.p., n.d., AOSB 1921–25.
10. See Pinehurst (N.C.) *Outlook*, April 20, 1922; and *New York Times*, March 6, 1922.
11. Pinehurst (N.C.) *Outlook*, nine-part series, "Memories of Annie Oakley," Winter 1917.
12. For Fred Stone's Motor Hippodrome, see New York *World*, June 28, July 4, 1922; New York *Herald*, July 4, 1922; New York *Tribune*, June 28, July 4, 1922; Hay, "Annie Oakley Still Pulls a Wicked Trigger"; "Society Applauds Stone's Big Show," "Fred Stone's Circus-Motor Hippodrome," and "Vaudeville on Wheels," n.p., n.d., AOSB 1921–25.
13. See Stone, *Rolling Stone*, 213–19; and Ketchum, *Will Rogers, His Life and Times*, 168.
14. Dayton (Ohio), n.p., n.d., AOSB 1912–on.
15. See Detroit *Free Press*, July 5, 1921; and *Billboard*, July 16, 1921.
16. Myles E. Connolly, "Annie Oakley Famous Woman Crack Shot Visits New England," n.p., n.d., AOSB 1921–25.
17. N.p., January 26, 1923, AOSB 1921–25.
18. See *Billboard*, November 11, 1922; and Newark (N.J.) *Sunday Call*, June 24, 1923.
19. For accounts of the accident, see Daytona (Fla.) *News*, November 10, 1922; Daytona (Fla.) *Journal*, November 11, 1922; and Claude R. Flory, "Annie Oakley in the South," *North Carolina Historical Review* 43 (Summer 1966):333–43. Accounts do not agree on the cause of the accident on the Dixie Highway. According to the Daytona *Journal*, quoted in Flory's article, the Cadillac turned over when Young tried to turn back on the road after he was forced into the sand by a passing car. Some accounts blame excessive speed on Young's part. In *Missie*, 293, Fern Campbell Swartwout said, "They went onto a soft shoulder on a new road and landed in the ditch."

20. Frank Butler, "'Dave' Annie Oakley's Wonder Dog Passes to Happy Hunting Grounds."

21. Annie's half-sister, Emily Brumbaugh Patterson was born on May 2, 1869, while Susan Shaw was married to her second husband, Daniel Brumbaugh.

22. See *American Field*, n.d., AOSB 1921–25; and n.p., January 26, 1923, AOSB 1921–25.

23. See Swartwout, *Missie*, 293–94; and Newark (N.J.) *Sunday Call*, June 24, 1923.

Chapter 24: Home to Darke County

1. Philadelphia *Evening Bulletin*, March 13, 1923.

2. Ibid.

3. *Billboard*, October 20, November 3, 1923; *American Field*, n.d., AOSB 1921–25; Philadelphia *Public Ledger*, October 28, 1923.

4. See Philadelphia *Public Ledger*, October 28, 1923; and AOSB 1921–25. Annie also had another motto: "You can do everything any one else can do. Start early, work for some definite aim and never give up, no matter how discouraged things may appear." See West Chester (Pa.) *Local Daily News*, n.d., AOSB 1921–25; and Greensboro (N.C.) *Daily News*, [1924?], AOSB 1921–25.

5. Darke County (Ohio) *Early Bird Supplement*, July 24, 1979. In this interview Rush Blakeley said the Butlers visited from the middle of September 1922 until the end of May 1923. Blakeley, recalling the visit fifty years after it happened, was a year off on his dates. Newspaper clippings in AOSB place Annie Oakley in Brockton, Massachusetts, in October 1922; in Daytona, Florida, in November 1922; and in Leesburg, Florida, in January, February, and March 1923.

6. See Charlotte (N.C.) *Observer*, July 9, 22, 1924.

7. See Dayton (Ohio) *Sunday Journal*, December 14, 1924; Greenville (Ohio) *Daily Advocate*, November 4, 1926; and Greenville (Ohio) *Early Bird Supplement*, July 20, 1981.

8. Dayton (Ohio) *Daily News*, August 26, 1925. Interestingly, when the clipping was pasted in Annie's scrapbooks, the word "old" was blotted out in ink. Annie had done that before when she read something she didn't like.

9. See unidentified clipping, AOSB 1921–25; and Dayton (Ohio) *Daily News*, August 26, 1925.

10. Shaw to Annie Oakley, March 3, 1926, Buffalo Bill Historical Center, Cody, Wyoming.

11. *Billboard*, May 9, 1925, AOSB 1921–25.

12. R. J. Middaugh to Annie Oakley, December 1, 1925, Buffalo Bill Historical Center, Cody, Wyoming.

13. Newark (N.J.) *Star-Eagle*, October 6, 1925.

14. See Dayton (Ohio) *Daily News*, August [?], 1925; and Rush Blakeley interview, May 13, 1981.

15. *Billboard*, January 17, 1925; Dayton (Ohio) *Daily News*, August 26, 1925.

16. Allene Stone to Annie Oakley, January 27, February 6, 1926, Buffalo Bill Historical Center, Cody, Wyoming.

17. Annie Oakley to Leonard Tufts, May 23, 1926, Given Memorial Library, Pinehurst, North Carolina.

18. Frank Butler to Leonard Tufts, May 15, 1926, Given Memorial Library, Pinehurst, North Carolina.

19. The letters reproduced here are in the Buffalo Bill Historical Center, Cody, Wyoming.

20. Frank Butler to Leonard Tufts, August 31, 1926, Given Memorial Library, Pinehurst, North Carolina; Swartwout, *Missie*, 295. Rush Blakeley also said that Annie

wanted Frank to go: "He hated winter up north and she felt going south was best for him."

21. Frank Butler to Leonard Tufts, August 31, 1926, Given Memorial Library, Pinehurst, North Carolina.

22. Swartwout, *Missie*, 295–96.

23. Darke County (Ohio) *Early Bird Supplement*, July 24, 1979.

24. See Stocker interview, Darke County (Ohio) *Early Bird Supplement*, Garst Museum; and Annie Oakley Butler, death certificate, Division of Vital Statistics, Ohio Department of Health, Columbus.

25. Swartwout, *Missie*, 296.

26. Stocker interview, Darke County (Ohio) *Early Bird Supplement*, Garst Museum. The urn was said to be a silver loving cup given to Annie by the people of France in 1889.

27. Frank E. Butler, death certificate, Circuit Court, Oakland County, Michigan.

28. According to Sayers, *Annie Oakley and Buffalo Bill's Wild West*, 86, the box containing Annie's ashes was buried with Frank's casket.

Bibliography

American Trapshooting Association. *The ATA Hall of Fame and Trapshooting Museum.* Vandalia, Ohio: Amateur Trapshooting Association, n.d.

Annie Oakley: Her Career and Experiences. Pinehurst, N.C., March 19, 1920.

Baldwin, Dick. "Trapshooting." In *The Expert's Book of the Shooting Sports,* ed. David E. Petzel, 169–78. New York: Simon & Schuster, 1972.

Bailey, M. B., ed. *Buffalo Bill's Wild West Route Book.* Buffalo, N.Y.: Courier, 1896.

Baker, Johnny. Scrapbooks. Western History Department, Denver Public Library.

Biographical History of Darke County, Ohio, Compendium of National Biography, A. Chicago: Lewis Publishing, 1900.

Blackstone, Sarah J. *Buckskins, Bullets, and Business: A History of Buffalo Bill's Wild West.* Westport, Conn.: Greenwood Press, 1986.

Bogardus, A. H. *Field, Cover and Trap Shooting.* New York: Orange Judd, 1874; rev. ed., ed. Colonel Prentiss Ingraham, 1884.

Branch, Douglas. *The Hunting of Buffalo.* New York: D. Appleton, 1929.

Brown, Gene, ed. *The New York Times Encyclopedia of Sport.* 15 vols. New York: Arno Press, 1979. Vol. 10: *Outdoor Sports.*

Buffalo Bill Wild West programs. Denver Public Library; University of Kansas Libraries, Lawrence.

Burke, John M. *Buffalo Bill, from Prairie to Palace.* Chicago: Rand, McNally, 1893.

Burton, Jack. *In Memoriam—Oldtime Show Biz.* New York: Vantage Press, 1965.

Butler, Frank. "Hunting and Fishing in Florida." N.p., n.d.

———. "The Life of Dave as Told by Himself." Newark (N.J.) *Sunday Call,* June 24, 1923.

———. "Two Hundred Miles from Broadway." *American Field,* n.d.

BIBLIOGRAPHY

Chapel, Charles Edward. *Field, Skeet and Trapshooting.* Rev. ed. New York: A. S. Barnes, 1962.

Clark, Ronald W. *Edison, the Man Who Made the Future.* New York: G. P. Putnam's Sons, 1977.

Clunn, Harold P. *The Face of London.* London: Spring Books, 1957.

Cody, Colonel W. F. *Buffalo Bill's Life Story, An Autobiography.* New York: Rinehart, 1920.

Cooper, Courtney Ryley. *Annie Oakley, Woman at Arms.* New York: Duffield, 1927.

Csida, Joseph, and June Bundy Csida. *American Entertainment: A Unique History of Popular Show Business.* New York: Watson-Guptill, 1978.

Deahl, William E., Jr. "Buffalo Bill's Wild West Show, 1885." *Annals of Wyoming* 47 (Fall 1975): 139–51.

Dedmon, Emmett. *Fabulous Chicago: A Great City's History and People.* New York: Atheneum, 1953; enlarged ed., 1981.

Durant, John, and Alice Durant. *Pictorial History of the American Circus.* New York: A. S. Barnes, 1957.

Durso, Joseph. *Madison Square Garden, 100 Years of History.* New York: Simon & Schuster, 1979.

Easton, Robert. "Guns of the American West." In *The Book of the American West,* Jay Monaghan, 377–426. New York: Bonanza Books, 1963.

Fellows, Dexter, and Andrew Freeman. *This Way to the Big Show.* New York: Viking, 1936.

Flory, Claude R. "Annie Oakley in the South." *The North Carolina Historical Review* 43 (Summer 1966): 333–43.

Garavaglia, Louis A., and Charles G. Worman. *Firearms of the American West, 1803–1865.* Albuquerque: University of New Mexico Press, 1984.

Gilbert, Douglas. *American Vaudeville: Its Life and Times.* New York: Dover, 1940.

Greener, W. W. *The Gun, and Its Development.* New York: Bonanza, 1881; rpt., 1910.

Halsey, Francis Whiting. *The Literary Digest History of the World War.* 10 vols. New York: Funk & Wagnalls, 1919. Vol. 4.

Harriss, Joseph. *The Tallest Tower, Eiffel and the Belle Epoque.* Boston: Houghton Mifflin, 1975.

Havighurst, Walter. *Annie Oakley of the Wild West.* New York: Macmillan, 1954.

History of Darke County, Ohio. Chicago: W. H. Beers, 1880.

Hoyt, Harlowe R. *Town Hall Tonight: Intimate Memories of the Grassroots Days of the American Theatre.* Englewood Cliffs, N.J.: Prentice-Hall, 1955.

Hughes, Glenn. *A History of the American Theatre, 1700–1950.* New York: Samuel French, 1951.

James, Edward T., ed. *Notable American Women 1607–1950: A Biographical Dictionary.* Vol. 2. Cambridge, Mass.: The Belknap Press of Harvard University Press, 1971.

Johnson, Allen, and Dumas Malone, eds. *Dictionary of American Biography.* New York: Charles Scribner's Sons, 1930.

Josephson, Matthew. *Edison.* New York: McGraw-Hill, 1959.

Keith, Elmer. *Shotguns by Keith.* 2nd ed. Harrisburg, Pa.: Stackpole, 1961.

Ketchum, Richard M. *Will Rogers, His Life and Times.* New York: American Heritage, 1973.

Kuhlhoff, Pete. *Kuhlhoff on Guns.* New York: Winchester Press, 1970.

Lancaster, Charles. *Illustrated Treatise on The Art of Shooting.* 4th ed. London: McCorquodale, 1892.

Leslie, Amy. *Some Players.* Chicago: Herbert S. Stone, 1899.

Lockwood, Charles. *Manhattan Moves Uptown.* Boston: Houghton Mifflin, 1976.

Lugs, Jaroslav. *A History of Shooting, Marksmanship, Duelling and Exhibition Shooting.* Feltham, Middlesex, England: Spring Books, 1968.

McCullough, Edo. *World's Fair Midways.* New York: Exposition Press, 1966.

McLaughlin, James. *My Friend the Indian.* Boston: Houghton Mifflin, 1910; rpt., Seattle: Salisbury Press, Superior Publishing, 1970.

Magnus, Philip. *King Edward the Seventh.* New York: E. P. Dutton, 1964.

"Memories of Annie Oakley." Pinehurst (N.C.) *Outlook,* December 9, 16, 23, 30, 1916; January 6, 20, 1917; February 3, 17, 1917.

Missildine, Fred, and Nick Karas. *Score Better at Trap and Skeet.* New York: Winchester Press, 1971.

National Cyclopaedia of American Biography. New York: J. T. White, 1935.

Oakley, Annie. "Annie Oakley's Story of Winter Hunting in Florida." Newark (N.J.) *Sunday Call,* n.d.

————. *A Brief Sketch of Her Career and Notes on Shooting.* N.p., n.d. [1899?].

————. "Coaching the 400." *American Shooter* (January 1, 1916).

————. "Facts and Fancies." N.p., n.d. [1912?].

————. "Hints on the Use of Firearms." *The Outer's Book* (January 1907).

————. *Powders I Have Used.* Wilmington: DuPont Powder, 1914.

————. "Speaking of Shooting." *New York Tribune,* February 8, 1917.

————. "Sports for Women." *Shooting and Fishing* (Christmas number, n.d. [1896?]).

————. *The Story of My Life.* N.p.: NEA Service, 1926.

————. "Why Ladies Should Shoot." (London) *Shooting Times and British Sportsman,* August 26, 1893.

————. "Why Women Should Shoot." *New York Sun,* June 3, 1894.

————. "Woman Can Shoot." Pinehurst (N.C.) *Outlook,* January 28, 1920.

Odell, George C. D. *Annals of the New York Stage.* 15 vols. New York: Columbia University Press, 1939. Vol. 11.

O'Neil, Paul. *The End and the Myth.* Alexandria, Va.: Time-Life, 1979.

Perry, Robert E. *Treaty City: A Story of Old Fort GreenVille.* Bradford, Ohio: By the author, 1945.

Pouska, Frank J. "Young Buffalo Wild West Show." *Bandwagon* (May–June 1959): 15–16.

————. "Young Buffalo Wild West Show Part II." *Bandwagon* (May–June 1960): 5–6, 19–20.

Rennert, Jack. *100 Posters of Buffalo Bill's Wild West.* New York: Darien House, 1976.

BIBLIOGRAPHY

Rifle Queen. London: General Publishing, 1887.

Robinson, Duane. *A History of the Dakota and Sioux Nation.* N.p.: State of South Dakota, 1904; rpt. Minneapolis: Ross & Haines, 1956.

Rogers, Will. *The Autobiography of Will Rogers.* Selected and ed. Donald Day. Boston: Houghton Mifflin, 1926.

Russell, Don. *The Lives and Legends of Buffalo Bill.* Norman: University of Oklahoma Press, 1960.

———. Speech to Chicago Corral of "The Westerners," January 26, 1970. Quoted in "The Golden Age of Wild West Shows," *Bandwagon* (n.d.).

———. *The Wild West: A History of the Wild West Shows.* Fort Worth, Tex.: Amon Carter Museum, 1970.

Rywell, Martin. *Fell's Collector's Guide to American Antique Firearms.* New York: Frederick Fell, 1963.

Salsbury, Nate. "The Origin of the Wild West Show," "Wild West at Windsor," "At the Vatican." *Colorado Magazine* 32 (July 1955): 204–15.

———. Scrapbooks. Western History Department, Denver Public Library.

Sayers, Isabelle S. *Annie Oakley and Buffalo Bill's Wild West.* New York: Dover, 1981.

Sell, Henry Blackman, and Victor Weybright. *Buffalo Bill and the Wild West.* New York: Oxford University Press, 1955.

Sells Brothers Circus Route Book. N.p., 1881, 1884. Circus World Museum, Baraboo, Wis.

Shapiro, Milton J. *A Beginner's Book of Sporting Guns and Hunting.* New York: Julian Messner, 1961.

Shirley, Glenn. *Pawnee Bill: A Biography of Major Gordon W. Lillie.* Lincoln: University of Nebraska Press, 1958.

Slosson, Preston W. *The Great Crusade and After.* New York: Macmillan, 1930.

Sobel, Bernard. *A Pictorial History of Vaudeville.* New York: Citadel Press, 1961.

Solomon, Saul. *Tuberculosis.* New York: Coward-McCann, 1952.

Speer Manual for Reloading Ammunition, Rifle, Pistol and Shotgun. Lewiston, Idaho: Speer, 1964.

Sports Illustrated Book of Shotgun Sports. Philadelphia: J. B. Lippincott, 1967.

Spring, Agnes Wright. *Buffalo Bill and His Horses.* Fort Collins, Colo.: B and M Printing, 1953.

Stone, Fred. *Rolling Stone.* New York: McGraw-Hill, 1945.

Story of American Hunting and Firearms, from Outdoor Life. New York: Sunrise Books, E. P. Dutton, 1976.

Swartwout, [Annie, pseud.] Fern. *Missie.* Blanchester, Ohio: Brown Publishing, 1947.

Thorp, Raymond W. *Doc W. F. Carver, Spirit Gun of the West.* Glendale, Calif.: Arthur H. Clark, 1957.

Toll, Robert C. *On with the Show: The First Century of Show Business in America.* New York: Oxford University Press, 1976.

"Tony Pastor and His Great Company." Scrapbooks, 1887. New York City Public Library.

Troy, Ann A., ed. *Nutley, Yesterday, Today.* Nutley, N.J.: Nutley Historical Society, 1961.

Turner, Katharine C. *Red Men Calling on the Great White Father*. Norman: University of Oklahoma Press, 1951.

U.S. Department of Commerce, Bureau of the Census. *Eighth Census of the United States, 1860:* Roll 956, vol. 16.

―――. *Ninth Census of the United Staes, 1870:* Roll 1194, vol. 15.

―――. *Tenth Census of the United States, 1880:* Roll 1011, vol. 17.

Vestal, Stanley. *Sitting Bull, Champion of the Sioux*. Norman: University of Oklahoma Press, 1932.

Viola, Herman J. *Diplomats in Buckskins: A History of Indian Delegations in Washington City*. Washington, D.C.: Smithsonian Institution Press, 1981.

Walsh, Richard J., with Milton S. Salsbury. *The Making of Buffalo Bill*. Indianapolis: Bobbs-Merrill, 1928.

Weinstein, Sheryl. "When Nutley Was Bloomsbury." *New Jersey Monthly* (December 1980): 139–40.

Wertheimer, Barbara Mayer. *We Were There: The Story of Working Women in America*. New York: Pantheon, 1977.

Wildes, Harry Emerson. *Twin Rivers: The Raritan and the Passaic*. New York: Farrar & Rinehart, 1943.

Wilson, Frazer E. *History of Darke County Ohio from Its Earliest Settlement to the Present Time*. Milford, Ohio: Hobart Publishing, 1914.

Yost, Nellie Snyder. *Buffalo Bill, His Family, Friends, Fame, Failures, and Fortunes*. Chicago: Sage Books Swallow Press, 1979.

Zellers, Parker. *Tony Pastor: Dean of the Vaudeville Stage*. Ypsilanti: Eastern Michigan University Press, 1971.

Index

279

INDEX

Lorillard, Pierre, 64
Luitpold, prince of Bavaria, 107, 110
Lynch, T. F., 165

McCarroll, Sylvester, 136
McClure, Bill, 169
McCormick, Langdon, 170, 173
MacKaye, Steele, 64
McKinley, William, 126, 214
McLaughlin, Maj. James, 26, 27
Madison Square Garden, 64, 65, 93, 190, 211
Mahzar, Fahreda, 123
Marsh, Mrs. Charles R., 212
Malone (train brakeman), 165
Manning, Cardinal Henry, 72
Manogue, D. H., 165
Marsh, Frederick Dana, 128
Marsh, Spencer S., 236–37
Marshall, Tom, 181
Matches and exhibitions, 109, 111, 188, 200, 221–22, 231–32; at army cantonments, 215–18; with Frank Butler, 16–17; at Fred Stone's Motor Hippodrome, 225; at Grand American Handicap, 182–85; with Grand Duke Michael of Russia, 85–86; at Lake Denmark, N.J., 166; at London Gun Club, 84–85; at Middlesex, N.J., Gun Club, 67; at Newton, N.J., Fair, 65–66; at Pinehurst, N.C., 207, 209; turkey shoots, 9; with Union Metallic Cartridge Company, 185–86; in Wild West arena, 41–48; with William Graham, 65–66, 93–95; at Wimbledon, 86–87; in year 1888, 95, 100. *See also* Butler, Frank; Feats and stunts; Guns; Hunting and hunters; Oakley, Annie; Shooting; Targets
Matchett, Dr. W. H., 242, 243
Matthews, James, 143
Mauzy. *See* Moses
Mayview Manor, N.C., 233
Means, Ambrose, 190
Medals, 64, 67, 111; from London Gun Club, 85; melting down of, 222; numbers of, 159; silver loving cup, 158–60
Merman, Ethel, 245, 246
Mexican Frank (cowboy), 100
Michael, grand duke of Russia, 85–86
Middaugh, R. J., 235
Miller, Raquel, 238
Miller & Arlington Wild West Show, 209

Miller Brothers 101 Ranch Wild West Show, 237
Miles, Gen. Nelson A., 262n.3
Missie, 39, 149–50, 252n.8. *See also* Oakley, Annie
Mitchell, Jim, 110
Mohawk (steamship), 117, 130
Molly (delivery horse), 132
Money, 7, 9, 24, 27, 65, 110, 112, 126, 200; importance of, 119–20; salary, 32, 119, 201, 260n.3
Montana Jack, 190
Montgomery and Stone. *See* Stone, Fred
Montgomery, Dave, 186, 197
Moody, Dwight, 123
Moore, Owen, 77
Morgan, W. L., 237
Morley, J. T., 166
Moses (family name), 23
Moses, C. G. and Lee (nephews), 247n.6
Moses, Elizabeth (sister), 221, 264n.7
Moses, Hulda (sister), 5, 155, 156, 158, 173, 236, 237, 263–64n.7
Moses, Jacob (father), 3, 5, 23, 200, 244
Moses, John (brother), 4, 149, 236, 247–48n.6, 263n.7
Moses, Lydia (sister), 221, 264n.7
Moses, Mary Jane (sister), 5, 264n.7
Moses, Phoebe Ann. *See* Oakley, Annie
Moses, Sarah Ellen (sister), 236, 242, 264n.7
Moses, Susan (mother), 3, 4, 5, 28, 68, 112, 113, 117, 149, 173, 188, 189, 200, 248n.10, 255n.30
Motor Hippodrome and Wild West Show, 223, 225
Moyer, George C., 226
Mozee, Bernard, Chelcy and Lee, 236. *See also* Moses, C. G. and Lee
Myrely, James, 162

Nelson, John, 39, 115
Newspapers and periodicals: *American Field*, 113; Baltimore *Sun*, 113; *Billboard*, 235; Bridgeport (Conn.) *Telegram Union*, 176; Brooklyn *Citizen*, 177; Brooklyn *Eagle*, 214; Brooklyn *Standard Union*, 174; Charleston (S.C.) *News and Courier*, 177; Chicago *Daily News*, 125, 169; Chicago *Examiner and American*, 173, 176, 177, 178; Cincinnati *Commercial*, 112; Cody (Wyo.) *Enterprise*, 152; Council Bluffs (Iowa)

Wiman, Erastus, 58, 64
Wimbledon (shooting range), 13, 86–87, 89, 90, 107, 110, 257n.44
Windecker, Mrs. (mindreader), 192
"The Wolves" (family), 6, 161, 175, 248n.10
Women: education of, 195; as feminists, 213; and guns, 213–15; and hunting, 154–55, 205; image as, 49–50, 82–83, 116, 213; prejudice faced as, 66–67; right to vote, 213; as shooters, 206–207, 214; and war, 212–13; in will, 236
Woodcott, E. W., 31
Woodland, Ohio, 3, 237, 245
World's Industrial and Cotton Exposition, 30–33

World War I, 114, 206, 211, 212, 219; at army cantonments, 215–18, 268–69n.39; women's regiment for, 212–13, 214, 215. *See also* Feats and stunts
Wright, Orville and Wilbur, 189
Wyndham, Charles, 72

"Yankeeries," 71, 72, 115; *See also* American Exhibition
Yellow Hair (Cheyenne warrior), 37, 41
Yellow Hand. *See* Yellow Hair
Young, Brigham, 39
Young Buffalo. *See* Smith, Joe R.
Young Buffalo Wild West, 190–93, 195–96, 202
Young, Mr. (chauffeur), 229

7305

DATE DUE

DE 21 '92			
FE 1 0 '93			
AC			
AG 1 '93			
MAY 1 1 1995			
JUL 2 5 1995			
NOV 2 2 1995			
		DISCARDED	

DEMCO 38-297